pwc

普华永道

普华永道国际财务报告准则实务指引系列（第六册）
PwC IFRS MOA Series (Volume Six)

Manual of Accounting — IFRS 2012

Chapter 15 – Intangible assets
Chapter 20 – Inventories

国际财务报告准则实务指引

第十五章—无形资产
第二十章—存货

中英文对照

U0823345

翻译组主要成员：金以文　张慧晞　黄志娜　林　燕　陈　闪

中国财政经济出版社

This book has been prepared for general guidance on matters of interest only, and does not constitute professional advice. You should not act upon the information contained in this book without obtaining specific professional advice. No representation or warranty (express or implied) is given as to the accuracy or completeness of the information contained in this book, and, to the extent permitted by law, PricewaterhouseCoopers does not accept or assume any liability, responsibility or duty of care for any consequences of you or anyone else acting, or refraining to act, in reliance on the information contained in this book or for any decision based on it.

This book covers one of the chapters of the English version and its Chinese translation, which the English version remains the definitive source of guidance. The publishers and the authors cannot accept any responsibility for any errors or misunderstandings arising from the English version and its Chinese translation. Neither can the publishers and the authors accept any responsibility for loss occasioned to any person acting or refraining from action as a result of the material in this book.

©2012 PricewaterhouseCoopers. All rights reserved. "*PricewaterhouseCoopers*" and "*PwC*" refer to the network of member firms of PricewaterhouseCoopers International Limited ("*PwCIL*"). Each member firm is a separate legal entity and does not act as agent of PwCIL or any other member firm. PwCIL does not provide any services to clients. PwCIL is not responsible or liable for the acts or omissions of any of its member firms nor can it control the exercise of their professional judgment or bind them in any way. No member firm is responsible or liable for the acts or omissions of any other member firm nor can it control the exercise of another member firm's professional judgment or bind another member firm or PwCIL in any way.

编写本书之目的是对感兴趣的事项给予一般性的指导，而非提供专业建议。未征得具体专业意见之前，不应依据本书所述内容采取任何行动。我们不对书中所述信息是否准确或完整作出任何明示或暗示的承诺或保证。除非法律另有明文规定，普华永道不对任何个人或单位因为阅读了本书而采取或未采取某项行动的后果、或基于本书所作出的任何决定承担任何责任。

本书内容为英文本中的一个章节及其中文译文，指导概以英文为准。出版社和编译者不对英文原文及中文译文的偏差或误解承担任何责任，也不对任何个人或单位因为阅读了本书而采取或未采取某项行动所发生损失承担任何责任。

ⓒ2012 普华永道（PricewaterhouseCoopers）版权所有。PricewaterhouseCoopers 及 PwC 泛指 PricewaterhouseCoopers International Limited（“*PwCIL*”）之成员机构网络。该机构网络中的每个成员均为独立的法律实体，不代表 PwCIL 或其他任何 PwCIL 的成员机构。PwCIL 不向客户提供任何服务。PwCIL 不为其成员机构的行为和疏忽担负责任，也不能影响成员机构的专业判断，对其不具有任何束缚。各成员机构不为其他成员机构的行为和疏忽担负责任，不影响他们的专业判断，对其他成员机构或 PwCIL 不具有任何束缚。

Preface

Businesses around the world are becoming more global and much of the accounting standard-setters' focus today is concerned with global harmonization of accounting requirements. Against this backdrop, International Financial Reporting Standards (IFRS) have become increasingly important as the global business language. IFRS aims to be a comprehensive set of neutral principles that produce consistent, comparable, relevant and reliable financial information useful for investors, lenders, creditors, and those who make decisions in the capital markets. PwC is strongly committed to a common goal of promoting these financial reporting standards to preparers and users.

The IFRS Manual of Accounting is a comprehensive practical guide to IFRS and provides straightforward explanations of how to prepare financial statements in accordance with IFRS, with hundreds of practical examples. The Manual was developed based on the extensive experience of the PwC's global network of firms.

Due to the importance of IFRS for many companies in China and the continued convergence of China Accounting Standards and IFRS, PwC China has undertaken a significant project to translate our IFRS Manual of Accounting into Chinese. We sincerely hope that our IFRS Manual of Accounting with Chinese Translation provides practical insights and can help finance directors, accountants, auditors, analysts and other users of financial statements to bridge the gap between accounting principles and their applications.

Ernest Ip
Senior Partner
PwC China and Hong Kong

© 2012 PricewaterhouseCoopers LLP. All rights reserved.

前 言

在营商环境日趋国际化的今天，会计规定的全球一致化已经成为会计准则制定者们关注的一个重点。在此背景下，国际财务报告准则（IFRS）作为全球商业语言变得愈发重要。IFRS 旨在成为一套全面的、中性的原则，向投资者、借款方、债权人及其他需在资本市场中作出决策的人士提供一致的、可比较的、相关的及可靠的财务信息。普华永道致力于将这些财务准则介绍给广泛的财务报表编制者及使用者。

英文版的《国际财务报告准则实务指引》（IFRS Manual of Accounting）是对 IFRS 的一份全面性实务指引，对如何按照 IFRS 编制财务报表提供了简明的阐述，并附有诸多实务示例。该指引是基于普华永道全球成员机构网络丰富的经验归纳而成。

鉴于 IFRS 对中国的许多公司的重要性，以及中国会计准则与 IFRS 的持续趋同，普华永道中国启动了这项具有重大意义的项目，即将《国际财务报告准则实务指引》译成中文，并分享给大家。我们诚挚地希望这套中英文对照的《国际财务报告准则实务指引》能够提供实用的见解，为财务总监、会计人员、审计人员、分析人员及其他财务报表使用者们在会计原则与其具体应用之间架起一座桥梁。

叶冠荣
首席合伙人
普华永道中国及香港

ⓒ 2012 普华永道（PricewaterhouseCoopers）版权所有。

Overview/Introduction

Recent years have seen major changes in financial reporting worldwide with the single most important change being convergence around IFRS. There has also been a keen focus to improve the long term development of the CPA profession within China. As the Ministry of Finance and other regulatory bodies continue to promulgate legislation to promote the development of the Chinese CPA profession, we hope the release of our IFRS Manual of Accounting with Chinese Translation will also contribute to this effort.

The Ministry of Finance issued the Accounting Standards for Business Enterprises (hereafter referred to as "China Accounting Standards" or "CAS") in 2006. CAS incorporates all of the principles of IFRS and there has been a continued focus on convergence over the last few years. Additionally, IFRS is becoming increasingly important for many companies in China, including domestic companies seeking to raise capital overseas, as well as for foreign companies that have operations in China. With the continued convergence of CAS and IFRS, the release of our IFRS Manual of Accounting with Chinese Translation brings to China the extensive collective experience of the PwC's global network of firms in applying IFRS.

We hope this Manual will play a part in promoting consistent, comparable, relevant and reliable IFRS financial information and will serve as a reference tool for accounting students, academics, practitioners and users of financial statements in better understanding and implementing IFRS. More importantly, we hope the advice given in this text will assist those dealing with the many issues faced in preparing IFRS financial statements and provide helpful insight to users of such statements.

Raymund Chao
Asia Pacific Assurance Leader
PwC

© 2012 PricewaterhouseCoopers LLP. All rights reserved.

概述/引言

近年来，全球财务报告领域发生了重大变化，其中最为重要的一项变化是与国际财务报告准则的趋同。同时人们也热切地关注着中国境内注册会计师行业的长期发展。财政部及其他监管机构不断完善法规，推动中国注册会计师行业的发展，我们希望这本中英文对照的国际财务报告准则实务指引能够对此作出贡献。

财政部于2006年颁布了《企业会计准则》（以下称为中国会计准则，或CAS）。CAS包含了IFRS中的所有原则，且在过去的几年里持续趋同。此外，IFRS对于中国的许多公司来说越来越重要，包括寻求筹集海外资本的国内公司，以及在中国境内运营的外国公司。随着CAS与IFRS的持续趋同，本书的发行将给中国读者带来普华永道全球成员机构网络在应用IFRS方面积累的丰富的经验。

我们希望本书能够在推广一致的、可比的、相关的以及可靠的IFRS财务信息方面起到作用，并且可以作为会计领域的学生、学者、从业人员及财务报表使用者更好地理解及运用IFRS的参考工具。更为重要的是，我们希望本指引中提出的建议能够帮助其处理在编制IFRS财务报表时遇到的问题，并向此类财务报表使用者提供有用的观点。

赵柏基
普华永道亚太区审计部主管合伙人

ⓒ 2012 普华永道（PricewaterhouseCoopers）版权所有。

How to use this publication

Given the increasing importance of IFRS in China and the continued convergence of CAS and IFRS, the accounting technical team of PwC China and Hong Kong have undertaken a significant project to translate the IFRS Manual of Accounting into Chinese.

The Manual is a practical guide in applying IFRS and the views are based on the extensive experience of the PwC's global network of firms. However, IFRS is not static and is continuously developing. The views on its interpretation and application will adapt and evolve. The views expressed in this Manual are a guide to applying IFRS rather than a set of definitive interpretations. The application of IFRS requires significant judgement and specific facts and circumstances should be carefully considered.

IFRS Manual of Accounting with Chinese Translation will be released in different volumes. Depending on the topic, each release may be a chapter or a combination of a number of chapters from the Manual.

Because of the interdependencies between individual IFRS, there are many cross references between different chapters of the Manual. Although the IFRS Manual of Accounting with Chinese Translation will be released in different volumes, the cross references have been maintained. Users are encouraged to refer to those cross references in other translated chapters or to the English version of the Manual if it helps in their understanding.

This book is the sixth volume of IFRS Manual of Accounting Series with Chinese Translation. The content covers Chapter 15 – Intangible assets, Chapter 20 – Inventories of the English version and its translation. While every effort has been made to ensure an accurate translation, reference should be made to the English version in the event there are any differences between the Chinese and English versions.

© 2012 PricewaterhouseCoopers LLP. All rights reserved.

使用说明

鉴于 IFRS 在中国愈发重要以及 CAS 和 IFRS 的持续趋同，普华永道中国及香港的会计专业技术支持部门已着手开始了一项具有重大意义的项目，即将国际财务报告准则实务指引译成中文。

国际财务报告准则实务指引是对应用 IFRS 的实务指引，其中的观点是基于普华永道全球成员机构网络丰富的经验。然而，IFRS 不是静止的，而是持续发展的；因此，对 IFRS 的解释和适用会有所改变和发展。本指引表达的观点是对应用 IFRS 的一种指引，而非一套具有决定性的解释。IFRS 的应用需要大量的判断，还应当谨慎考虑特定的事实及所处的环境。

IFRS 实务指引及其中文翻译版将分成多册发行。根据主题，每一册可能是本指引的某一章节或是包含某几个章节。

由于各个 IFRS 准则之间的相互依存，因此本指引中不同的章节会相互参照索引。尽管 IFRS 实务指引及其中文翻译版将分成多册发行，但仍保留此类相互参照索引。如果有助于理解，我们鼓励读者阅读此类相互参照索引时参考其他已翻译的章节或指引的英文版。

本书为普华永道国际财务报告准则实务指引系列（中英文对照）的第六册。内容为英文原版的《国际财务报告准则实务指引》中的《第十五章——无形资产》、《第二十章——存货》。我们已尽最大的努力来确保翻译的准确，但中文翻译版与英文版出现不一致时，应参考英文版。

ⓒ 2012 普华永道（PricewaterhouseCoopers）版权所有。

The English version of our IFRS Manual of Accounting Series includes 2 books: IFRS Manual of Accounting and IFRS Manual of Accounting – Financial Instruments with the following chapters.

IFRS Manual of Accounting

Accounting rules and principles

01 – Introduction
02 – Accounting principles and applicability of IFRS
03 – First-time adoption of IFRS
04 – Presentation of financial statements
05 – Accounting policies, accounting estimates and errors
06 – Hyper-inflation
07 – Foreign currencies
08 – Insurance contracts

Income statement and related notes

09 – Revenue and construction contracts
10 – Segment reporting
11 – Employee benefits
11A – Employee benefits
12 – Share-based payment
13 – Taxation
14 – Earnings per share

Balance sheet and related notes

15 – Intangible assets
16 – Property, plant and equipment
17 – Investment property
18 – Impairment of assets
19 – Lease accounting
20 – Inventories
21 – Provisions and contingencies
22 – Events after the reporting period and financial commitments

© 2012 PricewaterhouseCoopers LLP. All rights reserved.

英文原版的普华永道国际财务报告准则实务指引系列包括《国际财务报告准则实务指引》和《国际财务报告准则实务指引——金融工具》两本书，其所有章节列示如下：

国际财务报告准则实务指引

会计规则和原则

01 – 引言
02 – 会计原则和国际财务报告准则的适用性
03 – 首次采用国际财务报告准则
04 – 财务报表的列报
05 – 会计政策、会计估计和差错
06 – 恶性通货膨胀
07 – 外币
08 – 保险合同

利润表及相关附注

09 – 收入与建造合同
10 – 分部报告
11 – 职工福利
11A – 职工福利
12 – 以股份为基础的支付（“股份支付”）
13 – 所得税会计
14 – 每股收益

资产负债表及相关附注

15 – 无形资产
16 – 不动产、工厂和设备
17 – 投资性房地产
18 – 资产减值
19 – 租赁会计
20 – 存货
21 – 准备和或有事项
22 – 报告期后事项和财务承诺

ⓒ 2012 普华永道（PricewaterhouseCoopers）版权所有。

IFRS Manual of Accounting—Financial Instruments

© 2012 PricewaterhouseCoopers LLP. All rights reserved.

国际财务报告准则实务指引——金融工具

© 2012 普华永道（PricewaterhouseCoopers）版权所有。

Abbreviations and terms used

Accounts	financial statements
AG	Application Guidance
App	Appendix
ARC	Accounting Regulatory Committee
BC	Basis for Conclusions (to an accounting standard)
C	currency unit
Chp	Chapter
chapter (1)	'PricewaterhouseCoopers' Manual of accounting' – chapter (1)
CESR	Committee of European Securities Regulators
CPP	current purchasing power
DP	discussion paper
EBIT	earnings before interest and tax
EBITDA	earnings before interest, tax, depreciation and amortisation
ED	exposure draft
EFRAG	European Financial Reporting Advisory Group
EPS	earnings per share
EU	European Union
FASB	Financial Accounting Standards Board (US)
Framework	Framework for the preparation and presentation of financial statements
GAAP	generally accepted accounting principles (and practices)
IAS	International Accounting Standard (see also IFRS)
IASB	International Accounting Standards Board
IFRIC	International Financial Reporting Interpretations Committee
IFRS	International Financial Reporting Standard (see also IAS)
IG	Implementation Guidance (to an accounting standard)

© 2012 PricewaterhouseCoopers LLP. All rights reserved.

缩写及词汇对照

财务报表
实施指南
附录
会计监管委员会
（某一准则的）结论基础
货币单位
章
第一章（普华永道《国际财务报告准则实务指引》——第一章）

欧洲证券监管委员会
现行购买力
讨论稿
息税前收益
扣除利息、所得税、折旧和摊销之前的收益
征求意见稿
欧洲财务报告咨询组
每股收益
欧盟
（美国）财务会计准则委员会
编报财务报表的框架

公认会计原则
国际会计准则（亦请参见 IFRS）
国际会计准则理事会
国际财务报告解释委员会
国际财务报告准则（亦请参见 IAS）
（某一准则的）应用指南

ⓒ 2012 普华永道（PricewaterhouseCoopers）版权所有。

para(s)	paragraph(s) of Schedules to the Companies Acts, or IFRSs or IASs or FRSs, or SSAPs, or FREDs, or EDs, or DPs, or text
PPE	property, plant and equipment
US SEC	US Securities and Exchange Commission
SIC	Standing Interpretation Committee of the IASC (see IFRIC)
SPE	special purpose entity
UK	United Kingdom
US	United States of America

© 2012 PricewaterhouseCoopers LLP. All rights reserved.

段落（公司法、国际财务报告准则、国际会计准则、财务报告准则、会计实务准则、财务报告征求意见稿、征求意见稿、讨论稿或文章中的段落）

不动产、工厂和设备

美国证券交易委员会

国际会计准则委员会的常设解释委员会（参见 IFRIC）

特殊目的主体

英国

美国

ⓒ 2012 普华永道（PricewaterhouseCoopers）版权所有。

Content

IFRS Manual of Accounting

目　录

国际财务报告准则实务指引

Chapter 15 Intangible assets

Contents

© 2012 PricewaterhouseCoopers LLP. All rights reserved.

第十五章　无形资产

目　录

ⓒ 2012 普华永道（PricewaterhouseCoopers）版权所有。

© 2012 PricewaterhouseCoopers LLP. All rights reserved.

ⓒ 2012 普华永道（PricewaterhouseCoopers）版权所有。

Introduction

15.1 This chapter considers the accounting requirements affecting the different categories of intangible assets, which include:

- Separately acquired intangible assets.
- Intangible assets acquired as part of a business combination.
- Intangible assets acquired in exchange for non-monetary assets.
- Intangible assets acquired by way of government grant.
- Internally generated intangible assets.

The chapter covers the following matters:

- Identifying intangible assets.
- Recognition criteria.
- Initial measurement of intangible assets and subsequent expenditure.
- Measurement subsequent to initial recognition.
- Accounting for finite and infinite useful lives.
- De-recognition of intangible assets.
- Disclosure requirements.

15.2 This chapter considers the requirements of IAS 38, 'Intangible assets', published in 1998 by the IASC and revised in 2004 as well as the specific provisions relating to web site costs that are contained in SIC 32, 'Web site costs'. There are a number of consequential amendments to IAS 38 as a result of IFRS 3 (revised 2008) and from the IASB's annual improvements project. This chapter considers the currently applicable requirements of IAS 38, but also sets out the changes and when they become applicable.

15.3 The changes that arise from IFRS 3, 'Business combinations', are

© 2012 PricewaterhouseCoopers LLP. All rights reserved.

引言

15.1　针对不同类别的无形资产，本章考虑了影响它们的会计要求，这些类别包括：

■ 单独购买的无形资产。

■ 作为业务合并的一部分而取得的无形资产。

■ 通过非货币性资产交换而取得的无形资产。

■ 通过政府补助的方式而取得的无形资产。

■ 自创的无形资产。

本章包括以下事项：

■ 识别无形资产。

■ 确认的标准。

■ 无形资产的初始计量和后续支出。

■ 初始确认后的计量。

■ 使用寿命确定和不确定的会计处理。

■ 无形资产的终止确认。

■ 披露要求。

15.2　本章考虑了国际会计准则委员会 1998 年发布、2004 年修订的《国际会计准则第 38 号——无形资产》（IAS 38）的要求，以及常设解释委员会《解释公告第 32 号——网站成本》（SIC 32）中包含的与网站成本相关的具体规定。由于国际财务报告准则第 3 号（IFRS 3）（2008 年修订版）和国际会计准则理事会年度改进项目对 IAS 38 进行了大量修改，本章既考虑了目前适用的 IAS 38 的要求，也阐明了变化及其适用时间。

15.3　源于《国际财务报告准则第 3 号——业务合并》的变化对于 2009 年 7

ⓒ 2012 普华永道（PricewaterhouseCoopers）版权所有。

prospectively applicable to annual periods beginning on or after 1 July 2009. If an entity early adopts IFRS 3 for annual reporting periods beginning on or after 30 June 2007, the amendments to IAS 38 should be applied to the earlier period. The amendments changed the application of the probability criterion for separately acquired intangible assets and intangible assets acquired in a business combination. The presumption that the fair value of intangible assets acquired in a business combination can be reliably measured may no longer be rebutted and there is further guidance given on re-acquired rights (see chapter 25).

objective

15.4 The objective of IAS 38 is to set out the accounting treatment of intangible assets that are not dealt with by other standards. The standard specifies the rules for recognition, measurement and disclosure of intangible assets. [IAS 38 para 1].

Scope

15.5 IAS 38 applies to all intangible assets except:

- Intangible assets that are within the scope of another standard, including:
  - Intangible assets held-for-sale in the ordinary course of business dealt with in IAS 2, 'Inventories' – see chapter 20, and IAS 11, 'Construction contracts' – see chapter 9.
  - Deferred tax assets (dealt with in IAS 12, 'Income taxes' – see chapter 13).
  - Leases that fall within the scope of IAS 17, 'Leases' – see chapter 19.
  - Assets arising from employee benefits (dealt with by IAS 19, 'Employee benefits' – see chapter 11).
  - Goodwill (dealt with in IFRS 3, 'Business combinations' – see chapter 25).

© 2012 PricewaterhouseCoopers LLP. All rights reserved.

月 1 日或之后开始的会计年度未来适用。如果主体在 2007 年 6 月 30 日或之后开始的报告年度提前采用 IFRS 3，则对于 IAS 38 的修改也应当于同一的更早期间应用。这些修改改变了可能性标准在单独购买的无形资产和在业务合并中取得的无形资产中的应用。在业务合并中取得的无形资产的公允价值能够可靠计量的假设不再是可以推翻的，而且对于重新购得的权利提供了更多指导（参见第二十五章）。

目标

15.4　IAS 38 的目标是对没有在其他准则涉及的无形资产的会计处理进行规范。该准则明确了无形资产的确认、计量和披露的规则。[IAS 38 第 1 段]。

范围

15.5　IAS 38 适用于所有无形资产，除了：

- 在另一项准则范围内的无形资产，包括：
  - 在正常经营活动中的持有以备出售的无形资产，在《国际会计准则第 2 号——存货》（参见第二十章）和《国际会计准则第 11 号——建造合同》（参见第九章）中规范。
  - 递延所得税资产在《国际会计准则第 12 号——所得税》中规范（参见第十三章）。
  - 《国际会计准则第 17 号——租赁》范围内的租赁（参见第十九章）。
  - 来自职工福利的资产由《国际会计准则第 19 号——职工福利》中规范（参见第十一章）。
  - 商誉在《国际财务报告准则第 3 号——业务合并》中规范（参见第二十五章）。

ⓒ 2012 普华永道（PricewaterhouseCoopers）版权所有。

- Deferred acquisition costs and intangible assets arising from an insurer's contractual rights under insurance contracts (dealt with in IFRS 4, 'Insurance contracts'). IAS 38's disclosure requirements however, do apply to these intangible assets.

- Non-current intangible assets classified as held-for-sale in accordance with IFRS 5, 'Non-current assets held-for-sale and discontinued operations'—see chapter 26.

- Financial assets as defined in IAS 32, 'Financial instruments: Presentation'—see Manual of Accounting-Financial instruments.

- Exploration and evaluation assets (dealt with by IFRS 6, 'Exploration for and evaluation of mineral resources').

- Expenditure on the development and extraction of, minerals, oil, natural gas and similar non-regenerative resources. This scope exemption only applies to the exploration phase of a non-regenerative resource. Once the technical feasibility and commercial viability of extracting the non-regenerative resource has been determined (the development phase), the recognition criteria in IAS 38 for internally generated costs will need to be applied. [IFRS 6 pares 5, 10, BC 28].

[IAS 38 pares 2, 3].

15.6 Expenditure on advertising, training, start-up and research and development (R&D) are some of the activities that are within the standard's scope. The standard notes that although R&D may result eventually in a physical asset, it is directed primarily to the development of knowledge and any physical asset as a result of this is secondary in importance to the intangible element, that is, the knowledge embodied in the physical asset. Therefore, development expenditure is treated as an intangible asset. [IAS 38 para 5].

15.7 The underlying asset in a lease may be intangible or tangible in nature. After initial recognition of the asset in a lease transaction, the asset is accounted for under IAS 38 if it is intangible in nature. Such assets may include licensing agreements for films, videos, plays, manuscripts, patents and copyrights, all of which are specifically excluded from the scope of IAS 17, 'Leases'. [IAS 17

© 2012 PricewaterhouseCoopers LLP. All rights reserved.

- 在《国际财务报告准则第 4 号——保险合同》规范的保险合同中，由承保人的合同权利产生的递延取得成本和无形资产。然而，IAS 38 的披露要求确实适用于这些无形资产。

- 根据《国际财务报告准则第 5 号——持有待售的非流动资产和终止经营》分类为持有待售的非流动无形资产—参见第二十六章。

- 《国际会计准则第 32 号——金融工具：列报》定义的金融资产—参见《会计实务指引——金融工具》。
- 勘探和评价资产在《国际财务报告准则第 6 号——矿产资源的勘探和评价》中规范。
- 矿物、石油、天然气和类似的不可再生资源的开发和采掘支出。该范围免除仅适用于不可再生资源的勘探阶段。当采掘不可再生资源的技术可行性和商业可行性确定时（开发阶段），需要应用 IAS 38 中的内部产生成本的确认标准。[IFRS 6 第 5、10 段、结论基础第 28 段]。

[IAS 38 第 2、3 段]。

15.6 广告、培训、开办以及研究和开发支出是该准则范围内的一些活动。该准则表明，虽然研究和开发可能最终导致产生一项实物资产，但其主要指向知识的开发，作为其后果所产生的任何实物资产相对于无形资产，即实物资产中包含的知识，都是次要的。因此，开发支出作为一项无形资产处理。[IAS 38 第 5 段]。

15.7 一项租赁中的标的资产在性质上可能是无形的，也可能是有形的。在一项租赁交易中，在资产初始确认后，如果性质是无形的，则根据 IAS 38 进行会计处理。诸如此类的资产可能包括电影、视频、戏剧、手稿、专利和版权等的许可使用协议，所有这些明确排除在《国际会计准则第 17 号——租赁》之外。[IAS 17 第 2 段，IAS 38 第 6 段]。

ⓒ 2012 普华永道（PricewaterhouseCoopers）版权所有。

para 2, IAS 38 para 6].

15.8 The distinction between an intangible asset and a financial asset may be difficult to determine in practice. Generally where an entity has purchased the contractual right to receive cash, it would have acquired a financial asset as opposed to an intangible asset. [IAS 39 para 11]. Another area where it is necessary to distinguish between a financial asset and an intangible asset is the area of service concession arrangements, which are in the scope of IFRIC 12, 'Service concession arrangements'. See chapter 33.

Example – Purchase of the rights to a proportion of a football club's revenue as opposed to the rights to sell the underlying tickets

An entity that purchases the rights to a proportion of the revenue that a football club generates from ticket sales will generally have acquired a financial asset as opposed to an intangible asset. Where the entity has no discretion over the pricing or selling of the tickets and is only entitled to the cash generated from the sale of tickets, this would represent a financial asset, being a contractual right to receive cash. If on the other hand an entity has purchased the rights to sell tickets for a football club and was responsible for selling the tickets itself to generate revenue, this would represent an intangible asset.

15.9 IAS 38 excludes from its scope expenditure on certain specialised activities such as exploration for, development and extraction of, minerals, oil, natural gas and similar non-regenerative resources in the exploration phase and certain expenditure relating to insurance contracts. These activities are excluded from the scope of the standard as they are so specialised that they give rise to accounting issues that need to be dealt with in a different way. However, the standard does apply to any other non-specialised intangible assets used in such activities, such as computer software and to other expenditures such as start-up costs. [IAS 38 para 7].

Identifying intangible assets

15.10 Intangible assets may be purchased separately or as part of a business

© 2012 PricewaterhouseCoopers LLP. All rights reserved.

15.8 一项无形资产和一项金融资产之间的区别在实务中可能很难确定。一般说来，在一个主体已经购买了收取现金的合同权利的情况下，它应该是购买了一项金融资产，而不是一项无形资产。［IAS 39 第 11 段］。另一个要求在一项金融资产和一项无形资产之间进行区分的领域是服务特许权协议，由《国际财务报告解释公告第 12 号——服务特许权协议》规范。（参见第三十三章）。

示例——购买收取足球俱乐部部分收入的权利与购买出售标的票的权利

一个主体购买了一项权利，即收取足球俱乐部球票销售的部分收入，一般来说，主体获得了一项金融资产，而不是一项无形资产。在主体对球票的定价或出售没有自行决定权，而仅获得销售球票产生的现金的权利的情况下，则应该会将其视为一项金融资产，即收取现金的合同权利。另一方面，如果一个主体购买了为一个足球俱乐部销售球票的权利，并且负责自行销售球票以产生收入，则应该会将其视为一项无形资产。

15.9 IAS 38 从其范围中排除了某些专业化活动（例如在勘探阶段对矿产、石油、天然气和类似不可再生资源的勘探、开发和采掘）的支出，以及与保险合同相关的某些支出。由于这些活动专业性很强，它们所产生的会计问题需要以一种不同的方式处理，因此这些活动从该准则范围中被排除。然而，该准则适用于这些活动中的任何其他非专业化无形资产（例如计算机软件）和其他支出（例如开办成本）。［IAS 38 第 7 段］。

辨认无形资产

15.10 无形资产可以单独购买，或者作为业务合并的一部分取得、以其他非

ⓒ 2012 普华永道（PricewaterhouseCoopers）版权所有。

combination, exchanged for other non-monetary assets, acquired by way of government grant or created by an entity across the whole spectrum of its activities. IAS 38 gives examples of categories of expenditure on scientific or technical knowledge, design and implementation of new systems or processes, licences, intellectual property, market knowledge and trademarks. These categories include specific items such as computer software, patents, copyrights, motion picture films, customer lists, mortgage servicing rights, fishing licences, import quotas, franchises, customer or supplier relationships, customer loyalty programmes, market share and marketing rights. [IAS 38 para 9]. This is by no means an exhaustive list. IFRS 3, 'Business combinations', contains a further list of types of intangible asset that may be acquired in a business combination, which is discussed in paragraph 15.85 onwards.

15.11 The criteria that have to be satisfied before an item qualifies as an intangible asset under IAS 38 are discussed below. However, some items, such as internally generated intangible assets, may not be recognised as assets under the standard. Recognition is discussed from paragraph 15.26 below. Where an expenditure either does not qualify as an asset, or cannot be recognised as such, it is written off to the income statement as incurred.

Definition

15.12 IAS 38 defines an intangible asset as "*an identifiable non-monetary asset without physical substance*". [IAS 38 para 8]. The key characteristics of an intangible asset are that they:

- are resources controlled by the entity from which the entity expects to derive future economic benefits;
- lack physical substance; and
- are identifiable to be distinguished from goodwill.

15.13 The first of the key characteristics above establishes that there is an asset. An asset is defined under IFRS as a resource controlled by an entity as a result of past events and from which future economic benefits are expected to flow to the

© 2012 PricewaterhouseCoopers LLP. All rights reserved.

货币性资产交换、通过政府补助取得，或由主体在其经营活动范围中创立。IAS 第 38 号举例说明了下列支出类别：科学或技术知识、新系统或工艺的设计和实施、许可证，知识产权、市场知识、商标。这些类别包括具体项目，例如计算机软件、专利、版权、电影胶片、客户名单、抵押贷款服务权、捕鱼许可证、进口配额、特许权、客户或供应商关系、客户忠诚度计划、市场份额、营销权。[IAS 第 38 号第 9 段]。以上绝不是完整的清单。IFRS 第 3 号“业务合并”进一步列举了于业务合并中可能取得的无形资产类型，这在后面的第 15.85 段进行了讨论。

15.11 下面将讨论一个项目在 IAS 第 38 号下能够符合无形资产资格前必须满足的标准。然而，某些项目（例如内部产生的无形资产）在该准则下不一定能确认为资产。下面的第 15.26 段将讨论“确认”。如果一项支出不符合资产资格、或不能被确认为资产，则在发生时计入利润表。

定义

15.12 IAS 第 38 号将无形资产定义为“*没有实物形态的可辨认非货币性资产*”。[IAS 第 38 号第 8 段]。无形资产的关键特征如下：

- 是主体控制的资源，主体预期从其获得未来经济利益；
- 缺乏实物形态；
- 可辨认，从而与商誉区分开来。

15.13 以上第一项关键特征表明资产的存在。根据 IFRS，资产定义为主体由于过去事项而控制的资源，并且预期将从其获得未来经济利益流向主体。该定义本身包含两项要素：控制权和未来经济利益的预期。如果不能通过控

ⓒ 2012 普华永道（PricewaterhouseCoopers）版权所有。

entity. This definition itself contains two elements: control and expectation of future economic benefits. If the control test is not passed, no asset can be recognised.

Control

15.14 Control exists where an entity has the power to obtain the future economic benefits from an underlying resource and to restrict the access of others to those benefits. It is usually evidenced by legally enforceable contractual or other rights, such as legal title or a licence. It is more difficult to demonstrate control in the absence of legal rights. The entity may be able to control the future economic benefits in some other way, for example control over the benefits of know-how may be attained through secrecy. [IAS 38 para 13].

15.15 An entity is usually not considered to exercise sufficient control over the expected future economic benefits over its workforce for the workforce to be recognised as an intangible asset. [IAS 38 para 15].

Example – Sign-on bonuses paid to new employees

An entity is involved in retail banking. The bank's strategy is to diversify its services and expand its customer base. Management plans to establish an investment banking division. The bank is aware that it will need to recruit high-profile employees in order to attract new business quickly. The bank has made offers of employment to ten individuals. These offers have been accepted. The contracts are for a five year period and include substantial sign-on bonuses, without any claw back if the employee leaves during the term of the contract. The bank would like to recognise an intangible asset in respect the sign-on payments.

The sign-on payment may not be recognised as an intangible asset and should be expensed when incurred. The sign-on payment has not established a right to a future benefit over which the bank has control, as the new employees may leave during the contract period and use their skills elsewhere. An intangible asset could be recognised if there was an enforceable non-compete clause in the contract, enabling the entity to recover the sign-on payment in

© 2012 PricewaterhouseCoopers LLP. All rights reserved.

制权测试，则不能确认资产。

控制

15.14　如果主体有权力从标的资源获得未来经济利益并且限制他人获得这些利益，则主体拥有控制权。控制权一般由可依法执行的合同权利或其他权利证明，例如权利证书或许可证。如果缺乏权利证书，则证明控制权更加困难。主体也许能以其他方式控制未来经济利益，例如通过保密程序而获得对技术诀窍利益的控制权。[IAS 第 38 号第 13 段]。

15.15　主体通常不认为能够对劳动力所带来的预期未来经济利益行使足够的控制权以使得劳动力被确认为无形资产。[IAS 第 38 号第 15 段]。

示例——向新雇员支付的签约奖金

一家主体从事的是零售银行业务。该银行的战略是服务多样化和扩展客户基础。管理层计划建立投资银行部。该银行意识到需要雇用高素质的雇员以迅速获得新业务。银行雇用了十名雇员。合同期限为五年，包含高额的签约奖金。如果雇员在合同期间离职，无需支付任何补偿。该银行希望将签约奖金确认为无形资产。

签约奖金不能确认为无形资产，并应当在发生时费用化。签约奖金并没有为银行建立起对未来利益的权利的控制，因为新雇员可以在合同期间离职，然后在别处使用他们的技能。如果在合同中存在可执行的非竞争条款，使得该主体能够在雇员离职时收回签约奖金并使得竞争者不能使用该雇员，则可以确认无形资产。

ⓒ 2012 普华永道（PricewaterhouseCoopers）版权所有。

customer lists as both are resources controlled by the entity from which the entity expects to derive future economic benefit.

The entity should recognise the customer list acquired in the business combination as an intangible asset, provided its fair value can be reliably measured. The ability to sell the list or to exchange it provides evidence that it is separable from the goodwill arising in the acquisition.

The entity may not, however, recognise an intangible asset for the internally-generated customer list despite the fact that it clearly has satisfied the control criteria. IAS 38 specifically prohibits an entity from recognising internally generated intangible assets other than development expenditure that meets the conditions in the standard for recognition. This is because the cost of the list cannot be distinguished from the cost of developing the business as a whole. This is discussed further under 'Internally generated intangible assets' below (para 15.42).

Future economic benefits

15.17 Future economic benefits may include revenue from the sale of goods or the provision of services, cost savings, or other benefits derived by the entity from the use of the asset. [IAS 38 para 17]. The standard assumes that in certain types of transaction, such as the separate acquisition of an intangible asset or acquisition of intangible assets in a business combination, this element is always satisfied. See paragraphs 15.34 – 15.35 for further discussion.

Example – Capitalising expenses incurred

Entity A has acquired a license to distribute a branded fizzy drink in a new geographical area. The cost of the acquisition can be capitalised as an intangible asset in this example as it will lead to future economic benefit for entity A.

Lack of physical substance

15.18 Another essential characteristic of an intangible asset is that it lacks

© 2012 PricewaterhouseCoopers LLP. All rights reserved.

该供应商希望将以上客户名单确认为无形资产。

针对在业务合并中取得的客户名单，既然其公允价值能够可靠计量，该主体应当将它确认为无形资产。能够出售名单或将其用于交换证明它能够与收购中产生的商誉分离。

然而，针对内部产生的客户名单，尽管它明显满足控制标准，该主体不能将其确认为无形资产。除开发支出之外，IAS 第 38 号特别禁止主体确认除满足确认条件的开发支出之外的内部产生的无形资产。这是因为名单的成本不能与开发业务的整个成本区分开来。下面的“内部产生的无形资产”部分中将有进一步的讨论（第 15. 42 段）。

未来经济利益

15. 17　未来经济利益可能包括销售货物或提供服务的收入、成本节约，或主体从资产使用中获得的其他利益。［IAS 第 38 号第 17 段］。该准则假设在某些类型的交易中（例如单独购买无形资产或在业务合并中取得无形资产），该要素总能得到满足。参见第 15. 34—15. 35 段中的更多讨论。

示例——将发生的费用资本化

主体 A 购买了在一个新的地理区域分销某品牌发泡饮料的许可证。在此例中，购买成本可以资本化为无形资产，因为它将为主体 A 带来未来经济利益。

缺乏实物形态

15. 18　无形资产的另一项必要特征是缺乏实物形态。然而，可能很难将资产

ⓒ 2012 普华永道（PricewaterhouseCoopers）版权所有。

physical substance. It may, however, be difficult to categorise an asset as tangible or intangible. An intangible asset is often contained in or on a physical substance. Examples are a compact disc that contains computer software, legal documentation that evidences a patent or a licence, a building to which a trading licence attaches, a cassette containing a film recording or a computer system containing a database. The physical and non-physical elements may be incapable of separation in these instances and judgement is required to determine which element is the more significant. If the tangible element is the more significant, the asset should be treated as a tangible fixed asset and vice versa. [IAS 38 para 4].

15.19 The standard gives an example of the decision-making process in the situation where computer software and a physical asset are involved. If, for example, a machine cannot operate without a particular piece of software the software is regarded as an integral part of the machine and is treated as a tangible asset. By contrast, where a tangible asset is incidental to an intangible asset, both the tangible and intangible elements are treated as an intangible asset. This would include situations where the tangible asset is merely a means of containing the software or other intangible asset and has no other use, for example the compact disc on which software is contained.

15.20 There may also be situations where, although the tangible and intangible elements cannot operate independently of each other, their costs are each significant. It may be appropriate to account for each element separately in this case. For example, a database may be contained on expensive computer hardware and the costs of the hardware may be separately identifiable from those of the database. Each element may have a different useful life, for example the hardware may become obsolete and the database may be transferred to another computer system. It is appropriate in this situation to account separately for the two components of the computer database, classifying the hardware as tangible and the database itself as intangible, because they are both significant components.

Identifiability

15.21 The third essential characteristic of an intangible asset is that it must be identifiable. An intangible asset is identifiable when it:

© 2012 PricewaterhouseCoopers LLP. All rights reserved.

分类为有形资产或无形资产。无形资产通常以实物形态为载体。例如，包含计算机软件的光盘、证明专利或许可的法律文件、附带交易许可证的建筑物、录有电影的录像带，或包含数据库的计算机系统。在这些情况下，实物和非实物要素可能无法分开，需要判断哪项要素更为重要。如果有形要素更为重要，则该资产应当视为有形固定资产，反之亦然。[IAS 第 38 号第 4 段]。

15.19　该准则提供了涉及计算机软件和实物资产的决策过程的例子。比如，若一款机器在没有特定软件的情况下就不能运行，则该软件视为该机器的必要部分，因此视为有形资产。相反地，若有形资产对于无形资产来说是附带的，则有形和无形要素都被为无形资产。这会包括以下情况：有形资产仅为承载软件或其他无形资产的媒体而没有其他用途，例如承载软件的光盘。

15.20　可能还有以下情况：虽然有形和无形要素不能脱离对方独立运行，但各自的成本都很高。在这种情况下，分别处理个别要素是适宜的。例如，数据库可能包含在昂贵的计算机硬件中，而硬件的成本可以与数据库的成本分开辨认。每项要素可能有不同的使用寿命，例如硬件可能废弃，而该数据库可以转移至另一个计算机系统。在这种情况下，分别处理计算机数据库的两项要素是适宜的，即将硬件归类为有形资产，将数据库本身归类为无形资产，因为它们都是重要的组成部分。

可辨认性

15.21　无形资产的第三项必要特征是它的“可辨认性”。在以下情况中，无形资产是可辨认的：

ⓒ 2012 普华永道（PricewaterhouseCoopers）版权所有。

- is separable, that is it is capable of being separated or divided from the entity and sold, transferred, licensed, rented or exchanged, either individually or together with a related contract, asset or liability; or
- arises from contractual or other legal rights, regardless of whether the rights are transferable or separable from the entity or from other rights and obligations.

[IAS 38 para 12].

15. 22 Even if an asset is not individually separable, it is regarded as separable if it meets the definition of separability when combined with a related contract, asset or liability.

15. 23 For physical assets identifiability is straightforward, because they can be seen. For intangible assets identifiability is more difficult and requires clear and practicable principles. Intangible assets that can be separately identified are recognised separately from goodwill in a business combination.

15. 24 Intangible assets that can be separated and sold, individually or with another asset, are deemed to meet the criterion for identifiability. However, assets that arise from contractual or legal rights are also identifiable even if they cannot be separated from the business. [IAS 38 pares BC9, BC10]. For example, in some jurisdictions, some licences within the business may not be transferable except when the business is being sold as a whole.

15. 25 An asset may not, on its own, be separable or arise from contractual or legal rights. However, if there are exchange transactions in such assets, such as the sale of a portfolio of non-contractual customer relationships, they are deemed to meet the criterion for identifiability. Exchange transactions in the same or similar assets, would provide evidence that the entity had control and that the item was separable. [IAS 38 pares BC11 – 14]. For example, in some jurisdictions, some licences within the business may not be transferable except when the business is being sold as a whole.

Example – Maps of distribution network which cannot be sold or exchanged

An entity is involved in telecommunications and has an extensive distribution network that requires maintenance. Management maintains maps of the

© 2012 PricewaterhouseCoopers LLP. All rights reserved.

■ 可分离，即能够与主体分离并单独或与相关合同、资产或负债一起出售、转让、许可、出租或交换；或

■ 从合同权利或其他法律权利产生，无论这些权利是否能够转让，或是否能够与主体或其他权利和义务分离。

[IAS 第 38 号第 12 段]。

15.22 即使一项资产不可单独分离，如果它与相关合同、资产或负债合在一起时满足可分离性的定义，则它也被视为可分离的。

15.23 对于实物资产来说，可辨认性很明显，因为这些资产是能够被看见的。对于无形资产来说，可辨认性更加困难，需要清楚和可操作的原则。能够单独辨认的无形资产在业务合并中与商誉分开确认。

15.24 可分离并单独或与另一资产共同出售的无形资产被认定为满足可辨认性标准。然而，即使它们无法从业务中分离出来，产生于合同权利或法律权利的资产也是可辨认的。[IAS 第 38 号第 BC9、BC10 段]。例如，在某些辖区，业务中包括的一些许可证不可以转让，除非和整个业务一起出售。

15.25 一项资产自身可能不是可分离的或从合同权利或法律权利中产生的。然而，如果发生该类资产的交换交易（例如出售非合同性客户关系组合），则该类资产被认定为满足可辨认性标准。相同或类似资产的交换交易会证明主体拥有控制权并且该项目是可分离的。[IAS 第 38 号第 BC11—14 段]。例如，在某些辖区，业务中包括的一些许可证不可以转让，除非和整个业务一起出售。

示例——不能出售或交换的经销网络图

一家从事电信业务的主体，拥有广泛但需要维护的经销网络。管理人员以硬拷贝形式维护着经销体系图，使维护人员能够辨认和定位构成体系

ⓒ 2012 普华永道（PricewaterhouseCoopers）版权所有。

distribution system in hard copy form that enables maintenance crews to identify and locate the assets that form the system. The entity incurred substantial costs in developing these maps. The maps could not be sold or exchanged, as they are only of value to the entity. The entity would like to recognise an asset in respect of the expected future economic benefits to be derived from the maps.

Although the maps are not separable, management has control over the intellectual property that the maps represent. If a third party uses the maps without permission from management, the third party will be in breach of copyright law. The intellectual property, therefore, arises from contractual or legal rights and the criterion for identifiability is met. Economic benefits will further flow from the savings in maintenance costs that the entity will experience from having access to the maps. The costs incurred to develop the maps may, therefore, be recognised as an internally generated intangible asset (provided that all the criteria for capitalisation as development expenditure have been met). See paragraph 15.53 for the criteria for capitalisation of development expenditure.

Recognition

General rules

15.26 An item should be recognised in the financial statements as an intangible asset if it meets the definition of an intangible asset and it meets both the recognition criteria that it is probable that future economic benefits will flow to the entity and the cost of the asset can be reliably measured. [IAS 38 para 21]. The overriding recognition criteria apply to both initial costs and subsequent expenditure incurred in acquiring or internally generating an intangible asset. [IAS 38 para 18]. If the recognition criteria are not met, costs must be expensed.

15.27 'Probable', as used in 'probable economic benefit' is not defined in IAS 38. However, it is defined within other international standards. IAS 37 defines

© 2012 PricewaterhouseCoopers LLP. All rights reserved.

的资产。主体在开发这些体系图时产生了高昂的成本。这些体系图不能出售或交换，因为它们仅对该主体有价值。该主体希望将这些体系图能够带来的预期未来经济利益确认为资产。

虽然这些体系图是不可分离的，但管理层拥有对这些体系图所体现的知识产权的控制权。如果第三方未经管理层允许而使用这些体系图，第三方将违反版权法。因此，这些知识产权来自合同权利或法律权利，满足可辨认性标准。经济利益将来自主体由于拥有这些体系图而节约的维护成本。所以，开发体系图产生的成本可以确认为内部产生的无形资产（前提是满足开发支出资本化的所有标准）。参见第 15.53 段中的开发支出资本化的标准。

确认

总则

15.26　如果一个项目符合无形资产的定义以及同时满足以下两项确认标准，则应当在财务报表中确认为无形资产：未来经济利益很可能流向主体；资产成本能够可靠计量。［IAS 第 38 号第 21 段］。这些最重要的确认标准对于购买或内部产生无形资产时产生的初始成本和后续支出都适用。［IAS 第 38 号第 18 段］。如果不符合确认标准，则必须将成本费用化。

15.27　“很可能产生的经济利益”中的“很可能”在 IAS 第 38 号中没有定义。然而，在其他国际准则中对其进行了定义。IAS 第 37 号将“很可能”定

ⓒ 2012 普华永道（PricewaterhouseCoopers）版权所有。

'probable' as 'more likely than not'. It would seem reasonable to use this definition when considering what is probable for the purpose of interpreting the above requirement. Therefore, if management consider it more likely than not that the expected future economic benefits will flow to the entity, and this can be substantiated, then this criterion will be met.

15.28 An entity should assess the probability of expected future economic benefits using reasonable and supportable assumptions. These assumptions should represent management's best estimate of the set of economic conditions that will prevail over the asset's useful life. [IAS 38 para 22]. Judgement is required in assessing the degree of certainty to attach to the flow of economic benefits expected from the asset's use based on evidence available at the date of initial recognition. Management should place greater reliance on external evidence. [IAS 38 para 23].

15.29 The standard does not go into any greater detail than this on how the expected future economic benefits should be assessed. However, comparison may be made with IAS 36, 'Impairment of assets', which contains a similar requirement in respect of determining an asset's value in use. IAS 36 states:

"*In assessing value in use an entity shall*:

(*a*) *base cash flow projections on reasonable and supportable assumptions that represent management's best estimate of the range of economic conditions that will exist over the remaining useful life of the asset. Greater weight shall be given to external evidence*…" [IAS 36 para 33].

In assessing the future economic benefits attributable to an intangible asset, the guidance in IAS 36 may be helpful, see chapter 18. If the asset will generate economic benefits only when combined with other assets, the IAS 36 concept of cash generating units should be applied. [IAS 38 para 60].

15.30 The reference to the need to give greater weight to external evidence is important. Exchange transactions are referred to throughout the standard as providing evidence of the separability of intangible assets. Exchange transactions may also provide external evidence of the expected future economic benefits, but other external evidence might include industry forecasts, market and competitor

© 2012 PricewaterhouseCoopers LLP. All rights reserved.

义为“与不发生相比，更有可能发生”。看来为理解上述要求而考虑什么是“很可能”时，使用该定义是合理的。因此，如果管理层认为预期的未来经济利益更有可能流向主体，并且可以证实，则符合该标准。

15.28　主体应当使用合理和可支持的假设评价预期未来经济利益的可能性。这些假设应当体现管理层对于资产使用寿命期间经济状况的最佳估计。[IAS 第 38 号第 22 段]。在根据初始确认日期可获得的证据评价预期的资产使用经济利益流的确定程度时，需要进行判断。管理层应当更多地依靠外部证据。[IAS 第 38 号第 23 段]。

15.29　关于如何评价预期的未来经济利益，该准则未提供更多细节。不过，可以与 IAS 第 36 号“资产减值”进行比照。在确定资产使用价值方面，IAS 第 36 号“资产减值”包含类似的要求。IAS 第 36 号规定：

“*在评价使用价值时，主体应当：*

（*a*）*根据合理和可支持的假设进行现金流预测，这些假设体现管理层对于资产剩余使用寿命期间经济状况范围的最佳估计。应当更加重视外部证据*……”[IAS 第 36 号第 33 段]。

在评价无形资产产生的未来经济利益时，IAS 第 36 号中的指导可以提供帮助，参见第十八章。如果资产仅在与其他资产结合时才能产生经济利益，则应当应用 IAS 第 36 号中的现金产出单元概念。[IAS 第 38 号第 60 段]。

15.30　应当更加重视外部证据这一条十分重要。整个准则都表明交换交易提供了无形资产可分离性的证据。交换交易也可提供预期未来经济利益的外部证据，不过其他外部证据可能包括：行业预测、外部专家提供的市场和竞争者分析，以及有关预期通货膨胀和国家特定的增长率的一般信息。

ⓒ 2012 普华永道（PricewaterhouseCoopers）版权所有。

analysis provided by external experts as well as general information on expected inflation and country growth rates.

15. 31 An entity may obtain an intangible asset in a number of ways:

- By separate acquisition for monetary or other consideration.
- As part of a business combination.
- By exchange for other non-monetary assets.
- By way of government grant.
- By developing or generating the asset internally.

15. 32 The criteria for recognition are applied somewhat differently in each of these situations. This is because the extent and reliability of the evidence available to the entity in determining whether or not the criteria are met vary depending on which situation is involved. For example, in each of the first three situations there is an exchange transaction, which gives evidence that economic benefits are likely to flow to the entity.

15. 33 The nature of many intangible assets is that there are often no additions to the asset or replacements of parts of it. Therefore, most subsequent expenditure is likely to be incurred to maintain the asset and will not usually meet the criteria for recognition as an asset. It is often difficult to attribute subsequent expenditure to a particular intangible asset rather than to the business as a whole. Most subsequent expenditure will, therefore, not qualify as an asset and will be expensed as incurred. The standard requires specifically that subsequent expenditure on brands, mastheads, publishing titles, customer lists and items that are similar in substance is always expensed as incurred. This applies whether the asset was originally acquired or internally generated and is because such subsequent expenditure cannot be distinguished from expenditure to develop the business as a whole. [IAS 38 para 20]. Subsequent expenditure on artistic-related, contract-based and technology-based intangible assets may also have to be expensed if it does not meet the recognition criteria.

Assets acquired separately or as part of a business combination

15. 34 The probability recognition criterion is always assumed to be met for

© 2012 PricewaterhouseCoopers LLP. All rights reserved.

15.31　主体可以通过许多方式获得无形资产：

- 以货币或其他对价单独购买。
- 作为业务合并的一部分。
- 以其他非货币资产交换。
- 通过政府补助。
- 内部开发或产生。

15.32　在这些情况中对确认标准的应用略有不同。这是因为在确定是否满足标准时，取决于涉及哪种情况，主体可获得的证据的范围和可靠性会有所不同。例如，前三种情况通过交换交易来证明经济利益可能流向主体。

15.33　许多无形资产的性质是通常没有增加资产或替换其一部分。因此，后续支出大部分是用来维护资产的，因此通常不符合资产的确认标准。将后续支出归属于特定无形资产而不是整个业务通常很困难。因此，大多数后续支出将不符合资产资格，并在发生时被费用化。该准则特别要求品牌、刊头、出版标题、客户名单以及本质上类似的项目的后续支出都应在发生时费用化。这对于无论是购买还是内部产生的资产都适用，因为这些后续支出无法与开发整个业务的支出区分开来。[IAS 第 38 号第 20 段]。与艺术相关、基于合同和基于技术的无形资产的后续支出如果不满足确认标准，也不得不被费用化。

单独购买或作为业务合并的一部分取得的资产

15.34　单独购买的无形资产总是被认为满足可能性确认标准。支付的价格反

ⓒ 2012 普华永道（PricewaterhouseCoopers）版权所有。

separately acquired intangible assets. The price paid reflects expectations about the probability that the future economic benefits of the asset will flow to the entity. The greater the price paid the higher the expectations of future economic benefits to be derived from the asset. [IAS 38 para 25].

15.35 A business combination is also an exchange transaction. The price paid in a business combination reflects expectations about the future economic benefits expected from the acquired business as a whole. It does not directly reflect expectations about individual assets acquired as part of the combination. All intangible assets that can be reliably measured are recognised at fair value. [IFRS 3 para 37]. As noted in paragraph 15.85, under the revised IFRS 3 and the consequential amendment to IAS 38, the reliability of measurement criterion will always be met for intangible assets acquired in a business combination. The fair value of an intangible asset, like an arm's length price, reflects expectations about the probability that the future economic benefits of the asset will flow to the entity. The probability criterion for recognition is always assumed to have been satisfied for intangible assets acquired in a business combination.

15.36 Table 15.1 is an example where an entity has recognised intangibles acquired in a business combination involving the acquisition of a medical technology company.

Table 15.1 – Recognised intangibles acquired in a business combination

BTG plc – Report and accounts – 31 March 2011

	Developed technology £m	Contractual relationships £m	In-process research and development £m	Computer software £m	Patents £m	Repurchase of contractual rights £m	Total £m
Cost							
At 1 April 2009	120.3	36.1	7.7	0.5	14.7	–	179.3
Additions	–	–	–	–	1.2	–	1.2
Disposals	–	–	–	(0.5)	(2.8)	–	(3.3)
Currency movements	(2.9)	(0.9)	–	–	(0.1)	–	(3.9)

© 2012 PricewaterhouseCoopers LLP. All rights reserved.

映了资产的未来经济利益流向主体的可能性期望。支付的价格越高，对于从资产中获得的未来经济利益的期望越高。[IAS 第 38 号第 25 段]。

15.35　业务合并也是一种交换交易。业务合并中支付的价格反映对预计从所购的整个业务获得的未来经济利益的期望。它不直接反映对作为合并的一部分而取得的各资产的期望。能够可靠计量的所有无形资产以公允价值确认。[IFRS 第 3 号第 37 段]。如第 15.85 段所述，根据 IFRS 第 3 号和相应的对 IAS 第 38 号的修订，在业务合并中取得的无形资产总是被认为满足计量可靠性标准。无形资产的公允价值（如正常价格）反映对资产的未来经济利益将会流向主体的可能性的期望。在业务合并中取得的无形资产总是被认为满足确认的可能性标准。

15.36　在表 15.1 的例子中，主体确认了在一宗涉及收购一家医药技术公司的业务合并中所取得的无形资产。

表 15.1——确认在业务合并中取得的无形资产

BTG 公共有限公司——报告和账目——2011 年 3 月 31 日

	已开发的技术 百万英镑	合同关系 百万英镑	进行中的研发 百万英镑	计算机软件 百万英镑	专利 百万英镑	合同权利回购 百万英镑	合计 百万英镑
成本							
于 2009 年 4 月 1 日	120.3	36.1	7.7	0.5	14.7	–	179.3
新增	–	–	–	–	1.2	–	1.2
处置	–	–	–	(0.5)	(2.8)	–	(3.3)
外币变动	(2.9)	(0.9)	–	–	(0.1)	–	(3.9)

ⓒ 2012 普华永道（PricewaterhouseCoopers）版权所有。

Con.

At 1 April 2010	117. 4	35. 2	7. 7	–	13. 0	–	173. 3
Additions	–	–	–	–	0. 4	9. 7	10. 1
Acquired with Biocompatibles	118. 8	6. 7	11. 0	0. 3	–	–	136. 8
Disposals	–	–	–	–	(0. 1)	–	(0. 1)
Currency movements	(6. 0)	(1. 9)	0. 1	–	(0. 1)	(0. 2)	(8. 1)
At 31 March 2011	230. 2	40. 0	18. 8	0. 3	13. 2	9. 5	312. 0

[The next paragraph is 15. 38.]

15. 38 The recognition and measurement rules for accounting for subsequent expenditure on an acquired research and development project are discussed from paragraph 15. 162.

Assets acquired in an exchange for non-monetary assets

15. 39 The probability recognition criteria for intangible assets acquired separately in exchange for a non-monetary asset is also deemed to be satisfied, as in the acquisition for monetary consideration. The asset acquired in a non-monetary exchange is measured at fair value and the fair value reflects expectations about the probability of future economic benefits flowing to the entity. However, this assumes that the exchange transaction has commercial substance. See paragraph 15. 147.

Assets acquired by way of government grant

15. 40 An intangible may be acquired free of charge, or for nominal consideration, by way of a government grant. Where an intangible asset is acquired by way of a government grant there is no exchange transaction. Assets that may be acquired through government grant include airport landing rights, emission rights, radio or television station operating licences, import licences and quotas.

15. 41 No reference is made to the application of the recognition criteria for

© 2012 PricewaterhouseCoopers LLP. All rights reserved.

续表

于2010年4月1日	117.4	35.2	7.7	—	13.0	—	173.3
新增	—	—	—	—	0.4	9.7	10.1
在收购生物相容性公司时取得	118.8	6.7	11.0	0.3	—	—	136.8
处置	—	—	—	—	(0.1)	—	(0.1)
外币变动	(6.0)	(1.9)	0.1	—	(0.1)	(0.2)	(8.1)
于2011年4月1日	230.2	40.0	18.8	0.3	13.2	9.5	312.0

[下一段落为15.38。]

15.38　购买的研发项目的后续支出的确认和计量将从第15.162段起讨论。

在非货币性资产交换中取得的资产

15.39　与以货币对价购买一样，在非货币性资产交换中单独取得的无形资产也被认定为满足可能性确认标准。在非货币性交换中取得的资产以公允价值计量，并且公允价值反映对流向主体的未来经济利益的可能性的期望。然而，这假设了交换交易具有商业实质。参见第15.147段。

通过政府补助取得的资产

15.40　无形资产可以免费或以名义对价通过政府补助取得。如果通过政府补助取得无形资产，则不存在交换交易。可以通过政府补助取得的资产包括机场着陆权、排放权、无线电台或电视台经营许可证、进口许可证和配额。

15.41　在IAS第38号中没有提及通过政府补助取得的无形资产如何应用确

© 2012 普华永道（PricewaterhouseCoopers）版权所有。

intangible assets acquired by way of a government grant in IAS 38. IAS 20, 'Government grants', states, however, that a non-monetary grant at fair value is not recognised until there is reasonable assurance that the entity will comply with the conditions attaching to it and the grant will be received. [IAS 20 para 7, 8]. Receipt of a grant does not of itself provide conclusive evidence that the conditions attaching to the grant have been or will be met.

Internally generated intangible assets

15.42 Intangible assets that are developed or generated internally must satisfy the recognition criteria if they are to be regarded as intangible assets. It is sometimes difficult to determine whether costs incurred may be recognised as an intangible asset because:

- it may be uncertain whether the costs meet the definition of an intangible asset that will generate expected future economic benefits; and
- it may not be possible to establish the asset's cost reliably or distinguish the costs attributable to such an asset from costs of maintaining or increasing the entity's internally generated goodwill or the costs of carrying out the entity's day-to-day operations.

[IAS 38 para 51].

15.43 Generally, the difficulties associated with identifying internally generated intangible assets and with satisfying the recognition and measurement criteria mean that such assets either are indistinguishable from the rest of the business or cannot be reliably measured. There are specific procedures that must, therefore, be followed to determine whether certain internally generated intangible assets can be recognised. There is an outright prohibition against recognising specific types of intangible asset where the recognition criteria can never be satisfied.

Example – Research and development costs which cannot be attributed to a specific product

A major supplier that produces confectionery has two lines of business:

© 2012 PricewaterhouseCoopers LLP. All rights reserved.

认标准。然而，IAS 第 20 号“政府补助”规定，以公允价值计量的非货币性补助时方予确认，直至能够合理确信主体将遵守该补助的附加条件并获得补助。[IAS 第 20 号第 7、8 段]。获得补助自身不能证明该补助的附加条件已经或将要满足。

内部产生的无形资产

15.42　内部开发或产生的无形资产如果要被视为无形资产必须要满足确认标准。某些时候很难确定产生的成本是否可以确认为无形资产，因为：

- 可能不能确定成本是否符合将要产生预期未来经济利益的无形资产的定义；并且
- 可能不能可靠确定资产的成本，或将归属于该资产的成本与维护或提高主体内部产生的商誉的成本或主体日常运营成本区分开来。

[IAS 第 38 号第 51 段]。

15.43　一般来说，辨认内部产生的无形资产以及满足确认和计量标准的困难来自于该类资产无法与业务的其他部分区分开来，或不能可靠计量。因此，必须按照特定程序来确定是否能够确认某些内部产生的无形资产。某些特定类型的无形资产由于永远不可能满足确认条件，因此是直接禁止确认的。

示例——不能归属于特定产品的研究和开发成本

一家大型供应商生产甜食，拥有两个业务系列：巧克力和糖果。巧克力

© 2012 普华永道（PricewaterhouseCoopers）版权所有。

chocolates and candies. The chocolates unit comprises five brands, and the candies unit has three brands. Management is continually seeking to innovate and attract new customers. It incurs expenditure related to research and development of new products, such as investigation of customer preferences, design of variations to current products and designs of new products. Research and development expenditure of C1m for the chocolates unit, and C1.6m for the candies unit was incurred during the year. The expenditure cannot be allocated separately to any specific product, but can be associated with a line of business.

The research and development costs should not be capitalised as an internally generated intangible asset. An intangible asset must be identifiable and attributable to a specific product or project in order to meet the recognition criteria for an intangible asset. Management should be able to identify the future economic benefits that will flow from each separate intangible asset that it recognises. It is not possible to meet the recognition criteria for an intangible asset if management is unable to identify the individual product or project.

15.44 The standard sets out detailed rules for determining whether an internally generated intangible asset should be recognised. These rules preclude recognition of internally generated intangible assets except development expenditures. For development expenditures, in addition to complying with the general requirements for the recognition and initial measurement of an intangible asset, the stringent conditions set out in paragraph 57 of IAS 38 must also be met before internally generated development expenditure can be capitalised. See paragraph 15.53.

Research and development

15.45 The process of generating an intangible asset is divided into a research phase and a development phase. If the two phases are indistinguishable all the expenditure on the asset should be attributed to the research phase. [IAS 38 pares 52, 53].

15.46 'Research' is defined as "···*original and planned investigation undertaken*

© 2012 PricewaterhouseCoopers LLP. All rights reserved.

系列包含五个品牌，糖果系列包含三个品牌。管理层不断寻求创新和吸引新客户。新产品的研究和开发产生了支出，例如调查客户偏好，现有产品变化设计，以及新产品设计。巧克力系列当年产生了 100 万元的研发支出，而糖果系列当年产生了 160 万元的研发支出。这些支出不能分别分配到特定产品，但可以与一个业务系列相联系。

该研究和开发成本不应资本化为内部产生的无形资产。无形资产必须可辨认，并且可归属于特定产品或项目，才能满足无形资产的确认标准。管理层应当能够辨认来自所确认的每项单独无形资产的未来经济利益。如果管理层不能辨认特定的产品或项目，则不可能符合无形资产的确认标准。

15.44　该准则阐明了是否应当确认内部产生的无形资产的详细规定。除开发支出之外，这些规定禁止确认内部产生的无形资产。对于开发支出，除了要满足无形资产确认和计量的一般要求之外，内部产生的开发支出的资本化也必须满足 IAS 第 38 号第 57 段规定的严格条件。参见第 15.53 段。

研究和开发

15.45　产生无形资产的过程分为研究阶段和开发阶段。如果两个阶段不可区分，则该资产的所有支出应当归属于研究阶段。[IAS 第 38 号第 52、53 段]。

15.46　“研究”被定义为“……*为了获得新的科学或技术知识和理解而实施的*

ⓒ 2012 普华永道（PricewaterhouseCoopers）版权所有。

with the prospect of gaining new scientific or technical knowledge and understanding". 'Development' is defined as "…*the application of research findings or other knowledge to a plan or design for the production of new or substantially improved materials, devices, products, processes, systems or services before the start of commercial production or use*". [IAS 38 para 8]. The terms 'research phase' and 'development phase' have a broader meaning and are applied to a single project to distinguish the period of time and the quantum of the total project cost that is attributable to each type of activity.

15.47 Examples of research activities include:

- Activities aimed at obtaining new knowledge, such as biotechnology research aimed at discovering how the presence of particular genes may affect the incidence of particular illnesses in humans.

- Searching for suitable applications of research findings or other knowledge, evaluating the applications and making a final selection of suitable applications. For example, determining whether the discovery of the effect of a particular interaction of chemicals might be used in developing a treatment for a particular disease, using criteria that include the treatment's likely effectiveness, cost, and the alternative existing treatments available.

- Searching for alternatives for materials, devices, products, processes, systems or services. For example searching for alternatives that are more ecologically friendly as part of an entity's efforts to improve an entity's corporate social responsibility.

15.48 Examples of development activities include:

- Designing, constructing and testing of pre-production or pre-use prototypes and models.

- Designing tools, jigs moulds and dies involving new technology.

- Designing, constructing and operating a pilot plant that is not of a scale that is economically capable of commercial production.

- Designing, constructing and testing a selected alternative for new or improved materials, devices, products, processes, systems or services.

© 2012 PricewaterhouseCoopers LLP. All rights reserved.

独创性的和有计划的调查”。“开发”被定义为“……*在商业生产或开始使用之前将研究成果或其他知识应用到计划或设计中以生产新的或具重大改进的材料、设备、产品、工艺、系统或服务”*。[IAS 第 38 号第 8 段]。术语“研究阶段”和“开发阶段”具有更广泛的含义，并被应用于单个项目，以区分归属于每类活动的期间和项目成本。

15.47　研究活动的例子包括：

- 旨在获得新知识的活动，例如探索特定基因的存在如何影响人类特定疾病的发生的生物技术研究。

- 寻求研究成果或其他知识的适宜应用，评价这些应用并对适宜的应用进行最终选择。例如，确定对化学物质特定相互作用的效果的发现是否可以用来开发对于特定疾病的疗法，使用的标准包括疗法的可能的有效性、成本以及可用的现有替代疗法。

- 寻求材料、设备、产品、工艺、系统或服务的替代物。例如主体为提高企业社会责任而寻求更加环保的替代物。

15.48　开发活动的例子包括：

- 设计、建造和测试生产前或使用前的原型和模型。

- 设计含有新技术的工具、夹具模型和模具。

- 设计、建造和运营其规模不能进行经济性商业生产的试点厂。

- 设计、建造和测试新的或改进的材料、设备、产品、工艺、系统或服务的精选替代物。

ⓒ 2012 普华永道（PricewaterhouseCoopers）版权所有。

[IAS 38 para 59].

An entity may incur development expenditure in developing new products for sale, such as a new model of a car. It may also develop systems for its own use to enable it to keep up with changes in technology, such as design and construction of its own web site, or to enable it to remain competitive such as more efficient distribution, warehouse and electronic point of sale systems.

Research phase

15.49 Expenditure on the research phase of an internal project should be expensed as incurred. No intangible asset arising from research or from the research phase of an internal project can be recognised. [IAS 38 para 54]. During the research phase an entity is unable to demonstrate that there will be future economic benefits. The absence of probability of future economic benefits means that the expenditure does not meet the definition of an intangible asset, nor does it meet the criteria for recognition. Therefore, expenditure on research is expensed as incurred. [IAS 38 para 55]. However, research projects that are acquired as part of a business combination are treated differently and an asset will usually be recognised. See paragraph 15.162.

15.50 An entity may purchase patents and other rights over processes that are used in a research and development project. These rights would qualify for recognition as separately acquired intangible assets, even though they are used in the research activity. This is because the 'future economic benefits' criterion is assumed to be automatically satisfied in the separate acquisition of an intangible asset. However, using the patent in a research project may not give rise to future economic benefits, but the fact that it has been bought for value means that it is probable that it could also be sold again for value.

15.51 The standard defines research as related to scientific or technical knowledge. The same accounting treatment of expensing the costs as incurred would apply to other forms of enquiry, such as market or customer research.

Development phase

15.52 An internally generated intangible asset arising from the development phase

© 2012 PricewaterhouseCoopers LLP. All rights reserved.

[IAS 第 38 号第 59 段]。

主体在开发用于出售的新产品（例如新车型）时可能会产生开发支出。主体还可能开发自用系统，使其能够跟上技术变化，例如设计和建立自己的网站；或使其能够保持竞争力，例如更高效的经销、仓库和电子销售点系统。

研究阶段

15. 49　内部项目研究阶段的支出应当在发生时费用化。研究或内部项目研究阶段不能形成无形资产。[IAS 第 38 号第 54 段]。在研究阶段主体不能证明将会产生未来经济利益。未来经济利益可能性的缺乏意味着支出不符合无形资产的定义，也不满足确认标准。因此，研究支出在发生时应费用化。[IAS 第 38 号第 55 段]。然而，对于作为业务合并的一部分而取得的研究项目的处理方式有所不同，通常会确认资产。参见第 15. 162 段。

15. 50　主体可能会购买在研究和开发项目中使用的工艺的专利和其他权利。即使它们用于研究活动，这些权利也符合确认为单独购买的无形资产的资格。这是因为无形资产的单独购买被认为自动满足“未来经济利益”标准。然而，在研究项目中使用专利可能不会产生未来经济利益，但是已经被按价购买的事实意味着它也很可能可以再被按价出售。

15. 51　该准则将研究定义为涉及科学或技术知识。成本在发生时费用化的会计处理同样适用于其他形式的询问，例如市场或客户研究。

开发阶段

15. 52　如果满足确认标准，则应当确认来自项目开发阶段的内部产生的无形

ⓒ 2012 普华永道（PricewaterhouseCoopers）版权所有。

of a project should be recognised if the recognition criteria are satisfied.

15.53 The future economic benefits may become more apparent as a project progresses into the development stage. The measurement of development costs may become more reliable as this occurs. [IAS 38 para 58]. Therefore, the recognition criteria may be satisfied. The standard sets out criteria to assist in determining the point at which an entity moves from the research phase (when costs are expensed) to the development phase (when subsequent costs are recognised as an asset). If the criteria are met, then expenditure must be recognised as an asset. An entity must be able to demonstrate all of the following before an intangible asset is recognised:

(a) The technical feasibility of completing the intangible asset so that it will be available for use or sale.

(b) Its intention to complete the intangible asset and use or sell it.

(c) Its ability to use the intangible asset or to sell it.

(d) The way in which the intangible asset will generate probable future economic benefits. Amongst other factors, the entity must be able to demonstrate the existence of a market for the intangible asset's output or for the intangible asset itself or, if it is to be used internally, it must be able to demonstrate the usefulness of the intangible asset.

(e) The availability of adequate technical, financial and other resources to complete the development and to use or sell the intangible asset.

(f) Its ability to measure reliably the expenditure attributable to the intangible asset during its development.

[IAS 38 para 57].

15.54 Management should consider the product life cycle and then apply the above criteria at each stage of that cycle, as illustrated below.

© 2012 PricewaterhouseCoopers LLP. All rights reserved.

资产。

15.53 当项目进入开发阶段时，未来经济利益可能更加明显。开发成本在发生时更能可靠计量。[IAS 第 38 号第 58 段]。因此，可能能够满足确认标准。该准则阐明了帮助确定主体从研究阶段（成本费用化）转入开发阶段（后续成本确认为资产）的时点的标准。如果满足标准，则支出必须确认为资产。在确认无形资产前，主体必须能够证明以下各方面：

（a）完成无形资产使其能够使用或出售的技术可行性。

（b）主体完成无形资产并使用或出售的意图。

（c）主体使用或出售无形资产的能力。

（d）无形资产很可能产生未来经济利益的方式。主体必须能够证明无形资产的产出或无形资产本身存在市场；如果用于内部，主体必须能够证明无形资产的有用性。

（e）完成开发并使用或出售无形资产所需的足够的技术、财务和其他资源的可获性。

（f）主体可靠地计量开发期间归属于该无形资产的支出的能力。

[IAS 第 38 号第 57 段]。

15.54 如下例所述，管理层应当考虑产品生命周期，然后在生命周期的每个阶段应用以上标准。

ⓒ 2012 普华永道（PricewaterhouseCoopers）版权所有。

Example – Application of recognition criteria to each stage of the product life cycle

Consider the development of a new technology to be used in a manufacturing plant. The process could be split into the following stages:

1. Identify a need for/benefit of new technology.
2. Commission a project to investigate the new technology.
3. Investigate other technologies available in the market.
4. Investigate competitors' use of other technology.
5. Commission the design of alternative types of new technology and get input from the manufacturing floor for feasibility.
6. Prepare a shortlist of alternatives from commissioning stage and prepare costing.
7. Prepare a budget for the new technology and agree to the shortlist and the replacement of technology.
8. Send the shortlist to line managers for input and list three based on feedback.
9. Present the final three to the board for final selection.
10. Finalise a development plan for the final selection.
11. Develop new technology.
12. Test new technology.
13. Train staff on new technology.
14. Roll out new technology to the production line.

Management needs to determine at what stage it should start to capitalise the costs of the project. The recognition criteria should be considered at each stage to determine when the criteria have been met in full. From that point on the entity should capitalise all directly attributable costs. See paragraph 15. 152.

Stage 5: Criteria (a) and (c) have been met because the feasibility of

© 2012 PricewaterhouseCoopers LLP. All rights reserved.

示例——将确认标准应用到产品生命周期的每个阶段

考虑将在制造厂使用的新技术的开发。开发过程可以分成以下阶段：

1. 识别对于新技术的需求/新技术能带来的利益。
2. 启动调查新技术的项目。
3. 调查可在市场中获得的其他技术。
4. 调查竞争者对于其他技术的使用情况。
5. 委托设计新技术的备选类型，从制造厂获得可行性信息。
6. 通过委托阶段制订备选方案清单并进行成本核算。
7. 准备新技术的预算，同意清单及对老技术的更换。
8. 将清单发送至生产线经理评价，根据反馈挑选出三项方案。
9. 将最终的三项方案提交董事会最终决定。
10. 确定最终方案的开发计划。
11. 开发新技术。
12. 测试新技术。
13. 给员工培训新技术。
14. 新技术进入生产线。

管理层需要确定应当在哪个阶段开始将项目成本资本化。应当在每个阶段考虑确认标准，以确定何时完全满足标准。从这时起，主体应当将所有可直接归属的成本资本化。参见第 15.152 段。

阶段 5：已经满足标准（a）和（c），因为完成无形资产以供使用的可行

ⓒ 2012 普华永道（PricewaterhouseCoopers）版权所有。

completing the intangible asset for use and the entity's ability to use it has been confirmed.

Stage 7: Criteria (a), (c), (d) and (e) have been met at the end of this stage as a budget has been produced, it has been agreed to proceed with replacing the technology and adequate resources exist to complete the development.

Stage 10: All the criteria have been met at this stage as, in addition to the above, the board has approved the project (evidence of intention to complete the asset-criterion (b)) and the development plan, based on the budgets, evidences the ability to measure the expenditure reliably (criterion (f)).

15.55 Development expenditure that meets the recognition criteria must be capitalised.

15.56 Expenditure on research and development is significant in many industries, including the pharmaceutical industry and, as illustrated in Table 15.3, the engineering industry.

Table 15.3 – Expenditure on research and development

Rolls-Royce Group plc-Report and accounts-31 December 2010

Finance Director's review (extract)

Investments

The Group continues to subject all investments to rigorous examination of risks and future cash lows o ensure that they create shareholder value. All major investments require Board approval.

The Group has a portfolio of projects at different stages of their life cycles. Discounted cash flow an lysis of the remaining life of projects is performed on a regular basis. Sales of engines in production are assessed against criteria in the original development programme to ensure that overall value is enhanced.

Gross research and development (R&D) investment amounted to £923 million (2009 £864 million). Net research and development charged to the income statement was £422 million (2009 £379 million). The level of self-funded investment in research and development is expected to remain at approximately four to five per cent of Group revenues in the future. The impact of this investment on the income statement will reflect the mix and maturity of individual development programmes and will result in an increase in the level of net research and development charged within the income statement in 2011.

© 2012 PricewaterhouseCoopers LLP. All rights reserved.

性以及主体使用无形资产的能力已经确认。

阶段7：在本阶段末已经满足标准（a）、（c）、（d）和（e），因为已经制订预算，已经同意更换技术，并且有充足的资源完成开发。

阶段10：在本阶段已经满足所有标准，因为除了以上方面外，董事会已经批准项目（证明完成资产的意图 – 标准（b）），并且基于预算的开发计划证明了可靠计量支出的能力（标准（f））。

15.55 满足确认标准的开发支出必须资本化。

15.56 研究和开发支出在许多行业中是重大支出，包括制药行业以及表15.3中提及的工程行业。

表15.3——研究和开发支出

劳斯莱斯公司——报告和账目——2010年12月31日

财务总监的评述（摘录）

投资

集团持续对所有投资进行严格的风险和未来现金流检查，以确保它们创造股东价值。所有主要投资都需要董事会批准。

集团拥有处于生命周期不同阶段的各种项目，定期对项目进行剩余寿命现金流折现分析。根据初始开发计划中的标准对生产中的发动机的销售进行评价，以确保提高整体价值。

研发总投资达到9.23亿英镑（2009年为8.64英镑）。记入利润表的研发净额为4.22亿英镑（2009年为3.79亿英镑）。未来的自筹资金研发投资水平预期保持在集团收入的百分之四到五左右。该投资对于利润表的影响将反映各开发计划的组合和成熟度，并将导致2011年利润表中研发净额的增加。

ⓒ 2012 普华永道（PricewaterhouseCoopers）版权所有。

Con.

The continued development and replacement of operational facilities contributed to the total expenditure in property, plant and equipment of £361 million (2009 £291 million). Investment in 2011 is anticipated to be increased compared to the 2010 level as the investments in new facilities in the US and Singapore continues.

Investment in training was £33 million (2009 £24 million).

Intangible assets

The Group carried forward £2,884 million (2009 £2,472 million) of intangible assets. This comprised purchased goodwill of £1,108 million, engine certification costs and participation fees of £496 million, development expenditure of £630 million, recoverable engine costs of £346 million and other intangible assets of £304 million. Expenditure on intangible assets is expected to reduce modestly in 2011, largely as a result of the status of development programmes. Intangible assets of £211 million arose during the year as a result of the acquisition of ODIM ASA.

The carrying values of the intangible assets are assessed for impairment against the present value of forecast cash flows generated by the intangible asset. The principal risks remain reductions in assumed market share, programme timings, increases in unit cost assumptions and adverse movements in discount rates. There have been no impairments in 2010. Further details are given in note 8.

1 ACCOUNTING POLICIES (extract)

Research and development

In accordance with IAS 38 Intangible Assets, expenditure incurred on research and development, excluding known recoverable amounts on contracts, and contributions to shared engineering programmes, is distinguished as relating either to a research phase or to a development phase.

All research phase expenditure is charged to the income statement. For development expenditure, this is capitalised as an internally generated intangible asset only if it meets strict criteria, relating in particular to technical feasibility and generation of future economic benefits.

Expenditure that cannot be classified into these two categories is treated as being incurred in the research phase. The Group considers that, due to the complex nature of new equipment programmes, it is not possible to distinguish reliably between research and development

© 2012 PricewaterhouseCoopers LLP. All rights reserved.

续表

运营设施的持续开发和替换导致不动产、厂房和设备的总支出增加3.61亿英镑（2009年为2.91亿英镑）。由于美国和新加坡的新设施投资的继续，2011年的投资预期比2010年将有增加。

培训投资为3,300万英镑（2009年为2,400万英镑）。

无形资产

集团确认了28.84亿英镑（2009年为24.72亿英镑）的无形资产，包括购买的商誉11.08亿英镑，发动机认证成本和参与费4.96亿英镑，开发支出6.30亿英镑，发动机可收回成本3.46亿英镑以及其他无形资产3.04亿英镑。无形资产支出预计在2011年有适当减少，主要是因为开发项目的进展。对ODIM ASA的收购使得当年产生了2.11亿英镑的无形资产。

将无形资产的账面价值与无形资产将产生的预计现金流的现值相比较以评估是否存在减值。在假定的市场份额、项目时间、单位成本增加假设以及折现率的不利变化等方面的主要风险持续减少。2010年无减值。详见附注8。

1. 会计政策（摘录）

研究和开发

根据IAS第38号“无形资产”，研究和开发产生的支出（不包括已知的可收回合同金额和共享工程计划投入）区分为与研究阶段相关或与开发阶段相关。

所有研究阶段支出计入利润表。开发支出仅在满足严格标准时才资本化为内部产生的无形资产，这些标准特别涉及技术可行性和未来经济利益的产生。

不能划分为这两类的支出被视为在研究阶段发生。集团认为，由于新设备计划的复杂性，直到计划的晚期才能可靠地区分研究和开发活动。

© 2012 普华永道（PricewaterhouseCoopers）版权所有。

Con.

activities until relatively late in the programme.

Expenditure capitalised is amortised over its useful economic life, up to a maximum of 15 years from the entry into service of the product.

Consolidated income statement (extract)
For the year ended December 31, 2010

	Notes	2010	2009
		£ m	£ m
Revenue	2	**11,085**	10,414
Cost of sales		**(8,885)**	(8,303)
Gross profit		**2,200**	2,111
Other operating income		**95**	89
Commercial and administrative costs		**(836)**	(740)
Research and development costs		**(422)**	(379)
Share of results of joint ventures and associates	10	**93**	93
Operating profit		**1,130**	1,174

15.57 Many entities incur significant expenditure on development, but the amount that is recognised as an intangible asset varies considerably depending on the nature of the business and the nature of the products that are being developed. Consider, for example:

- An entity whose business is long-term contracting, where its business involves developing major computer or other systems for customers. Contract terms may provide for the entity to be reimbursed for development costs of the product or system as part of the contract price. These development costs would generally be accounted for, not under IAS 38, but as part of the cost of the contract under IAS 11, 'Construction contracts'.

- Another entity might make products for sale generally, such as cars. That entity might also incur significant expenditure on development of new models. Provided the recognition criteria were met, the entity would capitalise the

© 2012 PricewaterhouseCoopers LLP. All rights reserved.

续表

资本化的支出在其使用经济年限内摊销，最多为从产品投入服务起 15 年。

合并利润表（摘录）

截至 2010 年 12 月 31 日止年度

		2010	2009
	附注	百万英镑	百万英镑
收入	2	**11, 085**	10, 414
销售成本		**(8, 885)**	(8, 303)
毛利		**2, 200**	2, 111
其他经营收益		**95**	89
商业和管理成本		**(836)**	(740)
研究和开发成本		**(422)**	(379)
合营企业和联营企业经营成果的份额	10	**93**	93
经营利润		**1, 130**	1, 174

15. 57　许多主体都会产生高额开发支出，但确认为无形资产的金额因取决于业务性质和正在开发的产品性质而差别很大。例如：

- 主体的业务是长期承包，为客户开发大型计算机或其他系统。合同条款可能会规定在合同价中补偿主体的产品或系统开发成本。这些开发成本一般不应该根据 IAS 第 38 号进行处理，而是根据 IAS 第 11 号“建造合同”作为合同成本的一部分处理。

- 另一个主体可能制造用于日常销售的产品，例如汽车。主体也可能会产生新型开发的高额支出。如果满足确认标准，则主体将会资本化满足标准后产生的开发成本，因此会将高额开发成本确认为无形资产。

ⓒ 2012 普华永道（PricewaterhouseCoopers）版权所有。

development costs incurred after the criteria were met and thus might carry significant amounts of development costs as an intangible asset.

15. 58 Table 15. 4 is an example of a pharmaceutical entity that develops products that have to pass a number of regulatory hurdles that extend up to the time that the product is fully developed. Consequently, the entity capitalises few, if any, internal costs of development, because it considers that the probability criterion cannot be met until the final regulatory hurdle is passed.

Table 15. 4 – Research and development expenditure

Roche Holding Ltd-Report and accounts-31 December 2010

1. Summary of significant accounting policies (extract)

Research and development

Internal research costs are those costs incurred for the purpose of gaining new scientific or technical knowledge and understanding. These costs are expensed as incurred.

Internal development costs are those costs incurred for the application of research findings or other knowledge to plan and develop new products for commercial production. Such costs would qualify for capitalisation as intangible assets only if all of the following criteria can be demonstrated:

- The technical feasibility of completing the development project successfully so that it will be available for use or sale.
- The intention to complete the development project.
- The ability to use or sell the results of the development project.
- That the development project would generate economic benefits. This would normally be evidenced by the existence and size of a market for the results of the project itself or the products that would result from the project.
- The availability of adequate technical, financial and other resources to complete the development project.
- The ability to measure the development expenditure reliably that would qualify for capitalisation as an intangible asset.

The development projects undertaken by the Group are subject to technical, regulatory and other uncertainties, such that, in the opinion of management, the criteria for capitalisation are not met prior to obtaining marketing approval by the regulatory authorities in major markets. Internal development costs that do not meet these criteria are therefore expensed as incurred.

© 2012 PricewaterhouseCoopers LLP. All rights reserved.

15.58 表 15.4 以一家制药主体为例，该主体开发的产品必须通过许多法规障碍，直至产品完全开发为止。因此，主体几乎没有资本化开发的内部成本（如有），因为它认为只有通过最终的法规障碍才能满足可能性标准。

表 15.4——研究和开发支出

罗氏控股有限公司——报告和账目——2010 年 12 月 31 日

1. 重要会计政策概述（摘录）

研究和开发

内部研究成本是那些为取得新的科学或技术知识和理解而产生的成本。这些成本在发生时费用化。

内部开发成本是那些为应用研究发现或其他知识以计划和开发可供商业生产的产品而产生的成本。这些成本只有当所有以下条件都能论证的情况下才符合资本化为无形资产的资格：

- 完成无形资产使其能够使用或出售的技术可行性。
- 完成开发项目的意图。
- 使用或出售开发项目成果的能力。
- 开发项目将产生经济利益。这通常可以通过该项目成果或该项目可能得出的产品存在市场以及该市场的容量以证明。
- 完成开发项目所需的足够的技术、财务和其他资源的可获性。
- 可靠计量符合资本化为无形资产的资格的开发支出的能力。

本集团进行的开发项目取决于技术、监管以及其他不确定性。因此，管理层认为在取得监管机构对于主要市场的上市许可前不能满足资本化的条件。因此，不满足这些条件的内部开发成本在发生时费用化。

ⓒ 2012 普华永道（PricewaterhouseCoopers）版权所有。

Con.

> Post-marketing studies after regulatory approval, such as Phase IV costs in the pharmaceuticals business, are expensed as incurred. They generally involve safety surveillance and ongoing technical support of a drug after it receives marketing approval to be sold. They may be required by regulatory authorities or may be undertaken for safety or commercial reasons. The safety surveillance is designed to detect any rare or long-term adverse effects over a much larger patient population and longer time period than was possible during earlier stages of development. The costs of such post-marketing studies are not capitalised as intangible assets, as in the opinion of management, they do not generate separately identifiable incremental future economic benefits that can be reliably measured.
>
> In addition to its internal research and development activities, the Group is also party to in-licensing and similar arrangements with its alliance partners. The Group may also acquire in-process research and development assets, either through business combinations or through purchases of specific assets.
>
> In-process research and development resources acquired either through in-licensing arrangements, business combinations or separate purchases are capitalised as intangible assets if they are controlled by the Group, are separately identifiable and are expected to generate future economic benefits, even if uncertainty exists as to whether the research and development will ultimately result in a marketable product. Consequently, upfront and milestone payments to third parties for pharmaceutical products or compounds before regulatory marketing approval are recognised as intangible assets. Assets acquired through such arrangements are measured on the basis set out below in the 'Intangible assets' policy and are reviewed for impairment as set out below in the 'Impairment of property, plant and equipment and intangible assets' policy. Once available for use, such intangible assets are amortised on a straight-line basis over the period of the expected benefit and are reviewed for impairment at each reporting date. If research and development are embedded in contracts for strategic alliances, the Group carefully assess whether upfront or milestone payments constitute funding of research and development work or acquisition of an asset.

15.59 Entities involved in developing new drugs or vaccines are not normally able to capitalise development expenditure before obtaining regulatory authority for final approval of the drug (as they are not able to demonstrate the technical feasibility of completing project before this stage). These entities expense all research and development expenditure until they can demonstrate the feasibility of

© 2012 PricewaterhouseCoopers LLP. All rights reserved.

续表

在取得监管批准后的上市后研究，如制药业务中的第四阶段成本，在发生时费用化。它们通常包括在药物取得可出售的上市许可之后对其的安全监督和持续的技术支持。它们可能是监管机构要求的，或者是出于安全或商业的原因。安全监督被用来发现在开发的前期阶段不可能达到的大的病人总体和长时间的期间内任何稀有的或长期的副作用。这些上市后研究的成本不被资本化为无形资产，因为管理层认为它们并不产生单独的可辨认的并能够可靠计量的新增未来经济利益。
除内部研究和开发活动外，集团还与合作伙伴签订使用许可和类似协议。集团也可通过业务合并或购买特定资产来取得进行中的研究和开发资产。
通过许可协议、业务合并或单独购买取得的进行中的研究和开发资源如果能够被本集团控制、可单独辨认并且预期能够产生未来经济利益，则可以资本化为无形资产，即使对于研发是否能够最终得出一个可市场化的产品仍然存在不确定性。因此，为制药产品或化合物支付给第三方的预付款和阶段性的付款在获得监管上市许可之前就被确认为无形资产。通过这种安排取得的资产按照以下描述的“无形资产”政策进行计量，并按照以下描述的“物业、厂房和设备以及无形资产的减值”政策进行减值复核。一旦能够使用，则该无形资产根据直线法在预期利益期间内摊销，并在每个报告日进行减值复核。如果研究和开发被嵌入战略联盟的合同中，本集团仔细评估是否预付款和阶段性的付款是研发工作或收购一项资产的资金来源。

15.59　开发新药物或疫苗的主体在获得监管机构最终批准之前通常不能将开发支出资本化（因为它们在此阶段之前不能证明完成项目的技术可行性）。主体将全部研发支出费用化，直到他们能够证明产品的可行性。

ⓒ 2012 普华永道（PricewaterhouseCoopers）版权所有。

the products.

15. 60 Regulatory requirements are an important factor in restricting the ability of an entity to meet the recognition criteria in certain industries such as pharmaceuticals. However, the existence of such restrictions may have less impact in other industries. For example, the need for a new type of train to meet safety laws is in itself unlikely to prohibit an entity from concluding that it is probable that future economic benefits will flow to the entity. A train is an established form of transport, not a completely new product. Defects in design could be rectified to meet safety requirements. A failure to meet regulatory requirements with a completely new product, on the contrary, could mean that the entire project fails.

15. 61 An example of development costs in the aerospace industry is given in Table 15. 5. Although the entity recognises some development costs as an intangible asset, it states that it is unable to distinguish the development phase from the research phase in other projects and, therefore, expenses all costs on those projects.

Table 15. 5 – Research and development expenses

EADS NV-Report and accounts-31 December 2010

SIGNIFICANT ACCOUNTING POLICIES (extract)

Research and development expenses—Research and development activities can be: (i) contracted or (ii) self-initiated.

i) Costs for contracted research and development activities, carried out in the scope of externally financed research and development contracts, are expensed when the related revenues are recorded.

ii) Costs for self-initiated research and development activities are assessed whether they qualify for recognition as internally generated intangible assets. Apart from complying with the general requirements for an initial measurement of an intangible asset, qualification criteria are met only when technical as well as commercial feasibility can be demonstrated and cost can be measured reliably. It must also be probable that the intangible asset will generate future economic benefits and that it is clearly identifiable and allocable to a specific product.

Further to meeting these criteria, only such costs that relate solely to the development phase of a self-initiated project are capitalised. Any costs that are classified as part of the research

© 2012 PricewaterhouseCoopers LLP. All rights reserved.

15.60　在制药等某些行业中，法规要求是限制主体满足确认标准的能力的重要因素。然而，这些限制在其他行业中影响较小。例如，新型火车需要满足安全法本身不太可能禁止主体认为未来经济利益很可能流向主体。火车是成熟的运输形式，不是全新的产品。设计上的缺陷能够被改善以满足安全要求。相反，一个全新产品如不能满足法规要求则意味着整个项目的失败。

15.61　表 15.5 中提供了一个航天工业开发成本的案例。虽然主体将一些开发成本确认为无形资产，但它表示在其他项目中不能将开发阶段从研究阶段中区分出来，因此将那些项目的所有成本费用化。

表 15.5——研究和开发费用

欧洲航空防务及航天公司 – 报告和账目 – 2010 年 12 月 31 日

重要会计政策（摘录）

研究和开发费用——研究和开发活动可以是：(i) 承包的；或 (ii) 自行实施的。

i) 在外部融资研发合同的范畴下实施的承包研发活动成本在确认相关收入时费用化。

ii) 自行实施的研发活动成本需要评价是否能够符合确认为内部产生的无形资产的资格。除了满足无形资产的一般要求和初始计量外，仅在能够证明技术和商业可行性以及能够可靠计量成本时，才满足资格标准。无形资产还必须很可能产生未来经济利益、可清晰辨认，并且可分配至特定产品。

为了进一步满足标准，仅将只与自行实施项目的开发阶段相关的成本资本化。分类为自行实施项目的研究阶段的一部分的任何成本都在发生时费用化。如果研究阶段与

ⓒ 2012 普华永道（PricewaterhouseCoopers）版权所有。

Con.

phase of a self-initiated project are expensed as incurred. If the research phase cannot be clearly distinguished from the development phase, the respective project related costs are treated as if they were incurred in the research phase only.

Capitalised development costs are generally amortised over the estimated number of units produced. In case the number of units produced cannot be estimated reliably, capitalised development cost are amortised over the estimated useful life of the internally generated intangible asset. Amortisation of capitalised development costs is recognised in cost of sales. Internally generated intangible assets are reviewed for impairment annually when the asset is not yet in use and further on whenever events or changes in circumstances indicate that the carrying amount may not be recoverable.

Income tax credits granted for research and development activities are deducted from corresponding expenses or from capitalized amounts when earned.

15.62 Expenses incurred before a project meets the criteria for recognition as an intangible asset must be expensed as incurred. If the project has reached the stage when an asset must be recognised, previously written off costs may not be reinstated as part of the intangible asset. [IAS 38 para 71].

15.63 A new product or system may replace or makes obsolete an existing product or system owned by an entity. Thus as well as estimating the future economic benefits to be obtained from the new product or system, the entity should reassess the benefits from products or systems that are replaced or which are affected in other ways by the new product or system. IAS 36, 'Impairment of assets', contains several indicators of impairment, the existence of which require an entity to carry out an impairment review of existing assets. An example of where a new product may result in an impairment of existing assets or in the useful lives of the existing asset being shortened is the introduction of digital technology that replaces analogue technology, see paragraph 15.211.

Costs incurred under REACH (Registration, Evaluation, Authorisation and Restriction of Chemicals) EU legislation

15.64 The REACH legislation requires the registration of existing and new

© 2012 PricewaterhouseCoopers LLP. All rights reserved.

续表

开发阶段不能清晰区分，则相应的项目相关成本被视为仅在研究阶段产生。 资本化的开发成本一般按照产出单位的估计数目摊销。如果产出单位的数目不能可靠估计，则资本化的开发成本在内部产生的无形资产的估计使用寿命内摊销。资本化的开发成本的摊销确认为销售成本。当内部产生的无形资产未被使用时，每年对该资产进行减值复核。当重大事件或环境变化显示该资产账面价值可能不能收回时，也需进行减值复核。 研发活动享有的所得税减免在获得时从相应的费用或资本化金额中扣除。

15.62　在项目满足确认为无形资产的标准之前发生的费用在发生时必须费用化。如果项目已经到达必须确认资产的阶段，则以前冲销的成本不能恢复为无形资产的一部分。[IAS 第 38 号第 71 段]。

15.63　新产品或系统可以替代或废弃主体拥有的现有产品或系统。因此，在估计可从新产品或系统获得的未来经济利益后，主体应当重估被新产品或系统替代或以其他方式影响的产品或系统将可带来的利益。IAS 第 36 号“资产减值”包含若干减值迹象，这些迹象的存在要求主体对现有资产进行减值复核。数字技术的出现替代了模拟技术就是一个新产品可能导致现有资产减值或现有资产的使用寿命缩短的例子，参见第 15.211 段。

根据欧盟 REACH（化学品注册、评估、许可和限制）法规产生的成本

15.64　REACH 法规要求对已经进入或新进入欧洲市场的现有和新的化学品

© 2012 普华永道（PricewaterhouseCoopers）版权所有。

chemicals and substances currently or newly introduced to the European market. It requires manufacturers, importers, and downstream users to provide detailed information to the authorities concerning the properties and uses of the substances and their risks to both human health and the environment. The registration documentation and results of testing will be evaluated by the European Chemicals Agency and substances that exceed pre-defined risk thresholds may no longer be produced or traded. Failure of an entity to register a chemical means that the entity may not manufacture or import this chemical. Jurisdictions other than the EU have already developed or are in the process of developing regulations relating to similar environmental issues. The principles below may, therefore, be applied to similar legislation in these jurisdictions as well.

15. 65 The question arises as to whether the registration fees (akin to a license fee to sell a product as opposed to a patent) for each substance registered with the European Chemicals Agency may be capitalised as an intangible asset. As covered in paragraph 15. 12, the definition of an intangible asset is, "an identifiable non-monetary asset without physical substance"; and an asset is, "a resource controlled by an entity as a result of past events; and from which future economic benefits are expected to flow to the entity":

- Control and future economic benefits-With registration a manufacturer or importer obtains the right to manufacture or import a specific chemical. Future economic benefits are expected to arise on the future manufacture or import.
- Identifiability-The asset arising from the registration cannot be separated from the entity, but arises from a legal right.
- The asset is non-monetary and without physical substance.

The recognition criteria for an intangible asset are, therefore, met and it should be measured initially at cost. [IAS 38 para 24]. The cost of the intangible asset comprises any directly attributable cost. To determine which costs are to be capitalised, the individual facts and circumstances should be reviewed thoroughly to determine whether the costs incurred are directly attributable (that is, can be distinguished from the day to day costs of running the business) to registration, are reliably measurable and the development cost criteria are met.

© 2012 PricewaterhouseCoopers LLP. All rights reserved.

和物质进行注册。它要求制造商、进口商和下游用户向监管机构提供有关物质的属性和用途以及给人类健康和环境带来的风险的详细信息。注册文件和测试结果将由欧洲化学品管理局评估，超过预先设定的风险阀值的物质不能再生产或交易。主体注册某化学品失败意味着主体不能制造或进口该化学品。欧盟之外的地区也已经制订或正在制订与类似环境问题相关的规定。因此，以下原则也可能适用于这些地区的类似法律。

15. 65　相应产生的问题是，在欧洲化学品管理局进行注册的每种物质的注册费（类似于销售产品的许可费，而不是专利）是否可以资本化为无形资产。如第 15. 12 段如述，无形资产的定义是“没有实物形态的可辨认非货币性资产”；而资产的定义是“主体由于过去事项而控制的资源，并且预期将从其获得未来经济利益流向主体”：

■ 控制和未来经济利益——通过注册，制造商或进口商获得制造或进口特定化学品的权利。未来经济利益预期将从未来的制造或进口中产生。

■ 可辨认性——来自注册的资产不能与主体分离，但却产生于法律权利。

■ 该资产非货币，没有实物形态。

因此它符合无形资产确认标准，应当以成本初始计量。［IAS 第 38 号第 24 段］。无形资产成本包括任何可直接归属的成本。为了确定哪些成本应当资本化，应当彻底复核各个事实和环境，以确定所产生的成本是否可直接归属于（即可与运营业务的日常成本区分开来）注册、是否能够可靠计量，以及是否符合开发成本标准。

© 2012 普华永道（PricewaterhouseCoopers）版权所有。

15. 66 For substances of very high concern (according to list published by European Chemicals Agency) , an authorisation is required rather than registration. The costs incurred in achieving authorisation may be capitalised if the criteria listed in paragraph 15. 65 are met. It is likely to be more difficult to demonstrate the probability of future economic benefit flowing to the entity as a result of the required authorisation of a substance compared to the required registration of a substance, under the REACH legislation given authorisation may not be forthcoming.

15. 67 Similarly discretionary costs incurred by an entity to obtain a certification mark (defined in the Appendix to IFRS 3 as being "used to certify the geographical origin or other characteristics of a good or service", for example, British Standards recognition) may be capitalised as an intangible asset if the criteria listed in paragraph 15. 65 are met. Therefore, if the entity considers that it is probable that future economic benefits will flow from the asset to the entity (through increased sales), the cost of acquiring the specific certification may be recognised as an intangible asset if it is protected legally or through registration.

Expenditure which may not be capitalised as internally generated intangible assets

15. 68 The criteria for recognising internally generated intangible assets cannot be satisfied for some types of intangible asset. These include internally generated brands, mastheads, publishing titles, customer lists and items that are similar in substance. This is because it is extremely difficult to distinguish the costs of such items from the cost of developing the business as a whole. The standard, therefore, includes a specific prohibition on recognising those items as intangible assets. [IAS 38 paras 63, 64].

Example – Customer loyalty scheme

A supermarket is one of three large supermarket chains that dominate the market. Competition in the market is intense resulting in low product margins.

The supermarket has launched a customer loyalty scheme in an effort to boost

© 2012 PricewaterhouseCoopers LLP. All rights reserved.

15.66 非常重要的物质（根据欧洲化学品管理局发布的清单）需要“许可”而不是“注册”。如果满足第15.65段列出的标准，获得许可的成本可以资本化。与为物质“注册”相比，证明根据REACH法规为物质获得“许可”使得未来经济利益可能流向主体可能会更困难，因为不一定会获得许可。

15.67 类似地，主体获得认证标志（在IFRS第3号附录中定义为“用于证明货物或服务的地理原产地或其他特征”，例如“英国标准”确认）而产生的任意性成本可以资本化为无形资产，只要符合第15.65段列出的标准。因此，如果主体认为未来经济利益很可能从资产流向主体（通过销售增长），而前提是被法律保护或通过注册得到保护，则获得特定认证的成本可以确认为无形资产。

不能资本化为内部产生的无形资产的支出

15.68 某些类型的无形资产不能满足内部产生的无形资产确认标准，包括内部产生的品牌、刊头、出版标题、客户名单，以及实质上类似的项目。这是因为极难将该类项目的成本与开发整个业务的成本区分开来。因此，该准则特别禁止将这些项目确认为无形资产。[IAS第38号第63、64段]。

示例——客户忠诚度计划

一家超级市场是支配市场的三家大型连锁超市之一。市场竞争激烈，导致产品毛利很低。

该超市为提高市场份额而启动了客户忠诚度计划。签署该计划的客户获

ⓒ 2012 普华永道（PricewaterhouseCoopers）版权所有。

its market share. Customers who sign up for this scheme are issued loyalty cards that they can use to earn redeemable points based on the value of their purchases. Points can be redeemed against future purchases or to obtain prizes. The supermarket wishes to capitalise the cost of establishing the scheme as an intangible asset.

The customer loyalty scheme is internally-generated and cannot be recognised as an intangible asset. The expenditure on the scheme cannot be distinguished from the cost of developing the business as a whole.

15.69 Expenditure on intangible assets that cannot be capitalised should be expensed. However, such expenditure may be recognised as a pre-payment within current assets, where payment has been made in advance of delivery of goods or services. [IAS 38 para 70]. Expenditure on an intangible item must be recognised as an expense when it is incurred, unless it forms part of the cost of an intangible asset that meets the criteria for recognition as an internally generated or a separately acquired intangible asset. Pre-payment for such expenditure may only be recognised as an asset until the entity obtains right of access to the related goods or receipt of services.

15.70 IFRS 3 contains a list of items acquired in a business combination that meet the definition of intangible assets and which are recognised as such, separately from goodwill, if their fair values can be reliably measured. The following were specifically considered in drawing up this list and were excluded from the list as they are items that should not be recognised as intangible assets in a business combination:

- Customer service capability.

  An entity's customer service capability does not meet the identifiability criterion for separate recognition as an intangible asset. This is because an entity's customer service capability is dependent on its employees, which do not represent a resource controlled by the entity.

- A customer base, which is a group of customers not identifiable to the entity, such as the walk in customers of a retailer.

© 2012 PricewaterhouseCoopers LLP. All rights reserved.

得忠诚卡，可以用于根据购买价值获得返点。返点可用于未来购买或获得奖品。超市希望将建立计划的成本资本化为无形资产。

客户忠诚度计划为内部产生，不能确认为无形资产。在此计划上的支出无法与开发整个业务的成本区分开来。

15.69 不能资本化的无形资产支出应当费用化。然而，如在收到货物或服务之前付款，这些支出可以先确认为流动资产中的预付款。［IAS 第 38 号第 70 段］。无形项目支出在发生时必须确认为费用，除非构成符合内部产生或单独购买的无形资产确认标准的无形资产的成本的一部分。该类支出的预付款能确认为资产，但只到主体获得接收相关货物或服务的权利为止。

15.70 IFRS 第 3 号包含一份在业务合并中取得的符合无形资产的定义并且如果其公允价值能够可靠计量则可区别于商誉确认为无形资产的项目清单。以下是在拟订本清单时特别考虑并从清单中排除的项目，因为这些项目不应在业务合并中确认为无形资产：

■ 客户服务能力。

主体的客户服务能力不满足单独确认为无形资产的可辨认性标准。这是因为主体的客户服务能力取决于雇员，而这不是主体所控制的资源。

■ 客户基础。这是主体不可辨认的客户群体，例如零售商的无预约客户。

ⓒ 2012 普华永道（PricewaterhouseCoopers）版权所有。

The walk in customer base of a retailer does not meet the identifiability criterion for separate recognition as an intangible asset. The absence of contractual or legal rights plus the inability of the retailer to identify or contact the customer means that the entity has insufficient control over the economic benefits that it expects to derive from the customers.

- Presence in geographic markets or locations.

  Presence in geographic markets or locations does not meet the identifiability criterion for separate recognition as an intangible asset. As there is nothing to prevent other third parties entering the geographic markets or locations, the entity is not in a position to control the benefits associated with a specific location or geographic market.

- Non-union status or strong labour relations.

  Non-union status or strong labour relations do not meet the identifiability criterion for separate recognition as an intangible asset. Although an entity may be able to identify future economic benefits from non-union status such as reduced employee administrative and salary costs, employees do not represent a resource controlled by the entity.

- On-going training or recruiting programmes.

  Expenditure on training costs should be expensed as incurred, as these costs are indistinguishable from the costs of developing the business as a whole. See paragraph 15. 156. The entity may be able to identify incremental staff skills leading to future economic benefits from on-going training and recruiting programmes, but because employees do not represent a resource controlled by an entity it cannot recognise a separate intangible asset.

- Outstanding credit ratings or access to capital markets.

  Outstanding credit ratings or access to capital markets do not meet the identifiability criterion for separate recognition as an intangible asset. Credit ratings or a company's creditworthiness are not protected by contractual or legal rights. The entity has insufficient control over any economic benefits that it expects to derive as a result of favourable credit ratings/access to a capital

© 2012 PricewaterhouseCoopers LLP. All rights reserved.

零售商的无预约客户基础不满足单独确认为无形资产的可辨认性标准。缺乏合同或法律权利以及零售商不能辨认或联系客户意味着主体不能充分控制预期从客户获得的经济利益。

- 存在于地域市场或地点。

存在于地域市场或地点不满足单独确认为无形资产的可辨认性标准。因为无法预防其他第三方进入地域市场或地点，所以主体不能控制与特定地点或地域市场相关联的利益。

- 非工会状态或牢固的劳动关系。

非工会状态或牢固的劳动关系不满足单独确认为无形资产的可辨认性标准。虽然主体可能能够辨认来自非工会状态的未来经济利益（例如雇员管理和薪酬成本降低），但雇员不是主体控制的资源。

- 现行培训或招聘计划。

培训成本支出应当在发生时费用化，因为这些成本无法与开发整个业务的成本区分开来。参见第 15. 156 段。主体可能能够辨认来自现行培训和招聘计划而导致员工技能提高所带来的未来经济利益，但因为雇员不是主体控制的资源，所以不能确认为单独的无形资产。

- 高信用等级或资本市场通路。

高信用等级或资本市场通路不符合单独确认为无形资产的可辨认性标准。信用等级或公司的信用能力不受合同或法律权利保护。主体不能充分控制预期来自有利的信用等级或资本市场通路的预期经济利益。有利的信用等级或资本市场通路也不是可分离的，因为它们不能被出售给第三方。

ⓒ 2012 普华永道（PricewaterhouseCoopers）版权所有。

market. Favourable credit ratings or access to a capital market are also not separable as they cannot be sold to a third party.

■ Favourable government relations.

Favourable government relations do not meet the identifiability criterion for separate recognition as an intangible asset. The government does not represent a resource that is controlled by the entity. It is common practice in certain jurisdictions for entities to actively lobby government, which may result in certain economic benefits flowing to the company.

■ Assembled workforce.

The assembled workforce does not meet the identifiability criterion for separate recognition as an intangible asset. The benefits arising from an assembled workforce cannot be controlled by an entity, since it cannot prevent a change in the composition of the workforce.

15.71 IAS 38 gives examples of the types of cost that are indistinguishable from the costs of developing the business as a whole and that should, therefore, be expensed as incurred. These include:

■ Research expenditure, except where it forms part of the cost of a business combination.

■ Start-up costs, unless such costs (for example, costs of commissioning) are included in the cost of a tangible fixed asset under IAS 16, 'Property, plant and equipment'. Costs that should be expensed as incurred include preliminary expenses of establishing a legal entity, expenditure on opening a new facility or business (pre-opening costs) or expenditure on starting up a new operation or launching a new product or process.

■ Training costs.

■ Advertising and promotion costs (as part of the amendment to IAS 38 (see para 15.69) mail order catalogues are now included).

■ Relocation expenses.

■ Re-organisation costs for all or part of an entity.

© 2012 PricewaterhouseCoopers LLP. All rights reserved.

■ 良好的政府关系。

良好的政府关系不符合单独确认为无形资产的可辨认性标准。政府不是主体控制的资源。在某些管辖地主体积极游说政府已成惯例，这可能会导致某些经济利益流向公司。

■ 劳动力组合。

劳动力组合不符合单独确认为无形资产的可辨认性标准。来自劳动力组合的利益不受主体控制，因为不能预防劳动力组成的变化。

15.71　IAS 第 38 号举例说明不能与开发整个业务的成本区分开来因而应当在发生时费用化的成本类型。这些成本类型包括：

■ 研究支出，不包括构成业务合并成本的一部分的情况。

■ 开办费，除非该类成本（例如调试成本）根据 IAS 第 16 号“物业、厂房和设备”属于有形固定资本的成本。应当在发生时费用化的成本包括建立法律实体的初始费用，开办新设施或业务的支出（开业前成本），或启动新业务或发布新产品或工艺的支出。

■ 培训成本。

■ 广告和促销费用（作为 IAS 第 38 号修订的一部分（参见第 15.69 段），邮购目录现已纳入）。

■ 搬迁费用。

■ 主体的全部或一部分的重组成本。

ⓒ 2012 普华永道（PricewaterhouseCoopers）版权所有。

15. 72 Expenditure that does not meet the recognition criteria is recognised as an expense as incurred. This includes the general day-to-day expenditure on maintaining the business, such as wages and salaries, maintenance and so on. Some of the types of expenditure that might seem to be at the margin between intangible assets and such routine expenditure is specifically put into the latter category by IAS 38 and listed in paragraph 15. 71. The timing of recognition of an expense is clarified in IAS 38 (part of the 'Improvements to IFRSs' published in 2008). IAS 38 clarifies that services are received when they are performed by a supplier in accordance with a contract to deliver them and not when an entity uses them to deliver another service, for example to deliver an advertisement to customers. [IAS 38 para 69A]. Examples of policies are Tables 15. 5. A and 15. 5. B

Table 15. 5A – time of recognition of catalogue costs

Filtrona plc – Annual report – 31 December 2010

Accounting Policies (extract)

Catalogue costs

The costs associated with the production and printing of catalogues are expensed to the income statement when access is received to those goods.

Table 15. 5B – time of recognition of expense for advertising costs

Diageo plc – Annual report – 30 June 2010

Accounting policies of the group (extract)

Advertising and promotion costs

Advertising costs, point of sale materials and sponsorship payments are charged in the income statement when the company has a right of access to the goods or services acquired.

15. 73 Internally generated goodwill may not be recognised as an asset. [IAS 38 para 48]. The standard explains that internally generated goodwill is not recognised as an asset because it is not an identifiable resource, that is, it is not separable nor does it arise from contractual or other legal rights that are controlled by the entity and that are reliably measurable. [IAS 38 para 49].

© 2012 PricewaterhouseCoopers LLP. All rights reserved.

15.72 不符合确认标准的支出在发生时确认为费用。该类支出包括维持业务的一般性日常支出，例如工资薪金以及维护费等。看起来界于无形资产和上述常规支出之间的边缘支出类型被 IAS 第 38 号特别归于后者，在第 15.71 段列出。作为 2008 年发布的“国际财务报告准则改进”的一部分，IAS 第 38 号明确了费用的确认时点。IAS 38 明确了服务接受的时间是供应商根据合同执行并提供该服务的时间，而非主体利用该服务以提供其他服务的时间，例如，向客户提供广告。[IAS 第 38 号第 69A 段]。表格 15.5A 和 15.5B 为政策的示例。

表格 15.5A——目录成本的确认时点

菲尔创纳公司——年度报告——2010 年 12 月 31 日

会计政策（摘录）

目录成本

与目录编制和印刷相关的成本在收到商品时在利润表中记为费用。

表格 15.5B——广告成本的费用确认时点

帝亚吉欧公司——年度报告——2010 年 6 月 30 日

集团会计政策（摘录）

广告和推广成本

广告支出、销售点材料和赞助支出在收到商品或获得服务时计入利润表。

15.73 内部产生的商誉不能确认为资产。[IAS 第 38 号第 48 段]。准则解释了内部产生的商誉不确认为资产是因为它不是可辨认的资源，即它不可分离，也不来自主体控制并且能够可靠计量的合同或其他法律权利。[IAS 第 38 号第 49 段]。

ⓒ 2012 普华永道（PricewaterhouseCoopers）版权所有。

15.74 There may be a difference, sometimes large, between the market capitalisation of an entity and its net asset value. Such a difference can represent a wide variety of factors affecting the value of an entity, including management expertise or reputation, internally generated brand value, growth in acquired brand values carried at cost, bid speculation and so on. However, such differences do not represent identifiable intangible assets controlled by the entity. [IAS 38 para 50].

Initial measurement

15.75 Intangible assets should be measured on initial recognition at cost. [IAS 38 para 24]. Cost is defined as the amount of cash or cash equivalents paid, or the fair value of other consideration given, to acquire an asset at the time of its acquisition or construction. Alternatively, when applicable, cost is the amount attributed to that asset when initially recognised in accordance with the specific requirements of other IFRSs, for example IFRS 2, 'Share-based payment'. [IAS 38 para 8].

15.76 An entity may obtain an intangible asset in a number of ways:

- By separate acquisition for valuable monetary or other consideration.
- As part of a business combination.
- By exchange for other non-monetary assets.
- By way of government grant.
- By developing or generating the asset internally.

The method of determining cost in each of these situations is described below.

Separate acquisition

15.77 The cost of a separately acquired intangible asset (including in-process research and development projects) can usually be reliably measured. This is particularly so for assets acquired for cash. [IAS 38 para 26]. Cost for an intangible asset comprises:

© 2012 PricewaterhouseCoopers LLP. All rights reserved.

15.74　主体的市值与其净资产价值可能会存在差异，有时差异还较大。这种差异可以体现影响主体价值的多种因素，包括管理技术或声誉、内部产生的品牌价值、以成本计量的购买的品牌价值的增长、投标推测等。然而，这些差异不代表主体控制的可辨认无形资产。[IAS 第 38 号第 50 段]。

初始计量

15.75　无形资产应当在初始确认时以成本计量。[IAS 第 38 号第 24 段]。成本定义为在购买或建造资产时所支付的现金或现金等价物金额，或所提供的其他对价的公允价值。或者，如果适用，则成本为根据其他 IFRS（例如 IFRS 第 2 号“以股份为基础的支付”）的要求初始确认资产时归属于该资产的金额。[IAS 第 38 号第 8 段]。

15.76　主体可以通过许多方式获得无形资产：

- 以有价值的货币或其他对价单独购买。
- 作为业务合并的一部分。
- 以其他非货币性资产交换。
- 政府补助。
- 内部开发或产生。

针对每一种情况确定成本的方法如下所述。

单独购买

15.77　单独购买的无形资产（包括进行中的研发项目）的成本通常可以可靠计量，特别是现金购买的资产。[IAS 第 38 号第 26 段]。无形资产的成本包括：

© 2012 普华永道（PricewaterhouseCoopers）版权所有。

- the purchase price, including import duties and non-refundable purchase taxes. Trade discounts and rebates are deducted in arriving at the purchase price; plus
- any directly attributable cost of preparing the asset for its intended use.

[IAS 38 para 27].

15.78 Directly attributable costs include:

- The cost of employee benefits as defined in IAS 19, 'Employee benefits', that arise directly from bringing the asset into its working condition. There is no requirement for these costs to be incremental. Therefore, there is not a requirement for an employee who was specifically hired to prepare the asset for intended use, for the employee benefit costs to be capitalised. It is sufficient that the employee has incurred time working on the relevant project.
- Professional fees.
- Costs of testing whether the asset is working properly.

[IAS 38 para 28].

15.79 The directly attributable costs referred to above are more likely to arise where an intangible asset is internally generated, rather than acquired separately. Therefore, these types of cost are discussed in more detail under paragraph 15.153. An intangible asset that is acquired separately may sometimes still require expenditure to bring it into working condition, so the guidance in that section may be relevant in these circumstances.

15.80 Expenditure that does not form part of the cost of an intangible asset includes:

- The cost of introducing a new product or service, including advertising costs and promotional activities.
- Costs of conducting business in a new location or with a new class of customer, including training costs.
- Administration and other general overheads.

[IAS 38 para 29].

© 2012 PricewaterhouseCoopers LLP. All rights reserved.

■ 购买价格，包括进口关税和不能返还的购货税款。贸易折扣和折让在计算购买价格时扣除；加上

■ 为使资产能够用于预定用途而发生的可直接归属的成本。

[IAS 第 38 号第 27 段]。

15.78 可直接归属的成本包括：

■ 在将资产带入工作环境时直接产生的 IAS 第 19 号“职工福利”中定义的职工福利成本。没有要求这些成本必须是增量成本。因此，没有要求为使职工福利成本资本化，该员工必须是专门受雇于使资产能够用于预定用途的。员工在相关项目中工作并耗用时间就足够了。

■ 专业服务费。

■ 测试资产是否正常运转的成本。

[IAS 第 38 号第 28 段]。

15.79 上述可直接归属的成本在内部产生无形资产时比在单独购买时更可能会产生。因此，这些类型的成本在第 15.153 段中将更详细地讨论。将单独购买的无形资产引入工作状态，有时仍可能需要发生费用，因此那部分中的指导在这些情况中可能有用。

15.80 不构成无形资产成本的一部分的支出包括：

■ 推出新产品或服务的成本，包括广告成本和促销活动。

■ 在新地点营业或与新型客户进行交易的成本，包括培训成本。

■ 管理和其他的一般间接费用。

[IAS 第 38 号第 29 段]。

ⓒ 2012 普华永道（PricewaterhouseCoopers）版权所有。

15.81 Capitalisation of eligible costs should cease when the asset is capable of operating in the manner intended by management. Costs of using the asset or for redeploying it to other uses or another location are not capitalised. Such costs include any that are incurred while an asset is capable of operating in the manner intended by management and any initial operating losses, such as those that might be incurred while demand builds up for the asset's output. [IAS 38 para 30].

15.82 Some activities occur in the course of developing an intangible asset but are not necessary to bring the asset to its intended working condition. Income and expenditure relating to such non-essential incidental operations should not be capitalised, but instead should be expensed. [IAS 38 para 31]. This requirement is usually more relevant to internally generated intangibles, see paragraph 15.157.

15.83 If payment for an intangible asset is deferred beyond normal credit terms, the asset's cost is its cash price equivalent, which is the discounted amount. The difference between this amount and the total payment is treated as interest payable over the period of credit, unless it meets the conditions for capitalisation set out in IAS 23, 'Borrowing costs'. [IAS 38 para 32]. An example of a separately acquired intangible asset that would meet the definition of a qualifying asset for interest capitalisation purposes is in the pharmaceutical industry, where early stage research and development work is often sold several years from completion.

15.84 The fair value of an asset acquired for cash is usually equal to the asset's cost. Fair value is defined as the amount for which the asset could be exchanged between knowledgeable, willing parties in an arm's length transaction. For assets that are acquired for shares, the principles of IFRS 2, 'Share-based payment', apply. That standard requires that the goods or services received in exchange for shares should be measured at fair value of those goods or services. There is a rebuttable presumption that, for transactions with parties other than employees, fair value can be measured reliably. However, in rare cases where the fair value of the goods or services cannot be reliably measured, the entity should measure fair value indirectly by reference to the fair value of the equity instruments granted. [IFRS 2

© 2012 PricewaterhouseCoopers LLP. All rights reserved.

15.81 当资产能够以管理层预定的方式运营时，应当停止资本化符合条件的成本。使用资产或将其重新安排用于其他目的或另一地点的成本不能资本化。该类成本包括资产能够以管理层指定的方式运营时产生的成本和初始经营亏损，例如在对资产产出的需求形成规模的过程中可能产生的亏损。[IAS 第 38 号第 30 段]。

15.82 有些活动发生在开发无形资产的过程中，但却不是为使资产达到预定工作状态所必需的。与该类非必要的偶然运营相关的收益和支出不应资本化，而应费用化。[IAS 第 38 号第 31 段]。该要求对于内部产生的无形资产来说通常更为重要。参见第 15.157 段。

15.83 如果对于无形资产的支付延迟超过正常的信用期限，则资产的成本为其等值现金价格，即折现后的金额。除非符合 IAS 第 23 号“借款费用”中的资本化条件外，该金额和支付总额之间的差额应视为在信用期间的应付利息。[IAS 第 38 号第 32 段]。符合利息资本化所要求的合格资产定义的单独购买的无形资产在制药行业中有类似案例：早期研发工作通常在完成前几年就被出售。

15.84 现金购买的资产的公允价值通常等于资产的成本。公允价值定义为熟悉情况的自愿双方在正常交易中可用该资产换取的金额。以股份换取的资产适用 IFRS 第 2 号“以股份为基础的支付”。该准则要求以股份换取的货物或服务应当以货物或服务的公允价值计量。有一个可推翻的假设是：对于与不是雇员的各方进行的交易，公允价值可以可靠计量。然而，在货物或服务的公允价值不能可靠计量的罕见情况下，主体应当参考所授予的权益工具的公允价值间接计量公允价值。[IFRS 第 2 号第 10、13 段]。

© 2012 普华永道（PricewaterhouseCoopers）版权所有。

paras 10, 13].

Example – Shares issued as consideration for the acquisition of an intangible asset

An entity issues 100, 000 ordinary C1 shares for the acquisition of an intangible asset comprising certain rights. Similar intangible assets are regularly exchanged in cash transactions and the entity has been offered a similar asset for a cash price of C300,000, which is consistent with prices paid in similar transactions. The share price of the entity's ordinary shares at the date of the transaction is C2. 95. At what value should the intangible asset be recognised initially?

The asset should be recognised at the fair value of the rights acquired. The existence of exchange transactions and cash prices for similar assets means that the fair value of the rights can be determined reliably at C300,000. Therefore, the asset is recorded at this amount.

If the fair value of the rights had not been reliably measurable, the asset would be recorded at C295, 000, being the fair value of the equity instruments issued. Similarly, if the share price had been C3. 05 the asset's fair value would be C305,000.

Intangible assets acquired in a business combination

15. 85 IFRS 3 was revised in 2008 and there were amendments to IAS 38 as a result of this. IFRS 3 requires that in a business combination the acquirer should recognise an identifiable intangible asset if it's fair value can be reliably measured. [IFRS 3 para 37]. This is the only criterion that has to be satisfied as it is presumed that the probability criterion is satisfied. The condition is deemed to be satisfied, because the probability factor is reflected in the fair value attributed to the intangible asset. The cost of an intangible asset acquired in a business combination is its fair value at the acquisition date. [IAS 38 para 33]. The acquirer's intentions or specific circumstances are not relevant to the measurement of fair value as fair value is not entity specific. [IFRS 3 para B43]. But the

© 2012 PricewaterhouseCoopers LLP. All rights reserved.

示例——作为购买无形资产的对价而发行的股票

主体发行100,000股每股面值为1元的普通股股票以购买包含某些权利的无形资产。类似的无形资产经常以现金交易，主体已经得到过现金价格为300,000元的类似资产报价，与类似交易中支付的价格一致。主体的普通股股票价格在交易日为2.95元。无形资产应当以什么价值初始确认?

资产应当以所取得的权利的公允价值确认。交换交易的存在和类似资产的现金价格意味着这些权利的公允价值能够可靠确定为300,000元。因此，资产以该金额记录。

如果这些权利的公允价值不能可靠计量，则该资产应当以295,000元记录，即所发行的权益工具的公允价值。类似的，如果股票价格为3.05元，则该资产的公允价值应当为305,000元。

在业务合并中取得的无形资产

15.85 IFRS第3号在2008年进行了修订，IAS第38号也进行了相应的修订。IFRS第3号要求，如果可辨认无形资产的公允价值能够可靠计量，在业务合并中购买方应当予以确认。[IFRS第3号第37段]。可计量性是唯一必须满足的标准，因为可能性标准已经假定为满足。因为可能性因素在归属于无形资产的公允价值中已经反映。在业务合并中取得的无形资产的成本是其于购买日的公允价值。[IAS第38号第33段]。购买方的意图或特定环境与公允价值的计量无关，因为公允价值并不针对特定主体。[IFRS第3号第B43段]。但是根据IFRS第3号，在业务合并中取得的无形资产总是满足可靠计量标准。[IAS第38号第33段、BC第19B段]。不确定性的影响反映在资产公允价值的计量中。[IAS第38号BC第19A段]。这项对IAS第38号的修

ⓒ 2012 普华永道（PricewaterhouseCoopers）版权所有。

reliable measurement criterion will always be met for intangible assets acquired in a business combination under the IFRS 3. [IAS 38 para 33, BC19B]. The effects of uncertainty are reflected in measuring the asset's fair value. [IAS 38 para BC19A]. The consequence of the amendment to IAS 38 is that more intangible assets are likely to be identified in a business combination. The revised IFRS 3 is prospectively applicable to business combinations for which the acquisition date is on or after the beginning of the first annual reporting period beginning on or after 1 July 2009.

Types of identifiable intangible assets

15.86 The table below includes a list of intangible assets by major category and identifies whether the asset would typically meet the contractual-legal criterion or the separability criterion. In certain cases, an intangible asset may meet both identifiable criteria. However, the exhibit highlights the primary criterion under which the specific intangible asset would be recognised. The list is not intended to be all-inclusive, therefore, other acquired intangible assets might also meet the criteria for recognition apart from goodwill.

Intangible assets that generally meet the criteria for separate recognition. [IFRS 3 paras B31 – B40; IE16 – IE44].

Intangible asset	*Contractual-legal criterion*	*Separability criterion*
Marketing – related		
■ Trademarks, trade names.	√	
■ Service marks, collective marks, certification marks.	√	
■ Trade dress (unique colour, shape, or package design).	√	
■ Newspaper mastheads.	√	
■ Internet domain names.	√	
■ Non – competition agreements.	√	
Customer related		
■ Customer lists.		√
■ Order or production backlog.	√	

© 2012 PricewaterhouseCoopers LLP. All rights reserved.

订的结果是在业务合并中可能辨认出更多的无形资产。修订后的 IFRS 第 3 号对于购买日为开始于 2009 年 7 月 1 日或之后的第一个年度报告期的开始日或之后的业务合并未来适用。

可辨认无形资产的类型

15.86　下表包括了一个无形资产按照大类分类的清单，并辨认该资产是否应该一般地符合合同性—法律标准或可分离标准。在某些情况下，一项无形资产可能满足两项可辨认标准。然而，该表强调会据此确认特定无形资产的主要标准。该清单并不打算涵盖全部的无形资产，其他已购无形资产（除商誉外）可能也会满足确认标准。

一般符合单独确认标准的无形资产。［IFRS 3 附录 B 第 31 段至第 40 段 说明性示例第 16－44 段］。

	与市场营销相关的	
无形资产	**合同性—法律标准**	**可分离标准**
■ 商标，商号。	√	
■ 服务标志，团体标志，认证标志。	√	
■ 商业外观（独特的颜色、形状或包装设计）。	√	
■ 报头。	√	
■ 互联网域名。	√	
■ 非竞争协议。	√	
	与客户相关的	
■ 客户名单。		√
■ 订单或生产性积压	√	

ⓒ 2012 普华永道（PricewaterhouseCoopers）版权所有。

Con.

■ Customer contracts and related customer relationships.	√	
■ Non – contractual customer relationships.		√
Artistic-related		
■ Plays, operas, ballets.	√	
■ Books, magazines, newspapers, other literary works.	√	
■ Musical works, such as compositions, song lyrics, advertising jingles.	√	
■ Pictures, photographs.	√	
■ Video and audiovisual material, including motion pictures, music videos, television programmes.	√	
Contract-based		
■ Licensing, royalty, standstill agreements.	√	
■ Advertising, construction, management, service or supply contracts.	√	
■ Lease agreements.	√	
■ Construction permits.	√	
■ Franchise agreements.	√	
■ Operating and broadcast rights.	√	
■ Use rights, such as drilling, water, air, mineral, timber cutting, and route authorities.	√	
■ Servicing contracts (for example, mortgage servicing contracts).	√	
■ Employment contracts.	√	
Technology – based		
■ Patented technology.	√	
■ Research and development.		√
■ Computer software and mask works.	√	
■ Unpatented technology.		√
■ Databases, including title plants.		√
■ Trade secrets, such as secret formulas, processes, recipes.	√	

√Indicates the primary criterion under which the specific intangible asset would typically be recognised.

© 2012 PricewaterhouseCoopers LLP. All rights reserved.

续表

■ 客户合同和相关的客户关系。	√	
■ 非合同的客户关系。		√
与艺术相关的		
■ 戏剧，歌剧，芭蕾舞剧。	√	
■ 书籍，杂志，报纸，其他文学作品。	√	
■ 音乐作品，例如作曲，歌词，广告词。	√	
■ 图画，照片。	√	
■ 视频和视听材料，包括电影，音乐视频，电视节目。	√	
以合同为基础		
■ 使用许可，特许权，终止协议。	√	
■ 广告，建筑，管理，服务或供应合同。	√	
■ 租赁协议。	√	
■ 建筑许可证。	√	
■ 特许权协议。	√	
■ 运营和播放权。	√	
■ 使用权，例如钻井，水，空气，矿物，伐木，道路权限。	√	
■ 服务合同（例如，抵押贷款服务合同）。	√	
■ 雇佣合同。	√	
以技术为基础		
■ 专利技术。	√	
■ 研究和开发。		√
■ 计算机软件和掩膜作品。	√	
■ 非专利技术。		√
■ 数据库，包括产权档案库。		√
■ 商业秘密，例如保密公式、工艺、配方。	√	

√表示主要标准，特定的无形资产通常应该会据此确认。

© 2012 普华永道（PricewaterhouseCoopers）版权所有。

Marketing-related intangible assets

15. 87 Marketing-related intangible assets are primarily used in the marketing or promotion of products or services. They are typically protected through legal means and, therefore, generally meet the contractual-legal criterion for recognition separately as an intangible asset. [IFRS 3 para IE18]. The following paragraphs discuss common marketing-related intangible assets recognised and measured in a business combination.

15. 88 Trademarks, trade names, and other marks are often registered with governmental agencies or are unregistered, but otherwise protected. Whether registered or unregistered, but otherwise protected, trademarks, trade names, and other marks have some legal protection and would meet the contractual-legal criterion. If trademarks or other marks are not protected legally, but there is evidence of similar sales or exchanges, the trademarks or other marks would meet the separability criterion. [IFRS 3 para IE20].

15. 89 A brand is the term often used for a group of assets associated with a trademark or trade name. An acquirer can recognise a group of complementary assets, such as a brand, as a single asset apart from goodwill if the assets have similar useful lives and either the contractual-legal or separable criterion is met. [IFRS 3 para IE21].

15. 90 Trade dress refers to the unique colour, shape, or packaging of a product. [IFRS 3 para IE18]. If protected legally (as discussed above in relation to trademarks), then the trade dress meets the contractual-legal criterion. If the trade dress is not legally protected, but there is evidence of similar sales, or if the trade dress is sold in conjunction with a related asset, such as a trademark, then it would meet the separability criterion. Newspaper mastheads are generally protected through legal rights, similar to a trademark and, therefore, would meet the contractual-legal criterion. If not protected legally, a company would look at whether exchanges or sales of mastheads occur to determine if the separability criterion is met. Internet domain names are unique names used to identify a particular Internet site or Internet address. These domain names are usually registered and, therefore, would meet the contractual-legal criterion. [IFRS 3 para

© 2012 PricewaterhouseCoopers LLP. All rights reserved.

与市场营销相关的无形资产

15.87　与市场营销相关的无形资产主要在产品或服务的市场营销或促销中使用。它们通常会通过法律手段受到保护，因此一般符合单独确认为一项无形资产的合同性—法律标准。[IFRS 3 说明性示例第 18 段]。以下段落讨论在一项业务合并中确认和计量的与市场营销相关的常见无形资产。

15.88　商标、商号和其他标志通常在政府机构注册或者虽未注册，但却受到保护。无论是注册还是虽然未注册但是受到保护，这些商标、商号和其他标志都受到某些法律保护，应该会符合合同性—法律标准。如果商标或其他标志不受法律保护，但存在类似销售或交换的证据，则商标或其他标志应该会符合可分离标准。[IFRS 3 说明性示例第 20 段]。

15.89　品牌一词经常用于表示与一个商标或商号相关联的一组资产。购买方可以将一组互补性资产（如品牌）确认为除商誉外的一项单独的资产，前提是这些资产具有类似的使用寿命，并且符合合同性—法律标准或者可分离性标准。[IFRS 3 说明性示例第 21 段]。

15.90　商业外观系指一件产品独特的颜色、形状或包装。[IFRS 3 说明性示例第 18 段]。如果受到法律保护（如同上文关于商标的讨论），则商业外观符合合同性—法律标准。如果商业外观未受法律保护，但存在类似的销售证据，或如果商业外观是与一项相关的资产（例如商标）一起销售的，则它应该会符合可分离标准。报头一般通过法律权利保护，类似于商标，因此应该会符合合同性—法律标准。如果不受法律保护，则公司应该会考察报头的交换或销售是否存在，以确定是否符合可分离标准。互联网域名是用于识别一个特定互联网网站或互联网地址的唯一名称。这些域名通常进行了注册，因此应该会符合合同性—法律标准。[IFRS 3 说明性示例第 22 段]。

ⓒ 2012 普华永道（PricewaterhouseCoopers）版权所有。

IE22].

15.91 Non-competition ('non-compete') agreements are legal arrangements that generally prohibit a person or business from competing with a company in a certain market for a specified period of time. An acquiree may have pre-existing non-compete agreements in place at the time of the acquisition. As those agreements arise from a legal or contractual right, they would meet the contractual-legal criterion and represent an acquired asset that would be recognised as part of the business combination. The terms, conditions, and enforceability of non-compete agreements may affect the fair value assigned to the intangible asset, but would not affect their recognition. Other payments made to former employees that may be described as non-compete payments might actually be compensation for services in the post-combination period.

15.92 A non-compete agreement negotiated as part of a business combination generally prohibits former owners or key employees from competing with the combined entity. The agreement typically covers a set period of time that commences after the acquisition date or termination of employment with the combined entity. A non-compete agreement negotiated as part of a business combination will typically be initiated by the acquirer to protect the interests of the acquirer and the combined entity. Transactions are to be treated separately if they are entered into by or on behalf of the acquirer or primarily for the benefit of the acquirer. [IFRS 3 para 52]. As such, non-compete agreements negotiated as part of a business combination should generally be accounted for as transactions separate from the business combination.

15.93 A non-compete agreement will normally have a finite life requiring amortisation of the asset. The amortisation period should reflect the period over which the benefits from the non-compete agreement are derived. Determining the period is a matter of judgement in which all terms of the agreement, including restrictions on enforceability of the agreement, should be considered.

Customer-related intangible assets

15.94 Customer-related intangible assets include, but are not limited to: (i)

© 2012 PricewaterhouseCoopers LLP. All rights reserved.

15.91　非竞争协议是禁止个人或企业在规定期限内在特定市场与另一家公司竞争的法律安排。被购买方在收购时可能会具有预先存在的非竞争协议。因为这些协议来自法定或合同权利，所以它们应该会符合合同性—法律标准，并代表一项应该会确认为业务合并一部分的已购资产。非竞争协议的条款、条件和可执行性可能会影响分配至无形资产的公允价值，但应该不会影响它们的确认。向前雇员支付的其他款项可能被描述为非竞争支付，但实际上可能是合并后服务的报酬。

15.92　协商为业务合并一部分的非竞争协议一般禁止前所有者或重要员工与合并后的主体竞争。该协议一般涵盖一定期限，开始于收购日期之后或与合并后的主体雇佣关系终止之后。协商为业务合并一部分的非竞争协议一般由购买方发起，旨在保护购买方和合并后的主体的利益。如果非竞争协议是由购买方或代表购买方，为了购买方的利益而进行，则交易单独处理。[IFRS 3 第 52 段]。因此，协商为业务合并一部分的非竞争协议一般应当作为从业务合并中分离出来的交易进行会计处理。

15.93　一项非竞争协议一般具有有限的寿命，需要摊销该资产。摊销期间应当反映从非竞争协议获得利益的期间。确定该期间需要进行判断，应当考虑协议的所有条款，包括对于协议可执行性的限制。

与客户相关的无形资产

15.94　与客户相关的无形资产包括但不限于：（i）客户合同和相关的客户关

ⓒ 2012 普华永道（PricewaterhouseCoopers）版权所有。

customer contracts and related customer relationships, (ii) non-contractual customer relationships, (iii) customer lists, and (iv) order or production backlog. [IFRS 3 para IE23]. In many cases, the relationships that an acquiree has with its customers may encompass more than one type of intangible asset (for example, customer contract and related relationship, customer list and backlog). The inter-relationship of various types of intangible assets related to the same customer can pose challenges in recognising and measuring customer-related intangible assets. The values ascribed to other intangible assets, such as brand names and trademarks, may impact the valuation of customer-related intangible assets as well. Also, because the useful lives and the pattern in which the economic benefits of the assets are consumed may differ, it may be necessary to separately recognise intangible assets that encompass a single customer relationship. [IFRS 3 para IE27].

15.95 Additionally, customer award or loyalty programmes may create a relationship between the acquiree and the customer. Such programmes may enhance the value of a customer-related intangible asset. These programmes are expected to meet the term 'contractual' because the parties have agreed to certain terms and conditions, have had a previous contractual relationship, or both. In addition to evaluating the need to recognise and measure a customer-related intangible asset for these programmes, the acquirer must separately evaluate the need to recognise and measure any assumed liabilities related to these programmes on the acquisition date. Given the range of terms and conditions associated with these programmes, careful consideration should be given in assessing the recognition and measurement of any related intangible assets. The following paragraphs discuss the common customer-related intangible assets recognised and measured in a business combination.

15.96 A customer relationship exists between a company and its customer if (i) the company has information about the customer and has regular contact with the customer and (ii) the customer has the ability to make direct contact with the company. [IFRS 3 para IE28]. If the entity has a practice of establishing relationships with its customers through contracts, the customer relationship would meet the contractual-legal criterion for separate recognition as an intangible asset, even if no contract (for example, purchase order or sales order) is in place on the

© 2012 PricewaterhouseCoopers LLP. All rights reserved.

系；（ii）非合同客户关系；（iii）客户名单；（iv）订单或生产性积压。[IFRS 3 说明性示例第 23 段]。在许多情况下，被购买方与客户的关系可以包含一种类型以上的无形资产（例如客户合同和相关关系、客户名单和积压）。与同一客户相关的各种类型的无形资产之间的相互关系对确认和计量与客户相关的无形资产具有挑战。归属于其他无形资产的价值，例如品牌名称和商标，可能也会影响与客户相关的无形资产的评估。而且，因为资产使用寿命和经济利益消耗方式可能有所不同，所以可能有必要单独确认包含单一客户关系的无形资产。[IFRS 第 3 号说明性示例第 27 段]。

15.95　另外，客户奖励或忠诚计划可能创建了一种被购买方与客户之间的关系。该类计划可能提高与客户相关的无形资产的价值。这些计划预计符合“合同性”条件，这是因为双方已经同意某些条款或条件，或之前已经存在合同关系，或两者兼具。除了评估是否需要为这些计划确认和计量一项与客户相关的无形资产之外，购买方还必须单独评估是否需要在购买日确认和计量与这些计划相关的债务承担。在与这些计划相关联的条款和条件的范围既定的情况下，在评估任何相关无形资产的确认和计量时，应当仔细考虑。以下段落讨论在一项业务合并中确认和计量的与客户相关的常见无形资产。

15.96　在以下情况中，公司与其客户之间存在客户关系：（i）公司拥有客户信息，并定期与客户联系；（ii）客户有能力直接与公司联系。[IFRS 3 说明性示例第 28 段]。如果该主体具有通过合同与客户建立关系的惯例，则该客户关系应该会符合单独确认为无形资产的合同性—法律标准，即使在购买日没有合同（例如采购订单或销售订单）。通过销售或服务代表定期联系的惯例也可产生一项客户关系。客户关系可能表明一项无形资产的存在，如果它符合合同性—法律标准或可分离标准，应当被予以确认。[IFRS 3 说明性示例第

© 2012 普华永道（PricewaterhouseCoopers）版权所有。

acquisition date. A practice of regular contact by sales or service representatives may also give rise to a customer relationship. A customer relationship may indicate the existence of an intangible asset that should be recognised if it meets the contractual-legal or separable criteria. [IFRS 3 para IE28].

15.97 An acquirer may have relationships with the same customers as the acquiree (sometimes referred to as 'overlapping customers'). If the customer relationship meets the contractual-legal or separable criteria, an intangible asset should be recognised for the customer relationships of the acquiree, even though the acquirer may have relationships with those same customers. The valuation of such relationships may depend on a number of factors, including whether market participants would benefit from those same relationships. However, this is an evolving area in valuation practice.

Example 1 – Cancellable and non-cancellable customer contracts

An acquired business is a manufacturer of commercial machinery and related aftermarket parts and components. The acquiree's commercial machines, which comprise approximately 70% of its sales, are sold through contracts that are non-cancellable. Its aftermarket parts and components, which comprise the remaining 30% of the acquiree's sales, are also sold through contracts. However, the customers can cancel the contracts at any time.

The acquiree has a practice of establishing contractual relationships with its customers for the sale of commercial machinery and the sale of aftermarket parts and components. The ability of those customers that purchase aftermarket parts and components to cancel their contracts at any time would factor into the measurement of the intangible asset, but would not affect whether the contractual-legal criterion has been met from a recognition perspective.

Example 2 – Potential contracts being negotiated at the acquisition date

An acquiree is negotiating contracts with a number of new customers at the acquisition date for which the substantive terms, such as pricing, product specifications, and other key terms, have not yet been agreed to by both parties.

© 2012 PricewaterhouseCoopers LLP. All rights reserved.

28 段］。

15. 97 购买方、被购买方可能与同一群客户（有时称为“重叠客户”）有关系。如果该客户关系符合合同性—法律标准或可分离标准，则应当将被购买方的客户关系确认为一项无形资产，即使购买方可能也与那些同样的客户有关系。该类关系的评估可能取决于许多因素，包括市场参与者是否应该会受益于那些同样的关系。然而，这在评估实践中是一个不断发展的领域。

示例1——可撤销和不可撤销的客户合同

被购买业务是一个商用机器和相关的配件市场的部件和组件的制造商。被购买方的商用机器构成其销售额的70%左右，通过不可撤销的合同销售。其配件市场部件和组件占被购买方销售额的剩余30%，也通过合同销售。然而，客户能够随时撤销合同。

对于销售商用机器和销售配件市场部件和组件，被购买方具有与其客户建立合同关系的惯例。购买配件市场部件和组件的那些客户随时撤销合同的能力应该是在计量无形资产时考虑的因素，但是从确认方面看，应该不会影响是否合同性—法律标准已经满足。

示例2——于购买日正在协商的潜在合同

一个被购买方正在与许多新客户协商合同，于购买日双方尚未同意合同的实质条款，例如定价、产品规格以及其他关键条款。

ⓒ 2012 普华永道（PricewaterhouseCoopers）版权所有。

Although the acquirer may consider these prospective contracts to be valuable, potential contracts with new customers do not meet the contractual-legal criterion, because there is no contractual or legal right associated with them at the acquisition date. Potential contracts also do not meet the separability criterion, because they are not capable of being sold, transferred, or exchanged and, therefore, are not separable from the acquired business. In this fact pattern, the value of these potential contracts is subsumed into goodwill. Changes to the status of the potential contracts subsequent to the acquisition date would not result in a reclassification of goodwill to an intangible asset. However, the acquirer should assess the facts and circumstances surrounding the events occurring shortly after the acquisition to determine whether a separately recognisable intangible asset existed at the acquisition date.

15.98 Customer relationships that do not arise from contracts between an acquiree and its customers (that is, non-contractual customer relationships) do not meet the contractual-legal criterion. However, there may be circumstances in which these relationships can be sold or otherwise exchanged without selling the acquired business, thereby meeting the separability criterion. If a non-contractual customer relationship meets the separability criterion, the relationship is recognised as an intangible asset. [IFRS 3 para IE31].

15.99 Evidence of separability of a non-contractual customer relationship includes exchange transactions for the same or similar type of asset. These transactions do not need to occur frequently for a non-contractual customer relationship to be recognised as an intangible asset apart from goodwill. Instead, recognition depends on whether the non-contractual customer relationship is capable of being separated and sold, transferred, etc. [IFRS 3 para B33]. Non-contractual relationships that are not separately recognised, such as customer bases, market share, and unidentifiable 'walk-up' customers, should be included as part of goodwill.

15.100 A customer list represents a list of known, identifiable customers that contains information about those customers, such as name and contact information. A customer list may also be in the form of a database that includes other information about the customers (for example, order history and demographic

© 2012 PricewaterhouseCoopers LLP. All rights reserved.

虽然购买方可能认为这些未来合同具有价值，但与新客户之间的潜在合同不符合合同性—法律标准，这是因为在购买日不存在与其相关联的合同或法律权利。潜在合同也不符合可分离标准，这是因为它们不能被出售、转让或交换，因此不能从被购买业务中分离出来。在这种事实模式中，这些潜在合同的价值归入商誉。购买日后潜在合同状态的变化应该不会导致商誉重新分类为一项无形资产。然而，购买方应当评估购买后不久发生的事件的事实和环境，以确定在购买日是否存在可单独确认的无形资产。

15.98　不是来自被购买方与其客户签订的合同的客户关系（即非合同客户关系）不会符合合同性—法律标准。然而，可能会发生这些关系能够在不出售被购买业务的情况下被出售或交换的情况，从而符合可分离标准。如果一项非合同客户关系符合可分离标准，该关系确认为一项无形资产。[IFRS 3 说明性示例第 31 段]。

15.99　一项非合同客户关系的可分离性的证据包括相同或类似类型的资产的交换交易。对于非合同客户关系确认为除商誉外的一项无形资产来说，这些交易并不需要经常发生。相反地，确认是取决于非合同客户关系是否能够被分离和被出售、转让等。[IFRS 3 附录二第 33 段]。未单独确认的非合同关系（例如客户基础、市场份额以及不可辨认的无预约客户）应当被归为商誉的一部分。

15.100　客户名单是指已知、可辨认的客户的清单，包含这些客户的信息，诸如姓名和联系信息等。客户名单也可能为数据库的形式，包含客户的其他信息（例如，历史订单和人口统计信息等）。

© 2012 普华永道（PricewaterhouseCoopers）版权所有。

information).

15.101 A customer list does not usually arise from contractual or other legal rights and, therefore, typically does not meet the contractual-legal criterion. However, customer lists are frequently leased or otherwise exchanged and, therefore, generally meet the separability criterion, [IFRS 3 para IE24]. An acquired customer list does not meet the separability criterion if the terms of confidentiality or other agreements prohibit an acquiree from leasing or otherwise exchanging information about its customers. Restrictions imposed by confidentiality or other agreements pertaining to customer lists do not impact the recognition of other customer-related intangible assets that meet the contractual-legal criterion.

15.102 Customer list intangible assets may have a relatively low fair value and a reasonably short life, depending on the nature of the customer information, how easily it may be obtained by other sources, and the period over which the customer information may provide benefit.

15.103 A customer base represents a group of customers that are not known or identifiable (for example, persons who purchase newspapers from a news stand or customers of a fast-food franchise or petrol station). A customer base may also be described as 'walk-up' customers. A customer base is generally not recognised separately as an intangible asset, because it does not arise from contractual or legal rights and is not separable. However, a customer base may constitute a customer list if information is obtained about the various customers. For example, a customer list may exist, even if only basic contact information about a customer, such as name and address or telephone number, is available.

15.104 Order or production backlog arises from unfulfilled purchase or sales order contracts and may be significant in certain industries, such as manufacturing or construction. The order or production backlog acquired in a business combination meets the contractual-legal criterion and, therefore, may be recognised separately as an intangible asset, even if the purchase or sales order contracts are cancellable. However, the fact that contracts are cancellable may affect the measurement of the fair value of the associated intangible asset. [IFRS 3 para IE25].

© 2012 PricewaterhouseCoopers LLP. All rights reserved.

15.101　客户名单通常并不源于合同权利或其他法律权利，因此典型的客户名单不符合合同性—法律标准。然而，客户名单经常被租赁或交换，因此，一般符合可分离标准。[IFRS 3 说明性示例第 24 段]。但如果保密条款或其他协议禁止被购买方租赁或交换客户信息，则已购的客户名单不符合可分离标准。有关客户名单的保密条款或其他协议所施加的限制不会影响其他符合合同性—法律标准的与客户相关的无形资产的确认。

15.102　客户名单无形资产可能具有相对较低的公允价值及合理的短期的寿命，这取决于客户信息的性质、通过其他来源获得的容易程度以及客户信息能带来利益的期限。

15.103　客户基础是指一个未知或不可辨认的客户群体（例如，从一个报摊购买报纸的人，或一个快餐特许店或一个加油站的顾客）。客户基础也可描述为无预约客户（walk-up customers）。客户基础一般不单独确认为一项无形资产，这是因为它不源于合同或法律权利，并且不可分离。然而，如果获得了各种客户的信息，客户基础可以构成一个客户名单。例如，即使只有客户的基本联系信息（诸如姓名、地址或电话号码等），也可构成一个客户名单。

15.104　订单或生产性积压来自尚未履行完毕的购买或销售订单合同，在某些行业中可能比较重要，例如制造或建筑业。在一项业务合并中获得的订单或生产性积压符合合同性—法律标准，因此，即使购买或销售订单合同是可撤销的，也可以单独确认为一项无形资产。然而，合同可以撤销的事实可能会影响相关联的无形资产公允价值的计量。[IFRS 3 说明性示例第 25 段]。

ⓒ 2012 普华永道（PricewaterhouseCoopers）版权所有。

Example – Identification of customer-related intangible assets due to purchase orders

Entity M is acquired in a business combination by entity Y and has the following two customers:

- Customer A is a recurring customer that transacts with entity M through purchase orders, of which certain purchase orders are outstanding at the acquisition date.
- Customer B is a recurring customer that transacts with entity M through purchase orders, however, there are no purchase orders outstanding at the acquisition date.

Entity Y assesses the various components of the overall customer relationship that may exist for the acquired customers. As a result of this assessment, entity Y would recognise an intangible asset(s) for customers A and B based on the contractual-legal criterion. The customer relationship with customer A meets the contractual-legal criterion as there is a contract or agreement in place at the acquisition date. Customer B's customer relationship also meets the contractual-legal criterion as there is a history of entity M using purchase orders with this customer, even though there are no purchase orders outstanding on the acquisition date.

Artistic-related intangible assets

15.105 Artistic-related intangible assets are creative assets that are typically protected by copyrights or other contractual and legal means. Artistic-related intangible assets are recognised separately if they arise from contractual or legal rights, such as copyrights. [IFRS 3 para IE33]. Artistic-related intangible assets include (i) plays, operas, ballets; (ii) books, magazines, newspapers, other literary works; (iii) musical works, such as compositions, song lyrics, advertising jingles; (iv) pictures, photographs; and (v) video and audio-visual material, including motion pictures or films, music videos, and television programmes. [IFRS 3 para IE32]. Copyrights can be assigned or licensed, in part, to others. A

© 2012 PricewaterhouseCoopers LLP. All rights reserved.

示例——辨认由于采购订单而产生的与客户相关的无形资产

主体 M 被主体 Y 通过业务合并收购，主体 M 具有以下两家客户：

- 客户 A 是老客户，通过采购订单与主体 M 交易，在购买日某些采购订单未完成。
- 客户 B 是老客户，通过采购订单与主体 M 交易，然而，在购买日没有未完成的采购订单。

对于已获得的客户，主体 Y 评价全部客户关系内可能存在的各个组成部分。经评价的结果，主体 Y 应该会根据合同性—法律标准确认与客户 A 和 B 相关的一项或数项无形资产。因为在购买日存在一项合同或协议，与客户 A 的客户关系符合合同性—法律标准。即使在购买日没有未完成的采购订单，与客户 B 的客户关系也符合合同性—法律标准，这是因为存在主体 M 使用该客户采购订单的历史。

与艺术相关的无形资产

15.105　与艺术相关的无形资产是创造性资产，一般受到版权或其他合同和法律手段的保护。如果与艺术相关的无形资产来自于合同权利或法律权利，例如版权，则单独确认。[IFRS 3 说明性示例第 33 段]。与艺术相关的无形资产包括：(i) 戏剧，歌剧，芭蕾舞剧；(ii) 书籍，杂志，报纸，其他文学作品；(iii) 音乐作品，例如乐曲，歌词，广告词；(iv) 图画，照片；(v) 视频和视听材料，包括电影，音乐视频，电视节目。[IFRS 3 说明性示例第 32 段]。版权可以部分地转让或许可给他人。只要作为组成部分的资产具有类似的使用寿命，受到版权保护的无形资产和相关的转让或许可协议可以确认为一项单独的互补性资产。[IFRS 3 说明性示例第 32 段]。

ⓒ 2012 普华永道（PricewaterhouseCoopers）版权所有。

copyright-protected intangible asset and related assignments or license agreements may be recognised as a single complementary asset, as long as the component assets have similar useful lives. [IFRS 3 para IE33].

Contract-based intangible assets

15.106 Contract-based intangible assets represent the value of rights that arise from contractual arrangements. Customer contracts are one type of contract-based intangible assets. Contract-based intangible assets include (i) licensing, royalty, and standstill agreements; (ii) advertising, construction, management, service or supply contracts; (iii) construction permits; (iv) franchise agreements; (v) operating and broadcast rights; (vi) contracts to service financial assets; (vii) employment contracts; (viii) use rights; and (ix) lease agreements. [IFRS 3 para IE34]. Contracts whose terms are considered at-the-money as well as contracts in which the terms are favourable relative to market may also give rise to contract-based intangible assets. If the contract's terms are unfavourable relative to market, the acquirer recognises a liability assumed in the business combination.

15.107 Contracts to service financial assets may include:

- collecting principal, interest, and escrow payments from borrowers;
- paying taxes and insurance from escrowed funds;
- monitoring delinquencies;
- executing foreclosure, if necessary;
- temporarily investing funds pending distribution;
- remitting fees to guarantors, trustees and others providing services; and
- accounting for and remitting principal and interest payments to the holders of beneficial interests in the financial assets.

Although servicing is inherent in all financial assets, it is not recognised as a separate intangible asset unless (i) the underlying financial assets (for example, receivables) are sold or securitised and the servicing contract is retained by the seller; or (ii) the servicing contract is separately purchased or assumed. [IFRS 3

© 2012 PricewaterhouseCoopers LLP. All rights reserved.

以合同为基础的无形资产

15.106　以合同为基础的无形资产是指合同、安排所赋予的权利的价值。客户合同是以合同为基础的无形资产的类型之一。以合同为基础的无形资产包括：（i）使用许可，特许权，终止协议；（ii）广告，建筑，管理，服务或供应合同；（iii）建筑许可证；（iv）特许权协议；（v）运营和播放权；（vi）为金融资产提供服务的合同；（vii）雇佣合同；（viii）使用权；（ix）租赁协议。[IFRS 3 说明性示例第 34 段]。其条款视为平价的合同以及相对于市场来说条款优惠的合同可能也会产生以合同为基础的无形资产。如果合同条款相对于市场来说不优惠，则购买方确认一项业务合并中承担的负债。

15.107　为金融资产提供服务的合同可能包括：

■ 从借款人收取本金、利息和第三者保存契约款项；

■ 缴纳来自代管基金的税款和保险费；

■ 监控违约行为；

■ 如有必要，执行抵押品赎回权的取消；

■ 暂时投资于资金未决的经销；

■ 向保证人、受托人和提供服务的其他人汇款；

■ 向金融资产受益权持有人说明和汇出本金和利息。

虽然服务存在于所有金融资产中，但不确认为一项单独的无形资产，除非：（i）标的金融资产（例如应收款项）被出售或证券化，并且服务合同由卖方保留；或（ii）服务合同被单独购买或承担。[IFRS 3 说明性示例第 35 段]。

ⓒ 2012 普华永道（PricewaterhouseCoopers）版权所有。

para IE35].

15.108 If mortgage loans, credit card receivables, or other financial assets are acquired in a business combination along with the contract to service those assets, then neither of the above criteria has been met and the servicing rights will not be recognised as a separate intangible asset. However, the servicing rights are included in the measurement of the fair value of the underlying mortgage loans, credit card receivables, or other financial assets. [IFRS 3 para IE36].

15.109 Employment contracts may result in contract-based intangible assets or liabilities. [IFRS 3 para IE37]. An employment contract may be above or below market in the same way as a lease or a servicing contract. However, the recognition of employment contract intangible assets and liabilities are rare in practice, because employees can choose to leave employment with relatively short notice periods, employment contracts are usually not enforced and it is difficult to substantiate market compensation for specific employees.

15.110 An exception might be when a professional sports team is acquired. The player contracts may well give rise to employment contract intangible assets and liabilities. The athletes are often working under professional restrictions, such that they cannot leave their contracted teams at will and play with another team to maintain their professional standing. Player contracts may also be separable, in that they are often the subject of observable market transactions. Pre-existing employment contracts in the acquired business may also contain non-competition clauses. These non-competition clauses may have value and should be assessed separately as intangible assets when such contracts are part of a business combination.

15.111 An assembled workforce is defined as an existing collection of employees that permits an acquirer to continue to operate from the date of the acquisition. [IFRS 3 para B37]. Although individual employees may have employment agreements with the acquiree, which may, at least theoretically, be separately recognised and measured, the entire assembled workforce does not have such a contract. Therefore, an assembled workforce does not meet the contractual-legal criterion. Furthermore, the IASB concluded that an assembled workforce is not considered separable, because it cannot be sold or transferred without causing

© 2012 PricewaterhouseCoopers LLP. All rights reserved.

15.108 如果抵押贷款、信用卡应收款或其他金融资产是在在业务合并中与为这些资产提供服务的合同一起取得，则以上标准都不符合，并且服务权不会被确认为一项单独的无形资产。然而，服务权包含在标的抵押贷款、信用卡应收款或其他金融资产公允价值的计量中。[IFRS 3 说明性示例第 36 段]。

15.109 雇佣合同可能产生以合同为基础的无形资产或负债。[IFRS 3 说明性示例第 37 段]。雇佣合同可以高于或低于市场，其方式与一项租赁或服务合同相同。然而，在实务中很少确认雇佣合同无形资产和负债，这是因为雇员可以选择在相对较短的通知期内离职，雇佣合同通常不是强制性的，并且很难证实特定雇员的市场报酬。

15.110 购买一个专业运动队可能会是一个例外。队员合同很可能会产生雇佣合同无形资产和负债。运动员通常在专业限制下工作，使其不能随意离开签约队而转至另一队，以维护其专业声誉。队员合同也可分离，因为它们通常是可观察到的市场交易的对象。在已购业务中预先存在的雇佣合同也可包含非竞争条款。这些非竞争条款可能具有价值，当这些合同成为业务合并的一部分时，应当单独评价为无形资产。

15.111 劳动力组合被定义为使购买方能够从购买日起继续运营的雇员的现有组合。[IFRS 3 附录二第 37 段]。虽然单独的雇员可能会与被购买方签订雇佣协议，至少在理论上可以单独确认和计量，但整个劳动力组合没有这样的合同。因此，劳动力组合不符合合同性—法律标准。而且，国际会计准则理事会得出结论劳动力组合被认为是不可分离的，因为它不能在不中断被购买方业务的前提下被出售或转让。[IFRS 3 结论基础第 178 段]。因此，在一项业务合并（以及资产购买）中，劳动力组合不会单独被确认为可辨认无形资产，所以，归属于劳动力的任何价值归入商誉。

© 2012 普华永道（PricewaterhouseCoopers）版权所有。

disruption to the acquiree's business. [IFRS 3 para BC178]. As a result, in a business combination (as well as an asset acquisition), an assembled workforce is not an identifiable intangible asset that is to be separately recognised and, as such, any value attributable to the assembled workforce is subsumed into goodwill.

15.112 The intellectual capital that has been created by a skilled workforce may be embodied in the fair value of an entity's other intangible assets that would be recognised at the acquisition date as the employer retains the rights associated with those intangible assets. For example, in measuring the fair value of proprietary technologies and processes, the intellectual capital of the employee groups embedded within the proprietary technologies or processes would be considered. [IFRS 3 para BC180].

15.113 A collective bargaining or union agreement typically dictates the terms of employment (for example, wage rates, overtime rates and holidays), but does not bind the employee or employer to a specified duration of employment. The employee is still an at-will employee and has the ability to leave or may be terminated. Therefore, similar to an assembled workforce, no intangible asset would be separately recognised related to the employees covered under the agreement. However, a collective bargaining agreement of an acquired entity may be recognised as a separate intangible asset or liability if the terms of the agreement are favourable or unfavourable when compared to market terms.

15.114 Use rights, such as drilling, water, air, mineral, timber cutting and route authorities' rights, are contract-based intangible assets. Use rights are unique, in that they may have characteristics of both tangible and intangible assets. Use rights should be recognised based on their nature as either a tangible or intangible asset. [IFRS 3 para IE38]. For example, mineral rights, that are legal rights to explore, extract and retain all or a portion of mineral deposits, are tangible assets.

15.115 An intangible asset (or a liability) may be recognised at the acquisition date for the difference between the fair value of all assets and liabilities arising from the rights and obligations of any acquired insurance and reinsurance contracts and their carrying amounts.

© 2012 PricewaterhouseCoopers LLP. All rights reserved.

15.112　由熟练劳动力创造出的智力资本可以包含在购买日确认的主体的其他无形资产的公允价值中，这是因为雇主保留与那些无形资产相关联的权利。例如，在计量专有技术和工艺的公允价值时，应该会考虑专有技术或工艺中嵌入的雇员群体的智力资本。[IFRS 3 结论基础第 180 段]。

15.113　一个集体谈判或工会协议一般规定雇佣条款（例如工资等级、加班费、假期)，但不会将雇员或雇主绑定在规定的雇佣期限内。雇员仍然是随意的雇员，能够离职，也能够被解雇。因此，与劳动力组合类似，应该不会单独确认与协议所涵盖的雇员相关的无形资产。然而，如果被购买主体的一项集体谈判安排与市场条款相比是有利或不利的，则该安排可能被确认为一项单独的无形资产或负债。

15.114　使用权，诸如钻井、水、空气、矿物、伐木、道路权限的权利，是以合同为基础的无形资产。使用权是独特的，因为它们可能兼具有形和无形资产的特征。使用权应当根据性质被确认为一项有形资产或无形资产。[IFRS 3 说明性示例第 38 段]。例如，矿产权，即勘探、提取和保留所有或部分矿藏的法律权利，是有形资产。

15.115　在购买日，已购买的保险和再保险合同的权利和义务所产生的所有资产和负债的公允价值与其账面价值之间的差额，可以确认为一项无形资产（或负债)。

ⓒ 2012 普华永道（PricewaterhouseCoopers）版权所有。

15.116 Intangible assets or liabilities may be recognised for certain contracts, such as lease arrangements, whose terms are favourable or unfavourable to current market terms. In making this assessment, the terms of a contract should be compared to market prices at the date of acquisition to determine whether an intangible asset or liability should be recognised. If the terms of an acquired contract are favourable relative to market prices, an intangible asset is recognised. On the other hand, if the terms of the acquired contract are unfavourable relative to market prices, then a liability is recognised. [IFRS 3 para IE34]. The Board characterised the differences in contract terms relative to market terms as assets and liabilities, but these adjustments in value are unlikely to meet the definitions of an asset and liability under IFRS accounting framework. Within this chapter, these adjustments are referred to as assets and liabilities for consistency with the treatment by the Board.

15.117 A significant area of judgement in measuring favourable and unfavourable contracts is whether contract renewal or extension terms should be considered. The following factors should be considered whether to include renewals or extensions:

- Whether renewals or extensions are discretionary without the need to renegotiate key terms or are within the control of the acquiree. Renewals or extensions that are within the control of the acquiree are likely to be considered if the terms are favourable to the acquirer.

- Whether the renewals or extensions provide economic benefit to the holder of the renewal right. The holder of a renewal right, either the acquiree or the counterparty, will likely act in their best interest. For example, if the acquiree is the lessee of an operating lease that is favourable to the lessee, the renewals would likely be considered, because the acquirer, all things being equal, would plan to exercise the renewal right and realise the benefit of the favourable terms. On the other hand, if the acquirer is the lessor of an operating lease that is favourable to the lessor, the acquirer would usually not presume that the lessee would renew its unfavourable lease.

- Whether there are any other factors that would indicate a contract may or may not be renewed.

© 2012 PricewaterhouseCoopers LLP. All rights reserved.

15.116　对于某些合同，例如条款与当前的市场条款相比有利或不利的租赁安排，可能会确认无形资产或负债。在进行这种评价时，合同条款应当与购买日的市场价格进行对比，以确定是否应当确认一项无形资产或负债。如果一项已购入的合同的条款与市场价格相比有利，则确认一项无形资产。另一方面，如果已购入的合同的条款与市场价格相比不利，则确认一项负债。[IFRS 3 说明性示例第 34 段]。理事会将合同条款与市场条款之间的差异定性为资产和负债，但根据国际财务报告准则会计框架，这些价值调整不可能符合一项资产和负债的定义。在本章中，为了与理事会的处理一致，这些调整仍然称为资产和负债。

15.117　在计量有利和不利合同时，一个重要的判断领域是是否应当考虑合同续约或延期的条款。关于是否包括续约或延期，应当考虑以下因素：

- 续约或延期是否无需重新协商重要条款而自由决定，或是否在被购买方的控制之下。由被购买方控制的续约或延期，在条款对购买方有利的情况下可能予以考虑。
- 续约或延期是否给续约权持有人带来经济利益。续约权持有人（被购买方或交易对方）可能为自身最大利益而行事。例如，如果被购买方是一项经营租赁的承租人，该租赁是对承租人有利，则可能考虑续约，这是因为在一切条件相同的情况下，购买方应该会打算行使续约权并实现有利条款带来的利益。另一方面，如果购买方是一项经营租赁的出租人，该租赁对出租人有利，则购买方通常应该不会假定承租人应该会续约该不利租赁。
- 是否存在应该会表明合同可能会或不会续约的任何其他因素。

ⓒ 2012 普华永道（PricewaterhouseCoopers）版权所有。

15.118 Each arrangement is recognised and measured separately. The resulting amounts for favourable and unfavourable contracts are not offset. The fair value of an intangible asset or liability associated with favourable and unfavourable contract terms would generally be determined based on present-value techniques. For example, the difference between the contract price and the current market price for the remaining contractual term, including any expected renewals, would be calculated and then discounted to arrive at a net present-value amount. The fair value of the intangible asset or liability would then be amortised over the remaining contract term, including renewals, if applicable.

Example 1 – Favourable purchase contract

Entity N acquires entity O in a business combination. Entity O purchases electricity through a purchase contract, which is in year three of a five-year arrangement. At the end of the original term, Entity O has the option at its sole discretion to extend the purchase contract for another five years. The annual cost of electricity per the original contract is C80 per year and the annual cost for the five-year extension period is C110 per year. The current annual market price for electricity at the acquisition date is C200 and market rates are not expected to change in the future. (For the purpose of this example, assume that entity N does not account for the contract as a derivative.)

Entity O's purchase contract for electricity is favourable. Both the original contract and extension terms allow entity O to purchase electricity at amounts below the annual market price of C200 in this situation. While the contract is favourable based on the remaining two years of the original contractual term, entity N would likely consider the favourable five-year extension term as well.

Example 2 – Unfavourable purchase contract

Assuming the same facts above, except that the current annual market price for electricity at the acquisition date is C50 per year and market rates are not expected to change in the future.

Entity O's purchase contract is unfavourable. Both the original contract and extension term require it to pay amounts in excess of the current annual market

© 2012 PricewaterhouseCoopers LLP. All rights reserved.

15. 118 每项安排单独确认和计量。有利和不利合同的最终金额不抵销。与有利和不利合同条款相关联的无形资产或负债的公允价值一般应该根据现值技术确定。例如，剩余合同期限内（包括任何预期的续约）的合同价格和当前市场价格的差额应该会被计算，然后折现以获得净现值金额。无形资产或负债的公允价值应该会在剩余合同期限内（包括续约，如适用）摊销。

示例1——有利的购买合同

主体N通过一项业务合并并购了主体O。主体O通过一个购买合同购买电力，该合同处于五年期合同中的第三年。在原始合同结束时，主体O有权自行决定是否将购买合同延期五年。根据原始合同，电力年度成本为每年80元，五年的延期期间的年度成本为每年110元。购买日的电力现行市场价格为每年200元，并且预计未来的市场价格不会变化。（为了本例的目的，假设主体N不将合同视为衍生合同。）

主体O的电力购买合同是有利的。在这种情况下原始合同和延期条款使主体O能够以低于每年200元的市场价格购买电力。在原始合同期限的剩余两年内该合同是有利的，主体N也可能会考虑对其有利的五年的延期。

示例2——不利的购买合同

假设存在与以上内容相同的事实，除了于购买日的电力现行市场价格为每年50元，并且预计未来的市场价格不会变化。

主体O的购买合同是不利的。在这种情况下，原始合同和延期条款要求它支付的金额超过现行年度市场价格50元。尽管主体N应该会确认和计

ⓒ 2012 普华永道（PricewaterhouseCoopers）版权所有。

be identifiable if the terms of the lease contain purchase or renewal options. Lastly, leasehold improvements of the acquired entity would be recognised as tangible assets on the acquisition date at their fair value.

15. 122 No separate intangible asset or liability would typically be recognised for the lease contract terms if the acquiree is a lessee in a finance lease. Any value inherent in the lease (that is, fair value associated with favourable or unfavourable rental rents, renewal or purchase options, or in-place leases), is typically reflected in the amount assigned to the asset under capital lease and the capital lease obligation. In measuring the amount to record for the property under a finance lease, the acquirer should consider whether it is anticipated that the acquirer will obtain ownership of the leased property by the end of the lease term, because of a contractual requirement or pursuant to the exercise of a bargain purchase option. If it is anticipated that the acquirer will obtain ownership of the leased property, then the acquirer should record the property under capital lease at the fair value of the underlying property. If it is not anticipated that the acquirer will obtain ownership of the leased property, then the acquirer should record the property under capital lease at an amount equal to the fair value of the leasehold interest (that is, the value of the right to use the property until the end of the lease). In addition, any related leasehold improvements would be recognised and measured at fair value.

15. 123 A liability for the remaining rent payments due under a finance lease would also be recognised and measured at fair value. The assumptions used in measuring the liability should be consistent with the assumptions used in measuring the asset.

15. 124 The asset subject to the lease would be recognised at its fair value as encumbered by the existing lease, if the acquiree is a lessor in an operating lease. Therefore, a separate intangible asset or liability associated with the favourable or unfavourable terms, and any value associated with 'in-place' leases would not be separately recognised, but are included in the value of the leased asset. [IFRS 3 para B42]. However, it may be appropriate to amortise separately amounts related to favourable or unfavourable lease terms. [IAS 16 para 44]. Additionally, an intangible asset may be recognised for any value associated with the relationship the lessor has with the lessee. The acquired entity may also be a lessor in a lease other

© 2012 PricewaterhouseCoopers LLP. All rights reserved.

15.122 如果被购买方是一项融资租赁中的承租人，则对于租赁合同条款来说一般应该不会确认单独的无形资产或负债。租赁中的任何价值（即与有利或不利的租金、续约或购买选择权或适宜租赁相关联的公允价值）一般反映在分配给融资租赁资产的金额和融资租赁义务中。在计量一项融资租赁不动产的金额时，购买方应当考虑是否预期由于合同要求或根据廉价购买选择权的行使，购买方将在租赁期结束时获得租赁不动产的所有权。如果预期购买方将获得租赁不动产的所有权，则购买方应当以标的不动产的公允价值记录资本租赁不动产。如果预期购买方将不会获得租赁不动产的所有权，则购买方应当以等同于租赁权益的公允价值（即直至租赁结束为止使用不动产的权利的价值）的金额记录资本租赁不动产。另外，任何相关的租赁资产改良应该会以公允价值确认和计量。

15.123 在一项融资租赁下，剩余的租金支付负债也应该会以公允价值确认和计量。在计量负债时使用的假设应当与计量资产时使用的假设一致。

15.124 如果被购买方在经营租赁中是出租人，则租赁资产应该会以现有租赁具有的公允价值确认。因此，与有利或不利条款相关联的单独无形资产或负债以及与已执行租赁安排相关联的任何价值应该不会单独确认，而是包含在租赁资产的价值中。[IFRS 3 第 B42 段]。然而，单独摊销与有利或不利租赁条款相关的金额可能是适宜的。[IAS 第 16 号第 44 段]。另外，与出租人拥有的与承租人的关系相关联的任何价值可以确认为一项无形资产。被购买主体在一项非经营租赁的租赁中也可以是出租人，例如一项直接的融资租赁或销售型租赁。在那些情形中，购买方确认和计量一项代表其在租赁中的剩余投资的金融资产。该类投资应该根据 IAS 17 按照租赁安排的性质确认，一

ⓒ 2012 普华永道（PricewaterhouseCoopers）版权所有。

than an operating lease, such as a direct finance or sales-type lease. In those situations, the acquirer recognises and measures a financial asset that represents its remaining investment in the lease. Such investment would be recognised in accordance with IAS 17, based on the nature of the lease arrangement and would typically include any value associated with the existing in-place lease. Additionally, an intangible asset may be recognised for any value associated with the relationship the lessor has with the lessee.

15. 125 The table below summarises the typical items to consider in the recognition of assets and liabilities associated with lease arrangements in a business combination.

Lease classification	Item to consider
Acquired entity is a lessee in an operating lease.	■ Favourable or unfavourable rental rates. ■ Premium paid for certain at-the-money contracts. ■ Purchase or renewal options. ■ Leasehold improvements.
Acquired entity is a lessee of finance lease.	■ Property under finance lease (recognised at an amount equal to the fair value of the underlying property if ownership is reasonably certain to transfer to the lessee). ■ Property under finance lease (recognised at an amount equal to the fair value of the leasehold interest if ownership is not reasonably certain to transfer to the lessee). ■ Leasehold improvements owned. ■ Lease obligation recognised for remaining lease payments.
Acquired entity is lessor in an operating lease.	■ Leased asset (including tenant improvements) recognised, taking lease terms into account. ■ Customer (or tenant) relationships.
Acquired entity is lessor in a finance lease.	■ Financial asset that represents its remaining investment in the lease, measured in accordance with IAS 17, is recognised. ■ Customer (or tenant) relationships.

© 2012 PricewaterhouseCoopers LLP. All rights reserved.

般应该会包括与现已执行的租赁安排相关联的任何价值。另外，与出租人拥有的与承租人的关系相关联的任何价值都可能确认为一项无形资产。

15.125　下表汇总了在确认业务合并中与租赁安排相关联的资产和负债时应考虑的典型项目。

租赁类别	考虑的项目
被购买主体在经营租赁中是承租人。	■ 有利或不利的租金。 ■ 为某些平价合同支付的溢价。 ■ 购买或续约选择权。 ■ 租赁资产改良。
被购买主体在融资租赁中是承租人。	■ 融资租赁不动产（如果合理的确定所有权转让给承租人，以等同于标的不动产公允价值的金额确认）。 ■ 融资租赁不动产（如果不能合理的确定所有权转让给承租人，以等同于租赁权益公允价值的金额确认）。 ■ 拥有的租赁资产改良。 ■ 对于剩余租赁支付确认租赁义务。
被购买主体在经营租赁中是出租人。	■ 确认租赁资产（包括租户改良），考虑租赁条款。 ■ 客户（或租户）关系。
被购买主体在融资租赁中是出租人。	■ 按照 IAS 17 计量，确认代表其在租赁中的剩余投资的金融资产。 ■ 客户（或租户）关系。

ⓒ 2012 普华永道（PricewaterhouseCoopers）版权所有。

If the lease is classified as an operating lease and provides for non-level rent payments, the acquiree will have recorded an asset or liability to recognise rent expense or revenue on a straight-line basis. Such asset or liability would not be carried forward by the acquirer. Rather, the acquirer would recognise rent expense or revenue prospectively on a straight-line basis.

15.126 Assets and liabilities that arise on the acquisition date from leases assumed in a business combination are not exempt from the general fair value measurement principle. Accordingly, these assets and liabilities should be measured at their fair value on the acquisition date. The classification of a lease determined at lease inception should not be changed as a result of a business combination, unless the provisions of the lease are modified. [IFRS 3 para 17]. The determination of the lease term is important as this is a key assumption in establishing the classification of a lease at the inception of the contract. For example, including a renewal option in the lease term at inception may affect the initial lease classification.

Example – Recognisable intangible and tangible assets related to leases acquired in a business combination

Entity A, the lessor of a commercial office building subject to various operating leases, was acquired by entity G in 20X0. Included in the assets acquired is a building fully leased by third parties with leases extending through 20X9. As market rates have fluctuated over the years, certain of the leases are at above-market rates and others are at below-market rates at the acquisition date. All of the leases are classified as operating leases, as determined by the acquiree at lease inception.

Using the acquisition method, entity G would consider the following in recognising and measuring the assets and liabilities, if applicable, associated with the lease arrangements:

- *Building* – A tangible asset would be recognised and measured at fair value, taking into account the terms of the leases in place at the acquisition date. Therefore, the acquirer would not recognise separate intangible assets or liabilities related to the favourable/unfavourable leases or for the value of in-

© 2012 PricewaterhouseCoopers LLP. All rights reserved.

如果租赁被归类为一项经营租赁，并且租金的支付是非均衡的，则被购买方将已经按照直线法确认租赁费用或收入，并记录一项资产或负债。该类资产或负债应该不会被购买方结转后期。购买方应该是未来适用，根据直线法确认租赁费用或收入。

15.126　在购买日产生于在业务合并中承担的租赁的资产和负债不能免除一般的公允价值计量原则。因此，这些资产和负债应当在购买日以其公允价值计量。除非由于修改租赁条款，于租赁开始时已确定的租赁类别不应由于业务合并而发生改变。[IFRS 3 第 17 段]。确定租赁期限十分重要，因为这是合同开始时确定租赁类别的关键假设。例如，在开始时将续约选择权纳入租赁期限可能会影响初始租赁类别。

示例——与在业务合并中取得的租赁相关的可确认无形和有形资产

主体 A，是从事各种经营租赁的一个商业办公楼的出租人，在 20X0 年被主体 G 收购。在被购买资产中有一幢大楼，被第三方完全租用，租赁期延伸至 20X9 年。由于几年来市场价格一直波动，在购买日某些租赁的价格高于市场价格，某些租赁的价格低于市场价格。所有这些租赁都被购买方在租赁开始日分类为经营租赁。

采用购买法，主体 G 在确认和计量与租赁安排相关联的资产和负债时应该会考虑以下方面（如果适用）：

■ 大楼——在购买日考虑适宜的租赁的条款后，应该会以公允价值确认和计量一项有形资产。因此，购买方应该不会单独确认与有利/不利租赁相关的或具有适宜租赁价值的无形资产或负债。然而，根据 IAS 16 号，对于与市场条款相比有利或不利的租赁条款相关的金额单独计提

ⓒ 2012 普华永道（PricewaterhouseCoopers）版权所有。

place leases. However, it may be appropriate to depreciate separately amounts related to favourable or unfavourable lease terms relative to market terms in accordance with IAS 16.

- *Customer (tenant) relationships* – An intangible asset may be recognised, if applicable, for the value associated with the existing customer (tenant) base at the acquisition date. Such value may include expected renewals, expansion of leased space, etc.

Technology-based intangible assets

15.127 Technology-based intangible assets generally represent innovations on products or services, but can also include collections of information held electronically. [IFRS 3 para IE39]. The following paragraphs discuss the common technology-based intangible assets recognised and measured in a business combination.

15.128 Intangible assets used in research and development activities are initially recognised at fair value and classified as indefinite-lived (not available for use) assets until completion or abandonment. Research and development activities are not required to have an alternative future use to be recognised as an intangible asset. In subsequent periods, the intangible assets would be subject to periodic impairment testing. Additionally, research and development projects should be capitalised at the project level for purposes of recognition, measurement, and amortisation or subsequent impairment testing. Subsequent costs incurred for acquired projects that are in the development stage are capitalised, subject to impairment testing, if they meet the recognition criteria. If they do not, then subsequent costs are expensed.

15.129 Patented technology is protected legally and, therefore, meets the contractual-legal criterion for separate recognition as intangible assets. Unpatented technology is typically not protected by legal or contractual means and, therefore, does not meet the contractual-legal criterion. Unpatented technology, however, is often sold in conjunction with other intangible assets, such as trade names or secret formulas. As it is often sold with a related asset, the unpatented technology generally would meet the separability criterion.

© 2012 PricewaterhouseCoopers LLP. All rights reserved.

折旧可能是适宜的。

■ *客户（租户）关系*——如果适用，对于与现有客户（租户）基础相关联的购买日价值可以确认为一项无形资产。该价值可以包括预期续约、租赁空间扩展等。

以技术为基础的无形资产

15.127　以技术为基础的无形资产一般代表产品或服务创新，但也能包括电子信息收集。[IFRS 3 说明性示例第 39 段]。以下段落讨论在业务合并中确认和计量的常见的以技术为基础的无形资产。

15.128　研发活动使用的无形资产以公允价值初始确认，并且归为使用寿命不确定（尚不能使用）的资产，直至完成或废弃为止。研发活动不需要具有可选未来用途才能确认为无形资产。在后续期间，无形资产应该会接受定期减值测试。另外，为了确认、计量和摊销或后续减值测试的目的，研发项目应当在项目水平资本化。处于开发阶段的被购买项目产生的后续成本，如果符合确认标准则资本化，接受减值测试。如果不符合确认标准，则后续成本确认为费用。

15.129　专利技术受到法律保护，因此满足单独确认为无形资产的合同性—法律标准。非专利技术一般不受法律或合同手段保护，因此不满足合同性—法律标准。然而，非专利技术经常与其他无形资产共同出售，例如商号或保密配方。由于经常与相关资产共同出售，非专利技术一般应该会满足可分离标准。

ⓒ 2012 普华永道（PricewaterhouseCoopers）版权所有。

15. 130 Trade secrets are information, including a formula, pattern, recipe, compilation, programme, device, method, technique, or process, that derives independent economic value from not being generally known and is the subject of reasonable efforts to maintain its secrecy. If the future economic benefits from a trade secret acquired in a business combination are legally protected, then that asset would meet the contractual-legal criterion. Even if not legally protected, trade secrets acquired in a business combination are likely to be identifiable based on meeting the separability criterion. That is, an asset would be recognised if the trade secrets could be sold or licensed to others, even if sales are infrequent or if the acquirer has no intention of selling or licensing them. [IFRS 3 para IE44].

15. 131 Mask works are software permanently stored on read-only memory chips. Mask works, computer software, and programme formats are often protected legally, through patent, copyright, or other legal means. If they are protected legally, they meet the contractual-legal criterion. If they are not protected through legal or contractual means, these types of assets may still meet the separability criterion if there is evidence of sales or exchanges of the same or similar types of assets. [IFRS 3 para IE41].

15. 132 Databases are collections of information, typically stored electronically. Sometimes databases that include original works of authorship can be protected by legal means, such as copyrights, and if so, meet the contractual-legal criterion. More frequently, databases are information collected through the normal operations of the business, such as customer information, scientific data, or credit information. Databases, similar to customer lists, are often sold or leased to others and, therefore, meet the separability criterion. [IFRS 3 para IE42]. In the United States, title plants are an historical record of all matters affecting title to parcels of land in a specific area. These assets are sold or licensed to others and, therefore, meet the separability criterion. [IFRS 3 para IE43].

Complementary intangible assets and grouping of other intangible assets

15. 133 Sometimes, separate intangible assets work together or complement each

© 2012 PricewaterhouseCoopers LLP. All rights reserved.

15.130 商业秘密是信息，包括配方、样式、秘诀、汇编、程序、设计、方法、技术或工序，由于未被普遍知晓而产生独立的经济价值，是合理努力以保持其秘密的对象。如果在业务合并中取得的商业秘密产生的未来经济利益受到法律保护，则该资产应该会满足合同性—法律标准。即使未受法律保护，基于满足可分离标准，在业务合并中取得的商业秘密也可能是可辨认的。也就是说，即使销售活动并不频繁或购买方无意出售或许可，如果商业秘密能够出售或许可给他人，则应该会确认为一项资产。[IFRS 3 说明性示例第 44 段]。

15.131 掩膜作品是永久储存在只读存储芯片上的软件。掩膜作品、计算机软件和程序格式通常通过专利、版权或其他法律手段受到法律保护。如果它们受到法律保护，则符合合同性—法律标准。如果未受到法律或合同手段保护，但有相同或类似类型资产的销售或交换的证据，则这些类型的资产仍可符合可分离标准。[IFRS 3 说明性示例第 41 段]。

15.132 数据库是信息的集合，一般以电子方式储存。有时包含原始著作权作品的数据库能够通过法律手段保护，例如版权，如果这样，则符合合同性—法律标准。更常见的情况是，数据库是通过企业正常运营收集的信息，例如客户信息、科学数据或信用信息等。数据库与客户名单类似，经常出售或出租给他人，因此符合可分离标准。[IFRS 3 说明性示例第 42 段]。在美国，产权档案库是影响特定区域土地所有权的所有事宜的历史记录。这些资产出售或许可给他人，因此符合可分离标准。[IFRS 3 说明性示例第 43 段]。

互补性无形资产和其他无形资产的归类

15.133 有时，多项单独的无形资产一起运营或相互补充。在一些情况中，

ⓒ 2012 普华永道（PricewaterhouseCoopers）版权所有。

other. In some cases, an acquirer may wish to group these complementary intangible assets together for purposes of measuring their initial fair value at the acquisition date and for subsequent amortisation and impairment testing. An example is a brand or brand names. Only limited grouping is permitted under IFRS.

15.134 A brand is a general marketing term that refers to a group of complementary intangible assets, such as a trademark and its related trade name, formula, recipe, and technology. If the assets that make up that group meet the standards' identifiable criteria for separate recognition and have similar useful lives, an acquirer is not precluded from recognising them as a single intangible asset. [IFRS 3 para IE21]. An acquirer may also recognise other groups of complementary intangible assets as a single asset. The conclusion in the standards, with respect to a brand, may also be applied to other assets for which the underlying component assets have similar useful lives. Examples of assets that may be recognised as a single asset if the useful lives are similar include:

- A nuclear power plant and the license to operate the plant. [IFRS 3 para B32(b)].
- A copyright intangible asset and any related assignments or license agreements. [IFRS 3 para B34].
- A series of easements that support a gas pipeline.

In making this assessment, the acquirer would identify the component assets and determine each component asset's useful life to evaluate whether such lives are similar.

Intangible assets that the acquirer does not intend to use or intends to use differently than other market participants

15.135 IFRS 3 clarifies that the intended use of an asset by the acquirer does not affect its fair value. Rather, the acquirer should look to how other market participants may use the asset in recognising and measuring its fair value. [IFRS 3 para B43]. An intangible asset acquired in a business combination that the acquirer

© 2012 PricewaterhouseCoopers LLP. All rights reserved.

为了计量购买日的初始公允价值以及后续摊销和减值测试，购买方可能希望将这些互补性无形资产归到一起。一个案例是品牌或品牌名称。根据国际财务报告准则，仅在有限的情况下允许合并归类。

15.134　品牌是一个笼统的营销术语，系指一组相互补充的无形资产，例如一个商标及相关商号、公式、配方和技术。如果构成该组的资产符合准则的单独确认的可辨认标准，并且具有类似的使用寿命，则不能阻止购买方将其确认为一个单独的无形资产。[IFRS 3 说明性示例第 21 段]。购买方也可以将其他互补性无形资产组确认为一项单独资产。准则中有关品牌的结论也可应用于其他的其组成部分的资产具有类似的使用寿命资产。如果使用寿命类似就可以确认为一项单独的资产的案例包括：

- 核电站及运营核电站的许可证。[IFRS 3 第 B32(b) 段]。

- 版权无形资产及任何相关的转让或许可协议。[IFRS 3 第 B34 段]。

- 支持天然气管道的一系列地役权。

在进行这项评价时，购买方应该识别作为组成部分的资产，并确定每项作为组成部分的资产的使用寿命，以评估这些寿命是否类似。

购买方无意使用或准备以不同于其他市场参与者的方式使用的无形资产

15.135　IFRS 3 阐明，购买方对于一项资产的使用意图不影响该资产的公允价值。相反地，购买方在确认和计量其公允价值时应当考虑其他市场参与者可能如何使用该资产。[IFRS 3 第 B43 段]。在一项业务合并中取得，购买方无意积极使用但意在阻止他人使用的无形资产通常称为“防御性资产”或

ⓒ 2012 普华永道（PricewaterhouseCoopers）版权所有。

does not intend to actively use but does intend to prevent others from using, is commonly referred to as a 'defensive asset' or a 'locked-up asset'. The asset is likely contributing to an increase in the cash flows of other assets owned by the acquirer. Conversely, an intangible asset acquired in a business combination that the acquirer does not intend to actively use and does not intend to prevent others from using is not a defensive intangible asset.

Example 1 – Distinguishing defensive intangible assets from intangible assets

Entity A, a consumer products manufacturer, acquires an entity that sells a product that competes with one of entity A's existing products. Entity A plans to discontinue the sale of the competing product within the next six months, but will maintain the rights to the trade name, at minimal expected cost, to prevent a competitor from using it. As a result, entity A's existing product is expected to experience an increase in market share. Entity A does not have any current plans to re-introduce the acquired trade name in the future.

Because entity A does not intend to actively use the acquired trade name, but intends to hold the rights to the trade name to prevent its competitors from using it, the trade name meets the definition of a defensive intangible asset.

Example 2 – Distinguishing defensive intangible assets from intangible assets

Entity A acquires a business and one of the assets acquired is billing software developed by the selling entity for its own use. After a six month transition period, entity A plans to discontinue use of the internally developed billing software. In valuing the billing software in connection with the acquisition, entity A determines that a market participant would use the billing software, along with other assets in the asset group, for its full remaining economic life (that is, entity A does not intend to use the asset in a way that is its highest and best use). Due to the specialised nature of the software, entity A does not believe the software could be sold to a third-party without the other assets acquired.

Although entity A does not intend to actively use the internally developed billing software after a six month transition period, entity A is not holding the internally developed software to prevent its competitors from using it. Therefore, the internally developed software asset does not meet the definition

© 2012 PricewaterhouseCoopers LLP. All rights reserved.

“锁定资产”。该类资产可能有助于购买方拥有的其他资产增加现金流量。相反，在一项业务合并中取得而购买方无意积极使用也无意阻止他人使用的无形资产不是一项防御性无形资产。

示例 1——从无形资产中辨别防御性无形资产

主体 A 是一家消费品制造商，收购了一个主体，该主体销售的一个产品与主体 A 现有产品之一相竞争。主体 A 计划在未来的六个月内停止销售竞争产品，但将以最低预期成本维护对商号的权利，以防止竞争者使用。因此，主体 A 的现有产品的市场份额预期会增加。主体 A 目前没有计划在未来重新推出已购的商号。

因为主体 A 无意积极使用已购商标，但有意持有商号的权利以防止竞争者使用，所以该商号符合防御性无形资产的定义。

示例 2——从无形资产中辨别防御性无形资产

主体 A 购买了一个业务，所购买的资产之一是由卖方主体自行开发并自己使用的开票软件。六个月过渡期后，主体 A 计划停止使用该内部开发的开票软件。在评估该涉及收购的开票软件时，主体 A 确定一个市场参与者应该会在剩余的全部经济寿命中使用该软件以及资产组中的其他资产（即主体 A 无意以最佳使用方式使用该资产）。由于该软件的专门化，主体 A 认为没有其他已购资产该软件不能单独出售给第三方。

虽然主体 A 无意在六个月过渡期后积极使用该内部开发的开票软件，但主体 A 也不是为了防止竞争者使用而持有该内部开发的软件。因此，该内部开发的软件资产不符合防御性无形资产的定义。

ⓒ 2012 普华永道（PricewaterhouseCoopers）版权所有。

of a defensive intangible asset.

15.136 The table below highlights typical intangible assets found in major industries and their typical life characteristics. This table serves as a broad overview only, and is not intended to reflect all of the intangible assets that may be present for an industry participant or in a particular situation. In determining the useful lives of its recognised intangible assets, an entity must perform a thorough evaluation of the relevant facts and circumstances.

Summary of intangible assets and typical useful life characteristics found in major industries

Industry	Typical significant intangible assets	Typical life characteristics
Retail and consumer products	■ Trade and brand names. ■ Customer and supplier contracts. ■ Favourable/unfavourable contract or lease terms. ■ Process technology and know-how. ■ Liquor licenses. ■ Customer relationships (for example, pharmacy script files). ■ Customer lists. ■ Internet domain names.	Trade and brand names are likely to be long or possibly indefinite-lived if sustainable; otherwise, are short to moderate. Supplier arrangements are based on contractual terms, assuming renewals when appropriate (excluding a reacquired right). Contractual relationships are driven by contractual life or longer for low-cost renewals. Technology and know-how range from short-to long-term.
Industrial products	■ Trade names. ■ Customer and supplier contracts. ■ Favourable/unfavourable contract or lease terms. ■ Process technology and know-how.	Trade names are likely to be long or possibly indefinite-lived if sustainable; otherwise, are short to moderate. Contractual relationships are driven by contractual life or longer for low-cost renewals. Technology and know-how range from short-to long-term.
Real estate	■ Tenant relationships. ■ Favourable/unfavourable lease terms. ■ In-place leases.	Determined by lease life and expectation of tenant renewals.

© 2012 PricewaterhouseCoopers LLP. All rights reserved.

15.136 下表列示了在主要行业中发现的典型的无形资产及其典型的寿命特征。该表仅为一个宽泛的概述，并无意反映一个行业参与者的或在特定情况中存在所有无形资产。在确定已确认无形资产的使用寿命时，主体必须彻底评估相关事实和环境。

在主要行业中发现的无形资产和典型的使用寿命特征汇总

行业	典型的重要无形资产	典型的寿命特征
零售和消费产品	■ 商标和品牌名称。 ■ 客户和供应商合同。 ■ 有利/不利的合同或租赁条款。 ■ 加工工艺和技术诀窍。 ■ 酒牌。 ■ 客户关系（例如，制药正本文件）。 ■ 客户名单。 ■ 互联网域名。	商号和品牌名称可能会长，或者如果可持续，可能使用寿命不确定；否则时间短至适中。供应商安排依据合同条款，假设在适宜的时候续约（不包括重新购得的权利）。合同关系由合同寿命推动，如果低成本续约，则会更长久。技术和技术诀窍的范围为短期至中期。
工业产品	■ 商号。 ■ 客户和供应商合同。 ■ 有利/不利的合同或租赁条款。 ■ 加工工艺和技术诀窍。	商号可能会长，或者如果可持续，可能使用寿命不确定；否则时间短至适中。合同关系由合同寿命推动，如果低成本续约，则会更长久。技术工艺和技术诀窍的范围为短期至中期。
房地产	■ 租户关系。 ■ 有利/不利的租赁条款。 ■ 适宜的租赁。	由租赁期和租户续约的预期决定。

ⓒ 2012 普华永道（PricewaterhouseCoopers）版权所有。

Con.

Banking	■ Core deposit intangibles (CDI). ■ Distribution channels (for example, agents). ■ Brands and trade names. ■ Customer relationships (including purchased credit card relationships). ■ Customer lists.	CDI is short to moderate, based on customer churn, although may be longer for companies based outside the US. Brands and trade names are long and possibly indefinite-lived if sustainable. Others are typically short to moderate. Contractual relationships are driven by contractual life.
Insurance	■ Customer relationships, such as renewal rights on short-duration insurance contracts, cross-selling opportunities, and customer/member lists. ■ Distribution channels (including the distributor's ability to generate new business from new customers). ■ Insurance licenses. ■ Service contracts and provider contracts (particularly relevant for health insurers). ■ Brands and trade names. ■ Process technology and know-how.	Customer relationships and distribution channels are moderate. Trade names are long and possibly indefinite-lived if sustainable; otherwise, are short to moderate. Certain insurance licenses can be maintained indefinitely without substantial cost.
Investment management	■ Trade names. ■ Customer relationships. ■ Fund manager contracts.	Trade names are long and possibly indefinite-lived if sustainable; otherwise, are short to moderate. Customer relationships are moderate, but may be longer where focus is on institutional clients rather than

© 2012 PricewaterhouseCoopers LLP. All rights reserved.

续表

银行业	■ 核心存款无形资产（CDI）。 ■ 经销渠道（例如代理人）。 ■ 品牌名称和商号。 ■ 客户关系（包括已购买的信用卡关系）。 ■ 客户名单。	CDI，基于客户流失情况，短到适中，虽然对于总部在美国之外的公司可能更长。品牌名称和商号可能会长，如果可持续，则使用寿命也可能不确定。其他一般是短至适中。合同关系取决于合同期限。
保险	■ 客户关系，例如短期保险合同的续约权，交叉销售机会，客户/会员名单。 ■ 经销渠道（包括经销商从新客户获得新业务的能力）。 ■ 保险许可证。 ■ 服务合同和提供者合同（对于健康险保险人特别重要）。 ■ 品牌名称和商号。 ■ 加工工艺和技术诀窍。	客户关系和经销渠道适中。商号可能会长，如果可持续，则可能使用寿命不确定；否则就是持续时间很短至适中。某些保险许可证能够无需较高成本而无限期持有。
投资管理	■ 商号。 ■ 客户关系。 ■ 基金经理合同。	商号可能会长久保持，如果可持续，则可能使用寿命不确定；否则就是短至适中。客户关系适中，但是如果集中于机构客户而不是零售客户，则可能会更长久。基金经理合同和基金客户关系互相依存，需要

ⓒ 2012 普华永道（PricewaterhouseCoopers）版权所有。

Con.

		retail. Fund manager contracts and the customer relationships of the funds are interdependent and require special analysis. The lives of fund manager contracts are driven by the expectation of renewal with the funds and are likely to be moderate-to long-term, or possibly indefinite-lived.
Technology	■ Trade names. ■ Customer and supplier contracts. ■ Favourable/Unfavourable contract terms. ■ Process technology and know-how. ■ Computer software and mask works. ■ Internet domain names. ■ Databases. ■ IPR&D.	Trade names are likely to be long or possibly indefinite-lived if sustainable; otherwise, are short to moderate. Contractual relationships are driven by contractual life or longer for low-cost renewals. Technology and know-how range from short-to long-term. IPR&D would be an indefinite-lived (not available for use) intangible asset until the asset is put to use or in operation as a product, at which time, the life may be short to moderate, depending on the product
Life sciences and pharmaceuticals	■ Brands and trade names. ■ Patents, product rights and know-how. ■ Partnering and alliance arrangements. ■ IPR&D. ■ Customer relationships and customer base. ■ Supplier contracts.	Brands and trade names are likely short to moderate, depending on product portfolio (that is, remaining legal life of identifiable intangible assets). The exception is where brands and trade names have value and are sustainable, which could be long and possibly indefinite-lived. IPR&D would be an

© 2012 PricewaterhouseCoopers LLP. All rights reserved.

续表

		特殊分析。基金经理合同的寿命由基金续约的预期推动，可能为中期至长期，或可能不确定。
技术	■ 商号。 ■ 客户和供应商合同。 ■ 有利/不利的合同条款。 ■ 加工工艺和技术诀窍。 ■ 计算机软件和掩膜作品。 ■ 互联网域名。 ■ 数据库。 ■ 尚未完成的研究和开发项目。	商号可能会长，如果可持续，则使用寿命也可能不确定；否则就是短至适中。合同关系由合同期限推动，如果续约成本低，则会更长。技术和技术诀窍的范围为短至长。尚未完成的研究和开发项目应该是使用寿命不确定（尚不能使用）的无形资产，直至该资产投入使用或作为产品运营，此时，寿命可能为短至适中，取决于产品。
生命科学和制药	■ 品牌名称和商号。 ■ 专利，产品权利，技术诀窍。 ■ 合作和联盟安排。 ■ 尚未完成的研究和开发项目。 ■ 客户关系和客户基础。 ■ 供应商合同。	品牌名称和商号可能是短至适中，这取决于产品组合（即可辨认无形资产的剩余法定年限）。例外情况是在品牌名称和商号具有价值且可持续的情况下，则寿命延长，也可能使用寿命不确定。尚未完成的研究和开发项目应该是使用寿命不确定（尚不能使用）的无形资产，直至

ⓒ 2012 普华永道（PricewaterhouseCoopers）版权所有。

Con.

		indefinite-lived (not available for use) intangible asset until the asset is put to use or in operation as a product, at which time, the life may be short to moderate, depending on the product.
Entertainment and media	■ Trade names/trademarks. ■ Artistic properties (for example, cartoon characters, copyrights). ■ Licenses (for example, broadcast licenses, programme material licenses). ■ Favourable/unfavourable contract terms.	Trade names/trademarks and certain licenses and artistic properties likely to be longer term or possibly indefinite-lived if sustainable.
Telecommunications	■ Trade names. ■ Licenses and rights of use. ■ Installed base. ■ Technology.	Trade names likely to be long or possibly indefinite-lived if sustainable; otherwise, short to moderate. Other intangible assets range from short (technology) to long or indefinite (licenses), depending on ability to renew and risk of obsolescence.
Energy and resources (including oil and gas)	■ Trade and brand names where downstream operations are present (for example, retail front). ■ Contractual relationships. ■ Favourable/unfavourable contract terms (for example, drilling contract).	Trade or brand names likely to be longer term or possibly indefinite-lived, if sustainable; otherwise, short to moderate. Contractual relationships are driven by contractual life or longer for low-cost renewals.

© 2012 PricewaterhouseCoopers LLP. All rights reserved.

续表

		该资产投入使用或作为产品运营，此时，寿命可能为短至适中，取决于产品。
娱乐和媒体	■ 商号/商标。 ■ 艺术财产（例如卡通人物，版权）。 ■ 许可证（例如播放许可证，节目材料许可证）。 ■ 有利/不利的合同条款。	商号/商标和某些许可证和艺术财产可能寿命更长，或者如果可持续，则使用寿命不确定。
电信	■ 商号。 ■ 许可证和使用权。 ■ 安装基础。 ■ 技术。	商号可能会使用寿命长，或者如果可持续，则使用寿命也可能不确定；否则就是短至适中。其他无形资产寿命短（技术）到长或使用寿命不确定（许可证），这取决于更新能力和废弃风险。
能源和资源（包括石油和天然气）	■ 在存在下游业务（例如零售前沿）的情况下商号和品牌名称。 ■ 合同关系。 ■ 有利/不利的合同条款（例如钻井合同）。	商号和品牌名称可能会长，或者如果可持续，可能使用寿命不确定；否则时间短至适中。合同关系由合同期限推动，如果低成本续约，则会更长久。

ⓒ 2012 普华永道（PricewaterhouseCoopers）版权所有。

Con.

	■ Agreements (franchise service, inter-connection, operations and maintenance, railroad crossing). ■ Contracts (purchased power, fuel and other supply contracts). ■ Easements, rights of way, and rights of use. ■ Sitting, environmental, and other licenses.

15. 137 Table 15. 6 is an example that shows intangible assets acquired in a business combination.

Table 15. 6 – Intangible assets acquired in a business combination

Spectris plc – Report and accounts – 31 December 2010

28. Acquisitions (extract)

On 7 April 2010, the group acquired the trade and assets of Reologica Instruments AB, located in Sweden, for a consideration of £0. 5m. No goodwill arose on the Reologica Instruments AB acquisition, with the excess of the fair value of the consideration paid over the fair value of the net assets acquired represented by technology-based intangibles. This business has been integrated into the Materials Analysis segment.

On 6 July 2010, the group acquired 100% of the share capital of Zhuhai Omec Instruments Co. Ltd, a company based in China, which extends the group's capabilities in analytical systems for particle characterisation, for a total consideration of £9. 2m including £1. 9m contingent on the future performance of the acquired business. This forms part of the Materials Analysis segment. The excess of the fair value of the consideration paid over the fair value of the assets acquired is represented by customer-related and marketing based intangibles and the value of a non-compete agreement entered into with the previous owners of the business.

On 1 October 2010, the group acquired the trade and assets of a distributor in Japan where direct presence was sought for a consideration of £4. 6m including £1. 7m contingent on the

© 2012 PricewaterhouseCoopers LLP. All rights reserved.

续表

	■ 协议（特许权服务、互连、运营和维护、铁路交叉路口）。 ■ 合同（已购电力，燃料和其他供应合同）。 ■ 地役权、路权、使用权。 ■ 占用、环境和其他许可证。

15.137 表15.6举例说明了在一个业务合并中取得的无形资产。

表15.6——在一项业务合并中取得的无形资产

Spectris 上市有限公司报告和报表——2010年12月31日

28. 并购（节选）

2010年4月7日，本集团以0.5百万英镑的对价收购了坐落于瑞典的Reologica Instruments公司的商标和资产。并购Reologica Instruments公司没有产生商誉，支付的对价的公允价值超过所购入的净资产公允价值的部分代表了以技术为基础的无形资产。该业务被整合入原材料分析分部。

2010年7月6日，本集团收购了一家中国公司——珠海欧美克仪器有限公司100%股权，从而使本集团在粒子特性分析系统上的能力得以延伸，总对价为9.2百万英镑，其中包括基于被购买业务未来业绩的或有对价1.9百万英镑。该业务构成原材料分析分部的一部分。支付的对价的公允价值超过所购入的资产的公允价值的部分代表了与客户相关的以营销为基础的无形资产以及与该业务以前的所有者签订的非竞争协议的价值。

2010年10月1日，本集团收购一个日本经销商的商标和资产，对价为4.6百万英镑，其中包括基于被购买业务未来业绩的或有对价1.7百万英镑。该业务也构成原材料分

© 2012 普华永道（PricewaterhouseCoopers）版权所有。

Con.

future performance of the acquired business. This also forms part of the Materials Analysis segment. No goodwill arose on this acquisition with the excess of the fair value of the consideration paid over the fair value of the net assets acquired represented by customer-based intangibles. There was no material fair value attaching to the pre-existing relationships with the distributor.

Also on 1 October 2010, the group acquired the trade and assets of N-Tron Corp, a company based in the USA, which extends the group's capabilities in industrial networking products, for a consideration of £32.9m including deferred consideration of £0.1m. This forms part of the Industrial Controls segment. An analysis of the assets acquired is provided below. The excess of the fair value of the consideration paid over the fair value of the net assets acquired is represented by customer-related, technology and other intangibles of £9.1m, £2.5m and £2.1m, respectively, with residual goodwill arising of £16.7m. The goodwill arising is considered to represent the value of the acquired workforce and the ability to exploit the group's existing distribution arrangements to expand N-Tron's routes to market, particularly outside of North America where it currently makes limited sales.

On 24 November 2010, the group acquired 100% of the shares of the Delta F Corporation, a company based in the USA, which extends the group's capabilities in trace oxygen and water measurement, for a consideration of £15.8m, including deferred consideration of £0.4m. This forms part of the In-line Instrumentation segment. The excess of the fair value of the consideration paid over the fair value of the net assets acquired is represented by technology-based intangibles of £9.0m with residual goodwill arising of £7.6m. The goodwill arising is considered to represent the value of the acquired workforce and the ability to exploit the group's existing customer relationships and know-how to expand Delta F's routes to market, particularly into markets (both geographic and industry) where it currently makes limited sales.

The assets and liabilities acquired as a result of the above transactions, together with the aggregate purchase consideration, are summarised below. The revenue and operating profit contribution from the acquisitions in the year to the group's results for the year were £8.1m and £1.1m respectively. Group revenue and operating profit would have been £929.6m and £135.4m, respectively, had each of these acquisitions taken place on the first day of the year.

On acquisitions prior to 1 January 2010, the deferred and contingent consideration has been revised to reflect the increased earn-out payments amounting to £8.3m that were not accrued at 31 December 2009 with a corresponding increase to goodwill. The group also paid £4.5m in respect of prior period acquisitions, which had been accrued as deferred or contingent consideration at 31 December 2009.

© 2012 PricewaterhouseCoopers LLP. All rights reserved.

续表

析分部的一部分。这次并购也不产生商誉，支付的对价的公允价值超过所购入的净资产的公允价值的部分代表了以客户为基础的无形资产。没有重大的公允价值分配至与经销商相关的原已存在的关系。 也是在2010年10月1日，本集团收购了一家总部设在美国的公司——N - Tron公司的商标和资产，从而使本集团在工业网络产品的能力得以延伸，对价为32.9百万英镑，其中包括延迟支付的对价0.1百万英镑。该业务构成工业控制分部的一部分。对所购买的资产的分析详见下文。所支付的对价的公允价值超过购买的净资产的公允价值的部分分别代表了9.1百万英镑的与客户相关的无形资产、2.5百万英镑的技术和2.1百万英镑的其他无形资产，剩余的部分产生了16.7百万英镑的商誉。产生的商誉被认为代表了所购买的劳动力的价值以及拓展本集团现有的分销安排、扩大N - Tron市场，特别是在北美以外目前销售有限的市场的能力。 2010年11月24日，本集团收购了一家本部在美国的公司——Delta F公司100%的股份，以扩展本集团在微量氧和水测量方面的能力，对价为15.8百万英镑，其中包含延迟支付的对价0.4百万英镑。该业务构成在线仪器分部的一部分。支付的对价的公允价值超过所购买的净资产的公允价值的部分代表了以技术为基础的无形资产0.9百万英镑，剩余的部分产生了商誉7.6百万英镑。产生的商誉被认为代表了所购买的劳动力的价值以及拓展本集团现有客户关系和技术窍门、扩大Delta F市场，特别是目前销售有限的市场（既包含地域也包含行业）的能力。 作为上述交易的结果所购买的资产和负债，以及购买对价的合计汇总如下。这些并购在并购的当年对本集团收入和营业利润的影响分别为8.1百万英镑和1.1百万英镑。如果每个并购都发生在并购当年第一天，本集团的收入和营业利润将分别为929.6百万英镑和135.4百万英镑。 对于2010年1月1日之前的并购，已经对递延和或有对价进行了修改以反映增加的获利后支付的金额8.3百万英镑，同时增加商誉。该金额在2009年12月31日并没有预计。本集团还支付了与前期并购相关的在2009年12月31日已经预计的递延或者或有对价4.5百万英镑。

ⓒ 2012 普华永道（PricewaterhouseCoopers）版权所有。

Con.

Acquisition-related costs of £ 1. 9m have been recognised in the statement of income under IFRS 3 and included within administrative expenses.

The effect of the acquisition on the individual assets and liabilities of the group is as follows:

			2010
	Book value	Adjustments	**Fair value**
Net assets acquired under 2010 acquisitions	£ m	£ m	**£ m**
Intangible fixed assets	0. 1	36. 5	**36. 6**
Tangible fixed assets	0. 5	(0. 1)	**0. 4**
Inventories	4. 1	(0. 2)	**3. 9**
Trade and other receivables	4. 5	–	**4. 5**
Trade and other payables	(1. 7)	–	**(1. 7)**
Provisions	(0. 1)	–	**(0. 1)**
Deferred tax liabilities	–	(5. 7)	**(5. 7)**
Cash	0. 8	–	**0. 8**
Net assets acquired	8. 2	30. 5	**38. 7**
Goodwill			**24. 3**
Total consideration in respect of 2010 acquisitions			**63. 0**

Analysis of cash outflow in consolidated cash flow statement	
Total consideration in respect of 2010 acquisitions	**63. 0**
Adjustment for cash acquired on 2010 acquisitions	**(0. 8)**
Deferred and contingent consideration on 2010 acquisitions to be paid in future years	**(4. 1)**
Cash paid in 2010 in respect of 2010 acquisitions	**58. 1**
Prior year acquisitions	
Purchase price adjustment reprior year acquisition *	**8. 3**
Deferred and contingent consideration in relation to prior year acquisitions:	
Accrued at 31 December 2009	**4. 5**
Accrued during 2010 but not paid at 31 December 2010 *	**(8. 3)**
Cash paid in 2010 in respect of prior year acquisitions	**4. 5**
Net cash outflow relating to acquisitions	**62. 6**

* An additional purchase price of £ 8. 3m in relation to prior period acquisitions has been accrued (but not paid) during the year based on updated expectations of the amounts to be paid under contingent consideration arrangements.

© 2012 PricewaterhouseCoopers LLP. All rights reserved.

续表

与并购相关的费用 1. 9 百万英镑已经按照 IFRS 3 在利润表中确认，包含在管理费用中。

并购对本集团诸个资产和负债的影响如下：

			2010 年
	账面价值	调整	**公允价值**
2010 年并购取得的净资产	百万英镑	百万英镑	**百万英镑**
无形固定资产	0. 1	36. 5	**36. 6**
有形固定资产	0. 5	(0. 1)	**0. 4**
存货	4. 1	(0. 2)	**3. 9**
应收账款及其他应收款项	4. 5	–	**4. 5**
应付账款及其他应付款项	(1. 7)	–	**(1. 7)**
预计负债	(0. 1)	–	**(0. 1)**
递延税负债	–	(5. 7)	**(5. 7)**
现金	0. 8	–	**0. 8**
所购买的净资产	8. 2	30. 5	**38. 7**
商誉			**24. 3**
2010 年并购的总对价			**63. 0**

合并现金流量表中现金流出分析

2010 年并购总对价	**63. 0**
2010 年并购取得的现金的调整	**(0. 8)**
2010 年并购中未来将支付的递延和或有对价	**(4. 1)**
2010 年并购支付的现金	**58. 1**
以前年度的并购	
以前年度并购的价格调整*	**8. 3**
以前年度并购相关的递延和或有对价	
2009 年 12 月 31 日计提的金额	**4. 5**
2010 年计提但是尚未支付的金额*	**(8. 3)**
与以前年度并购相关的在 2010 年的现金支付	**4. 5**
有关并购的净现金流出	**62. 6**

* 与以前期间并购相关的增加的购买价格 8. 3 百万英镑已经按照或有对价协议根据最新的预期未来将要支付的金额在本年计提（但未支付）。

ⓒ 2012 普华永道（PricewaterhouseCoopers）版权所有。

Con.

Due to their contractual due dates, the fair value of receivables acquired (shown above) approximates the gross contractual amounts receivable. The amount of gross contractual receivables not expected to be recovered is immaterial.

There are no material contingent liabilities recognised in accordance with paragraph 23 of IFRS 3.

Contingent consideration exists on two of the acquisitions made in 2010. The maximum amounts payable (which will be settled in cash) total £4.1m and are contingent based on the future performance of the acquired businesses over periods of up to three years. Reflecting the levels of the performance targets set and expected business performance, these amounts have been accrued in full at the respective acquisition dates as the fair value of the contingent consideration is considered by the directors to approximate the full amounts potentially payable under the 'earn out' arrangements.

£16.7m of the goodwill arising on acquisitions in the year is expected to be amortised and deductible for tax purposes.

			2010
	Book value	Adjustments	**Fair value**
Net assets acquired for N-Tron	£m	£m	**£m**
Intangible fixed assets	0.1	13.6	**13.7**
Tangible fixed assets	0.1	–	**0.1**
Inventories	1.5	0.3	**1.8**
Trade and other receivables	1.8	–	**1.8**
Trade and other payables	(1.2)	–	**(1.2)**
Net assets acquired	2.3	13.9	**16.2**
Goodwill			**16.7**
Total consideration			**32.9**
Adjustment for cash acquired			–
Net consideration			**32.9**

© 2012 PricewaterhouseCoopers LLP. All rights reserved.

续表

考虑到合同的到期日，取得的应收款项（如上所述）的公允价值与合同应收总金额近似。合同应收总金额中预计将无法收到的金额不重大。

按照 IFRS 3 第 23 段确认的或有负债不重大。

2010 年并购中有两项并购存在或有对价。最高的应付金额（将以现金结算）总额为 4.1 百万英镑且其取决于所购买的业务在未来 3 年的业绩。反映业绩目标的水平和预期的业务的业绩，这些金额已经全额在其相应的购买日计提，这是因为董事们认为或有对价的公允价值与按照获利后支付协议潜在的应付总金额近似。

16.7 百万元并购产生的商誉预期将在税务上摊销和抵扣。

	账面价值	调整	**2010 年 公允价值**
购买 N-Tron 的净资产	百万英镑	百万英镑	**百万英镑**
无形固定资产	0.1	13.6	**13.7**
有形固定资产	0.1	–	**0.1**
存货	1.5	0.3	**1.8**
应收账款和其他应收款项	1.8	–	**1.8**
应付账款和其他应付款项	(1.2)	–	**(1.2)**
购买的净资产	2.3	13.9	**16.2**
商誉			**16.7**
总对价			**32.9**
对收到的现金的调整			–
净对价			**32.9**

ⓒ 2012 普华永道（PricewaterhouseCoopers）版权所有。

15. 138 The standard describes several methods that might be used to determine fair value of intangible assets acquired in a business combination.

15. 139 Where intangibles are traded on an active market the quoted market prices are the most reliable measure of fair value. An active market is a market where:

- The items traded are similar in kind or nature.
- Willing buyers and sellers are always available.
- Prices are publicly quoted.

The current bid price is the appropriate price to use for fair value. If the current bid price is not available, the price in the most recent and similar transaction may be used if there has been no material change in economic circumstances between the transaction's date and the date on which fair value is estimated. [IAS 38 para 39].

15. 140 Examples of intangible assets that may be quoted in an active market might include emission rights, taxi licences, fishing licences, telecommunications licences and production quotas, such as milk quotas.

15. 141 Where no active market exists for intangible assets, fair value should be the amount that an entity would have paid for the asset, at the acquisition date, in an arm's length transaction between knowledgeable willing parties. Fair value should be assessed taking into account any recent transactions for similar assets. [IAS 38 para 40].

15. 142 There are various techniques that might be used for assessing fair value in such circumstances. Paragraph 41 of IAS 38 clarifies the description of the valuation techniques for assets commonly purchased as part of a business combination. Some entities that buy and sell unique intangible assets may have developed techniques for valuing such assets. Similar techniques may be used to value intangible assets acquired in a business combination if they are consistent with current transactions and practices in the industry to which the intangible asset relates. These techniques include for example:

- Estimating the hypothetical costs the entity avoids by owning the intangible asset and note needing:
  - to license it from another party in an arm's length transactions (as in the relief

© 2012 PricewaterhouseCoopers LLP. All rights reserved.

15.138 准则描述了几种可以用于确定在一项业务合并中获得的无形资产的公允价值的方法。

15.139 如果无形资产在一个活跃市场中交易，则市场报价是最可靠的公允价值计量方式。一个活跃市场是指一个持有以下特征的市场：

■ 交易项目在类别或性质上类似。

■ 总是存在自愿的买方和卖方。

■ 有公开报价。

当前的报价是适用的用于确定公允价值的价格。如果不能获得当前报价，则可以使用最近的类似交易中的价格，前提是交易日期和估计公允价值的日期之间的经济环境没有重大变化。[IAS 第 38 号第 39 段]。

15.140 在活跃市场中有报价的无形资产的例子包括排放权、出租车执照、捕鱼执照、电信许可证和生产配额，例如牛奶配额。

15.141 如果无形资产不存在活跃市场，则公允价值应当等于购买日在公平交易中，熟悉情况的当事人自愿为资产支付的金额。在确定公允价值时应当考虑类似资产的近期交易。[IAS 第 38 号第 40 段]。

15.142 在这样的情况下，有各种技术可以用于评估公允价值。IAS 第 38 号第 41 段明确了作为一项业务合并一部分而购入的资产的估值技术的描述。有些购买和出售独特无形资产的主体可能已经开发评估该类资产的技术。类似的技术可以用于评估在业务合并中取得的无形资产，前提是它们符合无形资产所涉及行业的当前交易和惯例。这些技术例如：

■ 估计主体通过拥有该无形资产而避免发生的假定成本：

■ 在公平交易中从另一方获得特许权（如“权利金节省法”中所示）；或者

ⓒ 2012 普华永道（PricewaterhouseCoopers）版权所有。

from royalty approach); or

- to recreate or replace it (as in the cost approach).

- Discounting estimated future net cash flows from the asset.

[IAS 38 para 41].

15.143 This chapter does not provide detailed guidance on how to value intangible assets. There is limited authoritative guidance either in the accounting standards or the standards published by the International Valuation Standard Council. Entities may want to refer to their national professional association for guidance (if any). Many companies also choose to use specialist valuers.

15.144 Where discounted cash flow techniques are used, the guidance for determining fair value in the absence of a binding sale agreement or active market should be used. In the absence of a binding sale agreement or active market, the assumptions used in the cash flow forecasts should be consistent with those that a market participant would make and be further supported by external market data. The cash flows to be used in determining fair value are post tax cash flows. This approach is discussed more fully in chapter 18, which deals with the impairment of assets.

Intangible assets acquired in exchange for non-monetary assets

15.145 An intangible asset acquired in an exchange for a non-monetary asset or a combination of non-monetary and monetary assets should be recognised initially at its fair value, unless:

- the exchange transaction has no commercial substance; or
- the fair value of neither the asset received nor the asset given up can be reliably measured.

Example – Exchange of patents

Entity A is the holder of a patent with a carrying amount of C3,000. Entity A agreed to exchange its patent for that of entity B. The fair value of entity A's

© 2012 PricewaterhouseCoopers LLP. All rights reserved.

■ 重新创造或者取代它（如成本法中所示）。

■ 对资产产生的预计未来净现金流进行折现。

［IAS 第 38 号第 41 段］。

15.143　本章不对如何评估无形资产提供详细指导。在会计准则或国际评估准则理事会发布的准则中存在有限的权威性指导。主体可能会参考所处国家的专业团体的指引（如有）。许多公司也会选择使用评估专家。

15.144　在使用现金流量折现法的情况下，应当遵循在缺乏具有约束力的销售合同或积极市场时确定公允价值的指导。在缺乏具有约束力的销售合同或积极市场时，在现金流量预测中使用的假设应当符合市场参与者应该会作出的假设，并能够被外部市场数据进一步支持。在确定公允价值时使用的现金流量是税后现金流量。该方法在第 18 章讨论资产减值时有更充分的讨论。

在非货币性资产交换中取得的无形资产

15.145　以非货币性资产或以非货币性与货币性资产的组合交换取得的无形资产应当以其公允价值初始确认，除非：

■ 该交换交易没有商业实质；或

■ 所获得和所放弃的资产的公允价值都不能可靠计量。

示例——专利交换

主体 A 是账面价值为 3,000 元的专利的持有人。主体 A 同意以其专利交换主体 B 的专利。双方均将主体 A 的专利的公允价值评估为 5,000 元。

ⓒ 2012 普华永道（PricewaterhouseCoopers）版权所有。

patent has been assessed by both parties at C5,000. Entity B's patent cannot be measured reliably. No additional monetary or non-monetary consideration has been included in the exchange.

Entity A will record its acquired patent at a cost of C5,000, as the asset's fair value that can be measured reliably is used by both parties as the value of the consideration if the fair value of the other asset cannot be measured reliably. A gain arises on the transaction of C2,000 and is recognised by entity A in the income statement. This amount is the difference between the carrying amount of entity A's original patent (C3,000) and the fair value of the patent given up (C5,000). Patents are inherently unique and so the exchange has commercial substance.

15.146 Where the consideration received or given comprises a combination of non-monetary and monetary assets, the fair value is adjusted by the amount of the monetary assets (for example, cash) given or received.

Example – Exchange of distribution rights in a region for cash and distribution rights in another region

An entity exchanges the rights to distribute a product in Japan that have a carrying amount of C1m, but a fair value of C1.2m, for C0.5m cash and the rights to distribute the same product in Europe which are fair valued at C0.7m. The cash of C0.5m is effectively the difference between the fair value of the exchanged assets (C1.2m – C0.7m). The European distribution rights are, therefore, recorded at C0.7m, which is equivalent to the fair value of the Japanese rights of C1.2m less the cash received of C0.5m. A gain of C0.2m arises on the transaction and is recognised in the income statement.

15.147 The decision as to whether a transaction has commercial substance depends on the extent to which the entity's future cash flows are expected to change as a result of the transaction. An exchange transaction has commercial substance if the difference in the following is significant relative to the fair value of the assets exchanged:

- the configuration of the cash flows of the asset received differs from the configuration of the cash flows of the asset given up. 'Configuration of the cash

© 2012 PricewaterhouseCoopers LLP. All rights reserved.

主体 B 的专利不能可靠计量。在交换中没有包括额外的货币性或非货币性对价。

如果另一资产的公允价值不能可靠计量，则主体 A 将以 5,000 元的成本记录所取得的专利，因为能够可靠计量的资产的公允价值被双方用作了对价的价值。该交易产生 2,000 元的利得，由主体 A 在利润表中确认。该金额是主体 A 原始专利的账面价值（3,000 元）和所放弃的该专利的公允价值（5,000 元）的差额。专利具有内在独特性，因此交易具有商业实质。

15.146　如果所获得或给予的对价包含非货币性和货币性资产的组合，则该公允价值将按所给予或获得的货币性资产（例如现金）的金额进行调整。

示例——以某地区的经销权交换现金和另一地区的经销权

主体以账面价值为 1 百万元而公允价值为 1.2 百万元的某产品的日本经销权换取现金 0.5 百万元和公允价值为 0.7 百万元的同一产品的欧洲经销权。现金 0.5 百万元是所交换资产公允价值之间的差额（1.2 百万元 - 0.7 百万元）。因此，欧洲经销权以 0.7 百万元记录，等同于 1.2 百万元的日本经销权的公允价值减去所获得的 0.5 百万元现金。该交易产生 0.2 百万元的利得，在利润表中确认。

15.147　确定交易是否具有商业实质取决于主体的未来现金流量预期将由于交易而改变的程度。如果以下差异与所交换的资产的公允价值相比较为重大，则交换交易具有商业实质：

- 所获得资产的现金流量的构成不同于所放弃资产的现金流量的构成。“现金流量的构成”在这里表示现金流量的风险、时点和金额。例如，主体可能

© 2012 普华永道（PricewaterhouseCoopers）版权所有。

flows' in this sense means the risk, timing and amount of the cash flows. For example an entity might exchange a research and development project for the rights to market a developed product. The cash flows from the developed product are different in configuration from those (if any) from the research and development project; or

- the entity-specific value of the part of the entity's operations affected by the transaction changes as a result of the exchange. 'Entity-specific value' is defined as "...*the present value of the cash flows an entity expects to arise from the continuing use of an asset and from its disposal at the end of its useful life or expects to incur when settling a liability*". [IAS 38 para 8]. Entity-specific value is different from 'value in use', which is defined in IAS 36, 'Impairment of assets', as "...*the present value of the future cash flows expected to be derived from an asset or cash-generating unit*". [IAS 36 para 6]. One of the most significant differences is that entity-specific value is determined using post-tax cash flows and value in use is measured using pre-tax cash flows.

Example 1 – Exchange of licenses to provide telephone service

An entity provides fixed telephone services, operating under a licence acquired from the government five years ago. The entity is required, by the 7th year, to reach service coverage of at least 67% of a specific area under the licence terms. Failure to achieve it will result in a penalty payment and possible licence cancellation. Currently, the entity has only achieved 31% coverage. The government is offering new licences, under which both fixed and mobile services may be provided, to new entrants. No minimum coverage is required. Existing operators are entitled to exchange their licences for the new ones. Although management does not intend to expand into mobile phone services, it has decided to exchange its licence.

The exchange transaction is considered to have commercial substance. The fair value of the new fixed/mobile licence is expected to be higher than the fair value of the fixed licence. It is unlikely that the minimum required coverage ratio under the existing licence would be met by the entity. It would then incur a penalty payment and could have its licence cancelled. Therefore, the entity-specific value of the part of the entity's operations affected by the

© 2012 PricewaterhouseCoopers LLP. All rights reserved.

以研发项目交换销售已开发产品的权利。已开发产品的现金流量在构成上不同于研发项目的现金流量（若有）；或

■ 主体受该交换影响的部分经营的特定主体价值由于交换而改变。“特定主体价值”定义为“……*主体预期从一项资产的持续使用以及其使用寿命结束时的处置或预期将其用于结清一项负债时产生的现金流量的现值*”。[IAS 第 38 号第 8 段]。特定主体价值不同于“使用价值”，后者在 IAS 第 36 号“资产减值”中定义为“……*预期产生于一项资产或现金产出单元的未来现金流量的现值*”。[IAS 第 36 号第 6 段]。最重要的差别之一是特定主体价值通过税后现金流量确定，而使用价值通过税前现金流量计量。

示例 1——电话服务许可证的交换

主体提供固定电话服务，并根据五年前从政府取得的许可证运营。许可证条款要求主体截至第 7 年底在特定地区的服务覆盖率达到至少 67%。未实现该目标将导致罚款，并有可能被取消许可。目前，主体仅实现了 31% 的覆盖率。政府正在颁发新的许可证，在更新的许可证下，新进入者将可以同时提供固定和移动服务并且不要求最低覆盖率。目前的运营商有权以其许可证交换新许可证。虽然管理层无意进入移动电话服务领域，但已经决定交换许可证。

该交换交易被认定为具有商业实质。新的固定/移动许可证的公允价值预期高于固定许可证的公允价值。主体不太可能实现现有许可证所要求的最低覆盖率。这将会产生罚款，并将导致许可证被取消。因此，主体受该交换影响的部分经营的特定主体价值由于交换而改变。主体不打算在新的固定/移动许可证下将运营扩展至移动电话服务领域的意图是无关紧要的。

ⓒ 2012 普华永道（PricewaterhouseCoopers）版权所有。

transaction changes as a result of the exchange. The entity's intention not to expand its operations into mobile phone services under the new fixed/mobile licence is irrelevant.

Example 2 – Exchange of licenses to provide telephone services

An entity acquired a licence from the government to provide fixed telecommunication services four years ago. The government has now offered to exchange the original licence for another that will allow the entity to operate both fixed and mobile services. The entity's management has accepted the offer of exchange. Management does not believe that there is sufficient demand for mobile phone services by the country's residents at the present time to make the venture profitable and does not intend to provide this facility in the near future. Management believes that the exchange lacks commercial substance and proposes to record the acquired licence using the carrying value of the licence given up.

The transaction has commercial substance. The new licence provides management with the ability to obtain additional cash flows from the provision of mobile phone services. The decision not to capitalise on this opportunity is not relevant. The potential cash flows from the provision of mobile phone services will significantly increase the fair value of the new licence over that of the old fixed line licence. Therefore, the entity-specific value of the part of the entity's operations affected by the transaction changes as a result of the exchange. The new licence should be recorded at its fair value. The old licence should be derecognised with any difference between carrying amount of the old licence and fair value of the new licence recognised in the income statement.

15.148 The results of the above analysis may be clear without the entity having to perform detailed calculations. [IAS 38 para 46]. If, essentially, the entity is in the same position as it was before the transaction and no material change has taken place in its net assets, no gain or loss is recognised on the transaction and the cost of the new asset is the carrying amount of the asset given up. However, the fair value of the asset received may provide evidence of either a gain or an impairment in the asset given up. If the value of the asset received is different, then the

© 2012 PricewaterhouseCoopers LLP. All rights reserved.

示例2——电话服务许可证的交换

主体四年前从政府取得提供固定电信服务的许可证。政府现在提出以原始许可证交换新证，使主体能够同时运营固定和移动服务。主体的管理层接受了交换提议。管理层不认为该国居民目前对于移动电话服务的需求足以使这项业务有利可图，因此无意在近期提供该服务。管理层相信该项交换缺乏商业实质，提议使用所放弃的许可证的账面价值记录所取得的许可证。

该交易具有商业实质。新的许可证给管理层提供了从移动电话服务提供中获得额外现金流量的能力。不利用这次机会的决定是无关紧要的。与旧固定电话许可证的公允价值相比，来自移动电话服务提供的潜在现金流量将大幅度提高新许可证的公允价值。因此，主体受该交换影响的部分经营的特定主体价值由于交换而改变。新许可证应当以其公允价值记录。旧许可证应当终止确认，旧许可证账面价值与新许可证公允价值之间的差额于利润表中确认。

15.148　以上分析的结果可能很清晰，无需主体进行详细计算。[IAS 第38号第46段]。如果本质上主体的状况与交易前相同，净资产未发生重大变化，则对于该交易无利得或亏损确认，并且新资产的成本是所放弃资产的账面价值。然而，所获得资产的公允价值可能证明一项利得或所放弃资产的减值。如果所获得资产的价值不同，则该交换具有商业实质，所获得资产应当以公允价值记录。如果所获得资产的价值低于所放弃资产，则应当确认处置亏损。

ⓒ 2012 普华永道（PricewaterhouseCoopers）版权所有。

exchange has commercial substance and the asset acquired should be recorded at fair value. If the value of the asset acquired is less than that given up then a loss on disposal should be recognised.

15. 149 Where there are no comparable market transactions the fair value of either the asset given up or the asset received can still be reliably measured if:

- the range of reasonable estimates of fair value does not vary significantly, that is if the range is reasonably narrow; or
- the range of reasonable estimates is not narrow, but the probabilities of the various estimates within the range can be reasonably assessed and used in estimating fair values.

Where both the fair value of the asset given up and the fair value of the asset received can be estimated with equal reliability, the fair value of the asset given up is used to measure the cost of the asset received. [IAS 38 para 47].

Intangible assets acquired by way of government grant

15. 150 An intangible asset may sometimes be acquired for free or for a nominal amount by way of a government grant. Examples include allocations of airport landing rights and import quotas. Intangible assets such as these may be recognised either at fair value or nominal value. This is an accounting policy choice under IAS 20, 'Government grants'. Any expenditure incurred by the entity that is directly attributable to preparing the asset for its intended use is also included in the initial measurement of the intangible asset. If the entity chooses to recognise the asset at fair value, that fair value is determined using an appropriate method. [IAS 38 para 44].

Internally generated intangible assets

15. 151 Intangible assets are measured initially at cost. [IAS 38 para 24]. Cost for internally generated intangible assets that meet the recognition criteria is determined using similar principles as those used for separately acquired intangible assets.

© 2012 PricewaterhouseCoopers LLP. All rights reserved.

15.149　如果没有可比市场交易，在以下情况下，所放弃资产或所获得资产的公允价值仍能可靠计量：

- 公允价值合理估计的范围差异不大，即该范围合理的狭窄；或

- 合理估计的范围不狭窄，但范围内各种估计的可能性能够合理评估并在估计公允价值时使用。

如果所放弃资产和所获得资产的公允价值能以相同的可靠性估计，则所放弃资产的公允价值用于计量所获得资产的成本。[IAS 第 38 号第 47 段]。

通过政府补助获得的无形资产

15.150　无形资产有时可以通过政府补助免费或以名义金额获得。例如机场着陆权和进口配额的分配。这类无形资产可以以公允价值或名义价值确认。这是 IAS 第 20 号“政府补助”下的一项会计政策选择。主体产生的直接归属于使资产能够用于指定用途的任何支出也包含在无形资产的初始计量中。如果主体选择以公允价值确认资产，则使用适当的方法确定该公允价值。[IAS 第 38 号第 44 段]。

内部产生的无形资产

15.151　无形资产以成本初始计量。[IAS 第 38 号第 24 段]。符合确认标准的内部产生的无形资产成本使用与单独购买无形资产类似的原则确定。

ⓒ 2012 普华永道（PricewaterhouseCoopers）版权所有。

15.152 The cost of an internally generated intangible asset that meets the recognition criteria is the sum of directly attributable expenditure incurred to create, produce and prepare the asset so that it is capable of operating in the manner intended by management. [IAS 38 para 66].

15.153 Examples of directly attributable costs given in paragraph 66 of IAS 38 are:

- Costs of materials and services used or consumed in generating the intangible asset.
- The cost of employee benefits, as defined in IAS 19, 'Employee benefits', that arise directly from the generation of the asset.
- Fees paid to register a legal right, such as patent registration fees.
- Amortisation of patents and licences that are used in generating the asset.
- Borrowing costs to the extent that they are eligible for capitalisation as part of the cost. Borrowing costs are dealt with by IAS 23, 'Borrowing costs', see chapter 16.

15.154 Employee benefits are defined in IAS 19 as all forms of consideration given by an entity in exchange for service rendered by employees. [IAS 19 para 7]. The types of benefit include:

- Short-term employee benefits such as wages, salaries and social security contributions, paid annual leave and paid sick leave, profit-sharing and annual bonuses and non-monetary benefits such as medical care, housing and free or subsidised goods or services.
- Post-employment benefits such as pensions, other retirement benefits, post-employment life insurance and post-employment medical care.
- Other long-term employment benefits, including long service leave or sabbatical leave, jubilee or other long-service benefits, long-term disability benefit and deferred bonuses or profit-sharing and other deferred compensation.
- Termination benefits.

[IAS 19 para 4].

© 2012 PricewaterhouseCoopers LLP. All rights reserved.

15.152 符合确认标准的内部产生的无形资产成本是为了使资产能够以管理层指定的方式运营而创建、生产和准备资产所产生的可直接归属的支出的总额。[IAS 第 38 号第 66 段]。

15.153 IAS 第 38 号第 66 段提供的可直接归属的成本的例子如下：

- 在产生无形资产时使用或消耗的材料和服务的成本。
- 为产生资产而直接导致的在 IAS 第 19 号“职工福利”中定义的职工福利成本。
- 注册法律权利支付的费用，例如专利注册费。
- 在产生资产时使用的专利和许可证的摊销。
- 有资格作为成本的一部分予以资本化的借款成本。借款成本由 IAS 第 23 号“借款成本”提供指引，参见第十六章。

15.154 职工福利在 IAS 第 19 号中定义为主体为换取职工提供的服务而给予的所有形式的对价。[IAS 第 19 号第 7 段]。福利类型包括：

- 短期职工福利，例如工资、薪金、社会保障提存金、带薪年假、带薪病假、利润分享、年度奖金以及非货币性福利，例如医疗、住房和免费或有补贴的商品或服务。
- 离职后福利，例如退休金、其他退休福利、离职后人寿保险和离职后医疗。
- 其他长期在职福利，包括长期服务假或公休假、重要周年纪念或其他长期服务福利、长期伤残福利和递延奖金或利润分享和其他递延报酬。
- 终止福利。

[IAS 第 19 号第 4 段]。

© 2012 普华永道（PricewaterhouseCoopers）版权所有。

15.155 The types of costs described above are being incurred while an intangible asset is being generated. Further capitalisation may also be possible during the commissioning phase before an asset is capable of operating in the manner intended by management. The cost of testing whether an item is functioning properly is a directly attributable cost of a separately acquired intangible asset. [IAS 38 para 28]. Testing costs would also be a valid cost in relation to an internally generated intangible asset. However, not all of the above costs will always be eligible or relevant. For example, termination benefits will rarely, if ever, be relevant since they are provided to employees who, by definition, are leaving or have left and are unlikely to be contributing to the generating of an asset. The list is useful; however, in answering some frequently asked questions, such as whether the costs of an employee share scheme, social security costs and entity pension contributions may be considered to be directly attributable costs. These costs are directly attributable provided that they are incurred in bringing an asset to the condition necessary for it to operate in the manner intended by management.

15.156 Only the costs that are directly attributable to generating the intangible asset, and not the general costs of the operation, may be capitalised. The standard lists types of costs that are not 'directly attributable' and, therefore, are not components of the cost of an internally generated intangible asset as follows:

- Selling, administration and other general overhead costs, unless they can be directly attributed to preparing the asset for use.
- Inefficiencies and initial operating losses incurred before the asset achieves planned performance.
- Training costs for staff that will operate the asset.

[IAS 38 para 67].

Example – Promotion costs and operating losses related to entity database

An entity has developed a database of names and addresses of professional people who reach their twenty fifth birthdays between the years 2004 and 2010. Management intends to exploit this by selling the information to suppliers of life enhancement products and solutions for junior executives. The

© 2012 PricewaterhouseCoopers LLP. All rights reserved.

15.155　上述各类成本在产生无形资产时发生。在资产能够以管理层指定的方式运营之前的调试阶段可能会有进一步的资本化。测试项目是否正常运行的成本是单独购买的无形资产的可直接归属的成本。[IAS 第 38 号第 28 段]。测试成本也应该是与内部产生的无形资产相关的有效成本。然而，不是所有以上成本总是具有资格被资本化或相关。例如，终止福利极少相关，因为它们提供给根据定义正在离开或已经离开的雇员，这些费用不可能对资产的产生作出贡献。然而，在回答一些常见问题时，该清单是有用的，例如职工股权计划的成本、社会保障成本和主体退休金缴款是否可以视为可直接归属的成本。这些成本可直接归属的前提是它们是使资产达到能够以管理层指定的方式运营的必要状态而产生的成本。

15.156　只有可直接归属于无形资产的产生而发生的成本（而非一般运营成本）才能资本化。该准则列出了非“可直接归属”因而不是内部产生的无形资产成本的组成部分的各类成本：

■ 销售、管理和其他一般间接费用，除非可直接归属于使资产能够使用。

■ 在资产达到所计划的表现前产生的无效率和初始经营亏损。

■ 将要运营资产的员工的培训成本。

[IAS 第 38 号第 67 段]。

示例——与主体数据库相关的促销费用和经营损失

主体开发了在 2004 年至 2010 年期间满 25 周岁的专业人员的姓名和地址数据库。为了利用该数据库，管理层准备向针对初级管理人员提供生命提升产品和相应产品的供应商出售该信息。主体向这些产品的销售商（例如探险旅行供应商）宣传数据库时产生成本。因为管理成本很高，并

ⓒ 2012 普华永道（PricewaterhouseCoopers）版权所有。

entity is incurring costs of promoting the databases to vendors of such solutions, such as adventure holiday companies. It is also incurring losses as there are substantial administrative costs and no income as yet. Can it capitalise the promotion costs and the operating losses, as the database cannot work as intended by management unless a customer base is first established?

The promotional costs are not eligible for capitalisation as part of the cost of the intangible asset. The database is already capable of operating in the manner intended by management, that is, it can provide the information that management wish to exploit. Building up a customer base is not essential to the working of the database although it is essential to ensuring that the future economic benefits expected from the asset are achieved. The start-up losses are also not eligible for capitalisation as they are not directly attributable costs of the generation of the database.

15.157 The standard provides guidance on the period during which costs may be capitalised. The capitalisation of costs stops when the asset "*is capable of operating in the manner intended by management*". This means that if an asset is internally generated (constructed) and can operate in that manner immediately, but is not brought into use immediately, costs incurred whilst the asset is standing idle may not be capitalised. [IAS 38, para 30]. For example, staff costs in the development phase of a project may meet the capitalisation criteria. However, once the development project is complete, if the staff then commence work on another research project, their costs can no longer be capitalised. Costs incurred in using or redeploying an item are not included in its carrying amount. The standard also prohibits initial operating losses, such as those that may be incurred while demand for an item's output builds up, to be capitalised.

Web site costs

15.158 A web site that is developed for internal or external access is an internally generated intangible asset under IAS 38. SIC 32, 'Intangible assets – Web site costs', provides further guidance on this topic. To qualify for recognition as an asset the costs must satisfy the recognition criteria in IAS 38 for intangible assets. See paragraph 15.53.

© 2012 PricewaterhouseCoopers LLP. All rights reserved.

且尚未获得收益，所以也在亏损。除非首先建立客户基础，否则数据库不能按照管理层的意图运营，那是否能够因此将促销费用和经营亏损资本化？

促销费用没有资格作为无形资产成本的一部分而资本化。数据库已经能够以管理层指定的方式运营，即能够提供管理层希望利用的信息。虽然数据库对于确保实现预期从资产获得的未来经济利益十分重要，但建立客户基础对于数据库的运营并不重要。开办亏损也没有资格资本化，因为它们不是产生数据库而发生的可直接归属的成本。

15.157　该准则提供了关于成本资本化期间的指导。当资产“*能够以管理层指定的方式运营*”时，成本的资本化停止。这意味着如果一项资产是内部产生的（创立的）并能够立即以该方式运营但不立即进入使用，那么在资产闲置期间产生的成本不能资本化。[IAS 第 38 号第 30 段]。例如，项目开发阶段的员工成本可能符合资本化标准。然而，一旦开发项目完成后，如果员工开始实施另一研究项目，则其成本不再资本化。使用或重新配置项目产生的成本不包含在其账面价值中。该准则还禁止将初始经营亏损（例如在项目产出需求扩大时可能产生的亏损）资本化。

网站成本

15.158　根据 IAS 第 38 号，为向内部或外部开放而开发的网站是一项内部产生的无形资产。SIC 第 32 号“无形资产——网站成本”提供了有关该主题的更多指导。为符合确认为资产的资格，这些成本必须满足 IAS 第 38 号中的无形资产确认标准。参见第 15.53 段。

ⓒ 2012 普华永道（PricewaterhouseCoopers）版权所有。

15.159 Where the web site will be capable of generating revenues including direct revenues from enabling orders to be placed, an entity will be able to satisfy the requirement of how its website will generate future probable economic benefit in accordance with paragraph 57(d) of IAS 38. [SIC 32 para 8]. The web site itself may contain the product that is being sold (such as information) and access may be provided by way of a registration for a fee. However, a web site that is developed solely to promote or advertise an entity's products or services would not meet the condition in paragraph 57(d) of IAS 38 and, therefore, all expenditure on such a web site must be expensed as incurred. [SIC 32 para 8].

15.160 The costs incurred at each stage in developing the site must be evaluated to determine whether they should be expensed as incurred or capitalised. SIC 32 includes a detailed appendix that describes the nature of expenditure that may be incurred at each of the stages and the appropriate accounting treatment.

15.161 After initial recognition, a web site would normally be carried at cost less amortisation. The revaluation model permitted by IAS 38 would not apply, because there is no active market for websites. The amortisation period for a web site should be short, as rapid technological advances mean that web sites are susceptible to technological obsolescence. [SIC 32 para 10].

Subsequent expenditure on a research and development project acquired separately or in a business combination

15.162 Research and development projects acquired separately or as part of a business combination are recognised as an intangible asset if they can be reliably measured. This results in the recognition of many such assets at an earlier stage than if they were internally generated assets.

15.163 Subsequent costs related to acquired intangibles should be accounted for in accordance with the standard's rules relating to internally generated intangible assets. This means that the subsequent expenditure is accounted for as follows:

- Subsequent research expenditure is recognised as an expense as incurred.
- Subsequent development expenditure is recognised as an expense if it does not

© 2012 PricewaterhouseCoopers LLP. All rights reserved.

15.159 如果网站能够产生收入（包括能够下订单所产生的直接收入），则主体能够满足 IAS 第 38 号第 57（d）段的要求：证明网站如何产生未来经济利益。[SIC 第 32 号第 8 段]。网站本身可能包含正在销售的产品（例如信息），并且通过收费注册访问。然而，仅为了宣传主体的产品或服务而开发的网站不符合 IAS 第 38 号第 57（d）段的条件，因此，有关该网站的所有支出必须在发生时费用化。[SIC 第 32 号第 8 段]。

15.160 我们必须评估开发网站时每个阶段所产生的成本，以确定是否应当在发生时费用化或资本化。SIC 第 32 号包含详细的附录，描述了在每个阶段可能产生的支出的性质和其适当的会计处理。

15.161 经过初始确认后，网站一般以成本减摊销计量。因为不存在网站的活跃市场，IAS 第 38 号允许的重估模型不会适用。因为技术的迅速进步意味着网站容易在技术上过时，网站的摊销期应当较短。[SIC 第 32 号第 10 段]。

单独购买或在业务合并中取得的研究和开发项目的后续支出

15.162 如果能够可靠计量，则单独购买或作为业务合并的一部分取得的研究和开发项目应被确认为无形资产。这导致许多该类资产比其在作为内部产生的资产的情况下更早确认。

15.163 已购无形资产相关的后续成本应当根据内部产生的无形资产的相关准则规定进行会计处理。这意味着后续支出的会计处理如下：

- 后续研究支出在发生时确认为费用。
- 后续开发支出如不满足确认为资产的条件则确认为费用。参见第 15.45 段。

ⓒ 2012 普华永道（PricewaterhouseCoopers）版权所有。

satisfy the conditions for recognition as an asset. See paragraph 15. 45.

- Subsequent development expenditure that does satisfy the conditions for recognition as an asset is added to the carrying amount of the intangible asset.

[IAS 38 paras 42, 43].

Example – Separately acquired research project

Entity A has incurred C100, 000 of research expenditure on a project to develop a new type of fuel and has expensed these costs. Entity B purchases the research project, including certain patents that have been registered by entity A, for C150, 000 and recognises an intangible asset. Subsequently, entity B incurs C200,000 of expenditure on completing the research phase and decides to develop the product commercially. It incurs a further C300,000 of costs in bringing the product to a stage where the conditions for recognising development costs as an internally generated intangible asset are met. Further costs of C1m are incurred in bringing the product into a condition where it is ready for use in the manner that management intend. Initial marketing costs and losses are incurred of C200, 000 before the product reaches widespread distribution.

What costs can entity B capitalise?

- Entity B recognises C150,000 as the cost of the acquired research project. [IAS 38 paras 24, 25].
- The subsequent research costs of C200,000 may not be recognised and must be expensed as incurred. [IAS 38 paras 42, 54].
- The subsequent development costs incurred of C300, 000 do not meet the conditions for recognition and are expensed as incurred. [IAS 38 paras 42, 57].
- Further development costs of C1m must be recognised (there is no option of expensing these costs), because they meet the conditions for recognition as an intangible asset. [IAS 38 paras 42(b), 57]. The previously written off development costs are not reinstated. [IAS 38 para 71].
- The marketing costs and initial losses of C200, 000 are expensed as

© 2012 PricewaterhouseCoopers LLP. All rights reserved.

■ 满足确认为资产的条件的后续开发支出增加至该无形资产的账面价值。

[IAS 第 38 号第 42、43 段]。

示例——单独购买的研究项目

主体 A 在开发新型燃料的项目上产生了 100,000 元的研究支出并将其费用化。主体 B 以 150,000 元购买了该研究项目（包括主体 A 已经注册的某些专利），并确认为一项无形资产。之后，主体 B 为完成研究阶段产生了 200,000 元的支出，并且决定对产品进行商业开发。它将产品带入能够将开发成本确认为内部产生的无形资产的阶段又产生了 300,000 元的成本。将该产品带入能够以管理层指定的方式使用的状态又进一步产生了 1 百万元的成本。在产品能够广泛销售前产生了 200,000 元的初始营销成本和亏损。

主体 B 能够将哪些成本资本化？

■ 主体 B 将 150,000 元确认为已购研究项目的成本。[IAS 第 38 号第 24、25 段]。

■ 200,000 元的后续研究成本不能确认，必须在发生时费用化。[IAS 第 38 号第 42、54 段]。

■ 300,000 元的后续开发成本不符合确认条件，在发生时费用化。[IAS 第 38 号第 42、57 段]。

■ 1 百万元的进一步开发成本必须确认（没有将这些成本费用化的选择），因为它们符合确认为无形资产的条件。[IAS 第 38 号第 42（b）、57 段]。之前冲销的开发成本不予恢复。[IAS 第 38 号第 71 段]。

■ 200,000 元的营销成本和初始亏损在发生时费用化。[IAS 第 38 号第

ⓒ 2012 普华永道（PricewaterhouseCoopers）版权所有。

incurred. [IAS 38 paras 67, 69].

The intangible asset's carrying amount when production and sale of the product commences is, therefore, C1.15m. Had the asset been wholly internally generated by entity B the carrying amount would have been only C1m, with only the development costs incurred after the IAS 38 recognition criteria had been met being capitalised.

Measurement subsequent to initial recognition

Introduction

Internally generated intangible assets

15.164 Subsequent to initial recognition, an entity may adopt either the cost model or the revaluation model as its accounting policy. The revaluation model may only be adopted if the intangible assets are traded in an active market; hence it is not frequently used. The policy should be applied to the whole of a class of intangible asset and not merely to individual assets within a class, unless there is no active market for an individual asset. A policy of revaluation may be more onerous and involve more complex record keeping than using the cost model. [IAS 38 para 72].

15.165 The cost model requires that, after initial recognition, intangible assets should be carried at cost less accumulated amortisation and impairment losses. [IAS 38 para 74]. The revaluation model requires that, subsequent to initial recognition, intangible assets should be carried at fair value, determined by reference to an active market. Revaluations should be carried out with sufficient regularity that the carrying amount of the asset does not differ materially from that which would be determined using fair value at the balance sheet date. [IAS 38 para 75].

Classes of intangible assets

15.166 IAS 38 requires that if a single intangible asset is revalued, then the

© 2012 PricewaterhouseCoopers LLP. All rights reserved.

67、69 段］。

当产品的生产和销售开始时，无形资产的账面价值为 1.15 百万元。如果资产完全由主体 B 内部产生，则账面价值应该仅为 1 百万元（仅将符合 IAS 第 38 号确认标准后产生的开发成本资本化）。

初始确认后的计量

引言

内部产生的无形资产

15.164　初始确认后，主体可以采用成本模式或重估模式作为其会计政策。重估模式仅在无形资产在活跃市场交易时才能采用，因此不经常使用。除非该个别资产没有活跃市场，对于同一类无形资产应当全部应用同一政策，而不应仅对于一类中的个别资产应用该政策。与使用成本模式相比，重估政策可能更加繁琐，涉及更复杂的簿记。［IAS 第 38 号第 72 段］。

15.165　成本模式要求无形资产在初始确认后应当以成本减累计摊销和减值损失计量。［IAS 第 38 号第 74 段］。重估模式要求无形资产在初始确认后应当以参考活跃市场确定的公允价值计量。重估应当进行得足够规律，以使资产的账面价值不会与使用资产负债表日的公允价值确定的账面价值有重大差异。［IAS 第 38 号第 75 段］。

无形资产的类别

15.166　虽然重估政策无需应用于所有类别的无形资产，IAS 第 38 号要求，

ⓒ 2012 普华永道（PricewaterhouseCoopers）版权所有。

entire class of intangible assets to which that item belongs should be revalued, although the policy need not be applied to all classes of intangible asset. [IAS 38 para 72].

15.167 An entity may adopt classes of assets that meet the following definition that is given in the standard: "*A grouping of assets of a similar nature and use in an entity's operations*". [IAS 38 para 73]. Other than ruling out classes of assets determined on a geographical basis, this definition is reasonably flexible. An entity can adopt meaningful classes that are appropriate to its business. Separate disclosures must be made for each class of assets. For example, each class of assets must be presented as a separate category in the table of movements in intangible assets in the notes to the financial statements. [IAS 38 para 118]. Most companies have a few broadly drawn classes of intangible assets.

15.168 Examples of classes of intangible assets are:

- Brand names.
- Mastheads and publishing titles.
- Licences and franchises.
- Copyrights, patents and other industrial property rights, service and operating rights.
- Recipes, formulae, models, designs and prototypes.
- Intangible assets under development.
- Emission rights.

Items in this list might be further analysed or combined if that would give more relevant information to users of the financial statements. [IAS 38 para 119]. For example further categories resulting from aggregation or disaggregation of items in the above list that might sometimes be treated as separate classes of intangible asset include:

- Web site development costs.
- Computer software.
- Databases.

© 2012 PricewaterhouseCoopers LLP. All rights reserved.

如果重估单一无形资产，则该项目所属的整类无形资产都应当重估。[IAS 第 38 号第 72 段]。

15.167　主体可以采用符合准则提供的以下定义的资产类别：“*主体经营中具有类似性质和用途的一组资产*”。[IAS 第 38 号第 73 段]。除了排除掉根据地理区域确定的资产类别外，该定义具有合理的灵活性。主体可以采用适用于其业务的有意义的类别。对于每类资产必须作出单独披露。例如，每类资产必须在财务报表附注中的无形资产变动表中列报为单独的类别。[IAS 第 38 号第 118 段]。大多数公司有一些大致划分的无形资产类别。

15.168　无形资产类别示例：

■ 品牌名称。

■ 刊头和出版标题。

■ 许可证和特许权。

■ 版权、专利和其他工业产权，服务和经营权。

■ 配方、公式、模型、设计和原型。

■ 正在开发的无形资产。

■ 排放权。

可以对本表中的项目进行进一步的分析或汇总以向财务报表使用者提供更相关的信息。[IAS 第 38 号第 119 段]。例如将上述清单中的项目进行汇总或分离有时可以产生更多的无形资产的单独类别，包括：

■ 网站开发成本。

■ 计算机软件。

■ 数据库。

ⓒ 2012 普华永道（PricewaterhouseCoopers）版权所有。

- Aircraft landing rights.
- Picture or music libraries.
- Mobile phone licences.

Application of revaluation model

15.169 The revaluation model may not be applied to intangible assets that have not previously been recognised as intangible assets. [IAS 38 para 76]. For example, over the years an entity might have accumulated for nominal consideration a number of licences of a kind that are traded on an active market. The entity has not recognised an intangible asset as the licenses were individually immaterial when acquired. Market prices for such licences have recently risen significantly and the value of the licences held by the entity has substantially increased. The entity is, however, prohibited by IAS 38 from applying the revaluation model to the licences, because they have not previously been recognised as an asset.

15.170 The revaluation model may be applied to measure an intangible asset only subsequent to the asset's initial recognition and measurement at cost. The method cannot be used at initial recognition to record an intangible asset at a value other than cost. [IAS 38 para 76]. Recording assets acquired in a business combination at fair value is not the application of the revaluation model. It is a method of determining the 'cost to the group' of individual assets acquired in a business combination.

15.171 The revaluation model may also be applied to an asset that was acquired by way of government grant and measured on initial recognition at a nominal amount. [IAS 38 para 77]. The nominal amount could be nil if the asset was received free of charge.

15.172 Where a revalued asset's fair value can no longer be determined by reference to an active market, the carrying amount should be frozen at the revalued amount at the date of the last valuation. That carrying amount is then amortised and impaired as necessary in the normal way. The previous revaluation surplus is not reversed when the measurement by reference to an active market is no longer possible. The absence of an active market may be an indication of impairment that

© 2012 PricewaterhouseCoopers LLP. All rights reserved.

■ 飞机着陆权。

■ 图片或音乐资料库。

■ 移动电话许可证。

应用重估模式

15. 169　重估模式不能用于以前未确认为无形资产的无形资产。[IAS 第 38 号第 76 段]。例如，主体可能已经在若干年中以名义对价积累了在活跃市场上交易的大量某种许可证。因为在购买时单个许可证并不重大，主体未确认无形资产。该类许可证的市场价格最近显著提高，主体持有的许可证的价值大幅度增加。然而，IAS 第 38 号禁止主体将重估模式应用于这些许可证，因为它们之前没有被确认为资产。

15. 170　仅在以成本初始确认和计量资产后才能使用重估模式计量无形资产。在初始确认中不能使用这种方法以非成本的其他价值记录无形资产。[IAS 第 38 号第 76 段]。以公允价值记录在业务合并中取得的资产不是重估模式的应用。这是一种确定在业务合并中取得的各个资产的“针对该集团的成本”的方法。

15. 171　重估模式也可以应用于通过政府补助取得并且在初始确认时以名义金额计量的资产。[IAS 第 38 号第 77 段]。如果免费获得资产，则名义金额可以为零。

15. 172　如果重估的资产的公允价值不再能够参考活跃市场确定，则应当以最后一次评估日的重估金额冻结账面价值。之后以正常方式对账面价值进行必要的摊销和减值。当参考活跃市场计量不再可能时，之前的重估盈余无需冲回。缺乏活跃市场可能是一个减值迹象，因此需要对资产进行减值测试。如果之后资产再次能够参考活跃市场评估，则应当根据应用于其所属类别的重估模式从该日期起重估资产。[IAS 第 38 号第 81 至 84 段]。

© 2012 普华永道（PricewaterhouseCoopers）版权所有。

would require an impairment test to be carried out on the asset. If subsequently the asset is again able to be valued by reference to an active market, the asset should be revalued from that date in accordance with the revaluation model applied to the class of which it is part. [IAS 38 paras 81 to 84].

15.173 The only valuation basis permitted is fair value determined by reference to an active market. The definition of active market is a market in which all of the following conditions exist:

- The items traded in the market are homogeneous (similar in kind or nature);
- Willing buyers and sellers are always available; and
- Prices are publicly quoted.

[IAS 38 para 8].

15.174 An active market exists for only a few types of intangible asset and the revaluation model can only be used where such a market exists. The standard notes that in some jurisdictions an active market may exist for freely transferable taxi licences, fishing licences or production quotas. An example of the last of these might be emission rights, for which an active market is likely once a scheme is fully operational.

15.175 An active market cannot exist for brands, newspaper mastheads, music and film rights, patents or trademarks, because each such asset is unique. Although such unique intangibles may be bought and sold, the prices are negotiated between individual buyers and sellers rather than being quoted on an active market. Such purchase and sale transactions are fairly infrequent. The price paid for an asset in one transaction may not be a good guide to the fair value of another asset. [IAS 38 para 78]. An example might be the purchase and sale of a cigarette brand name. The price paid is not a reliable measure of the fair value of other cigarette brands as the asset is unique and there is no active market.

Frequency of revaluations

15.176 Valuations should remain up-to-date, as old valuations that do not reflect current values are less meaningful. There is no requirement for valuations to be performed every reporting period. However, revaluations should be made with

© 2012 PricewaterhouseCoopers LLP. All rights reserved.

15.173　唯一被允许的评估基础是参考活跃市场确定的公允价值。活跃市场的定义是存在以下所有条件的市场：

■ 市场中交易的项目是同质的（在类别或性质上类似）；

■ 总能有乐意的买方和卖方；

■ 公开报价。

［IAS 第 38 号第 8 段］。

15.174　活跃市场仅对几种无形资产存在，只能在存在该类市场时才能使用重估模式。该准则说明，在一些管辖区，可自由转让的出租车牌照、捕鱼许可证或生产配额存在活跃市场。最后一个例子是排放权，在有一个可充分运行的体系时，可能会存在活跃市场。

15.175　品牌、报头、音乐和电影版权、专利或商标不存在活跃市场，因为这类资产每项都是独一无二的。虽然该类独特的无形资产可以买卖，但价格在各个买方和卖方之间协商，而不是在活跃市场报价。该类买卖交易很不频繁。在一项交易中为某一资产支付的价格可能不是另一资产公允价值的良好参考。［IAS 第 38 号第 78 段］。例如在香烟品牌名称的买卖中，所支付的价格不是其他香烟品牌公允价值的可靠计量，因为该类资产是独特的，没有活跃市场。

重估频率

15.176　评估应当保持更新，因为不反映现时价值的旧评估值意义较小。准则没有要求每个报告期都进行评估，然而，重估应当进行得足够规律，以使资产的账面价值不会与资产负债表日的公允价值有重大差异。［IAS 第 38 号

ⓒ 2012 普华永道（PricewaterhouseCoopers）版权所有。

sufficient regularity that the carrying amount does not differ materially from fair value at the balance sheet date. [IAS 38 para 75].

15.177 The frequency of revaluations, therefore, depends on movements in the fair value of intangibles. If an intangible asset's fair value differs materially from its carrying amount a new valuation is needed. Market prices for some intangibles may suffer significant and volatile movements, such that annual valuations are needed. Intangibles with relatively stable market prices may not require such frequent valuations. [IAS 38 para 79]. A material change in value might be defined as one that "*would reasonably influence the decisions of a user of the accounts*". As a policy of revaluation is allowed only when there is an active market for the assets, market values should be relatively easy to obtain and keeping such values up to date on an annual basis should also be straightforward.

Treatment of accumulated amortisation when intangible assets are revalued

15.177.1 When an intangible asset is revalued, accumulated amortisation is treated in one of two ways:

- Eliminated against the asset's gross carrying amount with the net amount restated to equal the revalued amount; or
- Restated proportionately with the change in the asset's gross carrying amount such that the asset's net book value after revaluation equals its revalued amount.

[IAS 38 para 80].

15.177.2 The amount of the adjustment to accumulated amortisation forms part of the gain or loss on revaluation.

Revaluation gains and losses

Revaluation gains

15.178 A revaluation increase should be recognised in other comprehensive

© 2012 PricewaterhouseCoopers LLP. All rights reserved.

第 75 段]。

15.177 因此，重估频率取决于无形资产公允价值的变动。如果无形资产的公允价值明显不同于账面价值，则需要进行新的评估。某些无形资产的市场价格可能会发生剧烈而不稳定的变动，因此需要进行年度评估。而具有相对稳定的市场价格的无形资产不需要这样频繁的评估。[IAS 第 38 号第 79 段]。价值的重大变化可以定义为“*将合理影响账目使用者的决策*”的价值变化。因为仅在资产具有活跃市场时才允许使用重估政策，所以市场价值应当相对容易获得，每年更新这些价值也应当比较简单。

重估无形资产时对累计摊销的处理

15.177.1 在重估无形资产时，对累计摊销的处理有两种方式：

- 冲抵资产的账面原值，重述净值使其等于重估价值；或
- 与资产账面原值一起按比例重述，使重估后资产的账面净值等于重估价值。

[IAS 第 38 号第 80 段]。

15.177.2 对累计摊销的调整金额构成重估利得或亏损的一部分。

重估利得和亏损

重估利得

15.178 除非重估增值冲回了之前确认为费用的同一资产的重估减值，它应

ⓒ 2012 普华永道（PricewaterhouseCoopers）版权所有。

income and accumulated in equity under the heading of revaluation surplus, unless it reverses a revaluation decrease on the same asset previously recognised as an expense. Reversals of previous revaluation decreases are credited to profit or loss to the extent that the decrease was recognised as an expense. [IAS 38 para 85].

15.179 The revaluation surplus included in equity may be transferred directly to retained earnings when the surplus is realised (that is, when the asset is retired or disposed of). The transfer is made through other comprehensive income and is not made through profit or loss. [IAS 38 para 87].

15.180 Some of the surplus may also be transferred as the asset is used by the entity, that is, as the surplus is realised. The amount transferred is the difference between amortisation based on the revalued carrying amount of the asset and amortisation based on the asset's original cost. This amount may, therefore, be transferred from revaluation surplus to retained earnings each year, by means of a reserve transfer through other comprehensive income. [IAS 38 para 87].

Revaluation losses

15.181 A revaluation decrease should be recognised in profit or loss. However, the decrease should be recognised in other comprehensive income if there is a credit balance in the revaluation surplus on the same asset. The decrease in other comprehensive income also decreases the amount accumulated in equity under the heading of revaluation reserve. [IAS 38 para 86].

Amortisation

15.182 Amortisation is defined in IAS 38 as the systematic allocation of the depreciable amount of an intangible asset over its useful life. The depreciable amount is defined as the asset's cost, or other amount substituted for cost, less its residual value. [IAS 38 para 8].

15.183 The method of amortisation that is used should reflect the pattern in which the asset's future economic benefits are expected to be consumed by the entity. If that pattern cannot be determined reliably, the straight-line method of

© 2012 PricewaterhouseCoopers LLP. All rights reserved.

以重估盈余的名称确认为其他综合收益计入权益。之前的重估减值的冲回以之前确认为费用的减值为限计入损益。[IAS 第 38 号第 85 段]。

15.179 在重估盈余实现时（即当停用或处置资产时），包含在权益中的重估盈余可以直接转移至留存收益。这种转移通过其他综合收益进行，不通过损益。[IAS 第 38 号第 87 段]。

15.180 在主体使用资产时（即盈余实现时）一些盈余也可转移。转移的金额是以资产的重估账面价值为基础的摊销和以资产的原始成本为基础的摊销之间的差额。因此，该金额可以通过其他综合收益以准备转移的方式每年从重估盈余转移至留存收益。[IAS 第 38 号第 87 段]。

重估亏损

15.181 重估减值应当确认为损益。然而，如同一资产在重估盈余中有贷方余额，那么减值应当确认为其他综合收益。在其他综合收益中记录的减值也同时减少了在权益中的重估储备项下累计的金额。[IAS 第 38 号第 86 段]。

摊销

15.182 摊销在 IAS 第 38 号中定义为将无形资产的可折旧金额在使用寿命内的系统分配。可折旧金额定义为资产的成本（或替代成本的其他金额）减去其残值。[IAS 第 38 号第 8 段]。

15.183 所使用的摊销方法应当能够反映主体消耗资产的未来经济利益的预期方式。如果该方式不能可靠确定，则必须使用直线法摊销。摊销费用应当确认为费用，除非 IAS 第 38 号或另一项准则允许或要求它们包含在另一项资

ⓒ 2012 普华永道（PricewaterhouseCoopers）版权所有。

amortisation must be used. Amortisation charges should be recognised as an expense, unless they are permitted or required by IAS 38 or another standard to be included in the carrying amount of another asset. [IAS 38 para 97].

15.184 Amortisation applies to all intangible fixed assets, whether held at cost or fair value, except intangible assets with indefinite useful lives. An intangible asset with an indefinite useful life should not be amortised. [IAS 38 para 107].

15.185 Amortisation should begin as soon as an asset is available for use, that is, when it is in the location and condition necessary for it to be capable of operating in the manner intended by management. [IAS 38 para 97].

Example – Amortisation of product distribution rights

An entity acquires licences and trademarks including product distribution rights on 1 January 20X0. The licences and product distribution rights still require some regulatory approval at this date. On 1 March 20X0 the entity receives regulatory approval to distribute the products. Management proposes that amortisation of these rights begins on the 1 March 20X0, therefore, the amortisation will match when the intangibles were available for use.

The amortisation of an acquired intangible can be delayed only to the point where the intangible asset becomes available for use. The acquired rights will be consumed over a fixed period from 1 March 20X0 and so should be amortised over that period.

15.186 Amortisation should stop at the earlier of the date when the intangible asset is derecognised and the date when it is classified as held-for-sale under IFRS 5, 'Non-current assets held-for-sale and discontinued operations'. [IAS 38 para 97]. An intangible asset is derecognised on disposal or it is impaired when no future economic benefits are expected from its use. An intangible asset is classified as held-for-sale in accordance with IFRS 5 when it meets the conditions in that standard for such classification. See chapter 26. Amortisation does not stop when an asset is retained but no longer used, unless it has been fully depreciated or classified as held-for-sale under IFRS 5. [IAS 38 para 117]. However, if the asset were no longer used because no future economic benefits were expected from it or if an asset is temporarily unused, this would be an indication of impairment for the relevant

© 2012 PricewaterhouseCoopers LLP. All rights reserved.

产的账面价值中。[IAS 第 38 号第 97 段]。

15.184　除非是具有不确定使用寿命的无形资产，摊销适用于所有无形资产，无论是以成本还是公允价值计价。具有不确定使用寿命的无形资产不应摊销。[IAS 第 38 号第 107 段]。

15.185　资产可供使用时（也就是说，当它处于能够以管理层预定的方式运营所需的必要地点和情况时），就应立即开始摊销。[IAS 第 38 号第 97 段]。

示例——产品经销权的摊销

主体于 20X0 年 1 月 1 日获得执照和商标以及产品的经销权，但此时执照和产品经销权还需要监管部门审批。20X0 年 3 月 1 日，主体获得了产品经销审批。管理层提出这些权利的摊销开始于 20X0 年 3 月 1 日，因此，摊销将与无形资产可供使用的时间一致。

购买的无形资产的摊销只能被推迟至其可供使用日。购买的权利将在 20X0 年 3 月 1 日起的固定期间内消耗，因此应当在该期间内摊销。

15.186　摊销应当于以下日期的较早者停止：无形资产终止确认的日期和根据 IFRS 第 5 号“持有待售的非流动资产和终止经营”分类为持有待售的日期。[IAS 第 38 号第 97 段]。无形资产在处置时终止确认，或在预期不能从其使用或处置中获得未来经济利益时减值。当无形资产符合 IFRS 第 5 号中的持有待售的分类条件时被分类为持有待售。参见第 26 章。除非资产已经提足折旧或根据 IFRS 第 5 号分类为持有待售，当保留无形资产但不再使用该资产时，摊销不应停止。[IAS 第 38 号第 117 段]。然而，如果因为预期不能从其获得未来经济利益而不再使用资产或如果资产暂时未用，这些应是相关现金产出单元的减值迹象，应当进行减值复核。

ⓒ 2012 普华永道（PricewaterhouseCoopers）版权所有。

cash-generating unit and an impairment review should be carried out.

15.187 Amortisation charges are usually included in the income statement. However, where the intangible asset is used in producing another asset, the amortisation charge may qualify for inclusion in the cost of that other asset. The standard gives the example of intangible assets used in the production process for inventories and states that in such a situation the amortisation charges relating to the intangible asset would be included in the cost of the inventories. [IAS 38 para 99].

Useful lives-finite and indefinite

15.188 The useful life of an intangible asset is the period over which the depreciable amount of the asset is allocated. Therefore, estimating the useful life is a key factor in determining the periodic charge for amortisation. Useful life is defined as:

- the period over which an asset is expected to be available for use by an entity; or
- the number of production or similar units expected to be obtained from the asset by an entity.

[IAS 38 para 8].

15.188.1 The definition makes it clear that the useful life includes any period after acquisition when the asset is capable of operating in the manner intended by management, but has not yet been brought into use.

15.189 The end of the asset's useful life is not necessarily the end of its economic life. The economic life is the period during which the asset produces economic benefits, no matter who is using it at the time. The useful life is the period when the asset is used by the entity. If the entity buys an asset for C100 that has an economic life of ten years, but the entity intends to use the asset for only six years, the useful life that the entity assigns to the asset will be six years and not ten years. It would then be necessary to estimate the residual value at the end of six years. See paragraph 15.202.

15.190 Management should assess whether an intangible asset's useful life is finite or indefinite. An intangible asset should be regarded as having an indefinite

© 2012 PricewaterhouseCoopers LLP. All rights reserved.

15.187　摊销费用通常包含在利润表中。然而，如果无形资产被用于生产另一资产，则摊销费用可以包含在该另一资产的成本中。该准则举例说明在存货的生产过程中使用的无形资产的摊销费用在这种情况下应当包含在存货成本中。[IAS 第 38 号第 99 段]。

使用寿命——确定和不确定

15.188　无形资产的使用寿命是分配资产的可折旧金额的期间。因此，估计使用寿命是确定定期摊销费用的关键因素。使用寿命定义为：

- 主体预期能够使用资产的期间；或
- 主体预期从资产获得的产品或类似单位的数目。

[IAS 第 38 号第 8 段]。

15.188.1　该定义表明使用寿命包括购买后的任何资产能够以管理层预定的方式运营但尚未投入使用的期间。

15.189　资产使用寿命的结束不一定是其经济寿命的结束。无论哪个主体在这期间使用资产，经济寿命是资产产生经济利益的期间。使用寿命是主体使用资产的期间。如果主体以 100 元购买经济寿命为十年的资产，但主体准备仅使用六年，则主体分配给该资产的使用寿命为六年，而不是十年。那么还需要估计六年结束时的残值。参见第 15.202 段。

15.190　管理层应当评价无形资产的使用寿命是确定还是不确定的。在以下情况下无形资产应当视为具有不确定的使用寿命：根据所有相关因素，对于

ⓒ 2012 普华永道（PricewaterhouseCoopers）版权所有。

useful life if, based on all the relevant factors, there is no foreseeable limit to the period over which the asset is expected to generate net cash inflows for the entity. [IAS 38 para 88].

15.191 IAS 38 contains guidance on factors to be taken into account when estimating useful lives which includes:

- Expected usage by the entity of the asset and whether it could be managed efficiently by another management team.
- The typical product life cycle for the asset and published information about useful lives of similar assets that are used in a similar way. This might include comparison with useful lives disclosed in the financial statements of companies that have a similar business using similar assets.
- Technical, technological, commercial and other types of obsolescence.
- The stability of the industry in which the asset operates and changes in market demand for the products or services from or related to the asset.
- Expected actions by actual or potential competitors.
- The level of maintenance required to maintain the asset's operating capability and whether management intends to perform that level of maintenance. For example, management may have to spend on advertising to maintain the value of a trademark.
- The period for which the entity has control of the asset and any legal or similar limits on the asset's use, including for example, expiry dates of leases or licences or geographical restrictions.
- Whether the asset's useful life is dependent on the useful life of other assets of the entity. For example, use of a trademark or brand may cease if production of the goods represented by the trademark or brand is discontinued.

[IAS 38 para 90].

15.192 An intangible asset that is determined to have an indefinite useful life is not amortised. [IAS 38 paras 89, 107]. Indefinite is not the same as infinite (limitless in extent). Indefinite means that there is no foreseeable limit

© 2012 PricewaterhouseCoopers LLP. All rights reserved.

资产预期为主体产生净现金流入的期间没有可预见的限制。[IAS 第 38 号第 88 段]。

15.191 IAS 第 38 号包含对估计使用寿命时需要考虑的因素的指导，包括：

- 主体预期对资产的使用，以及另一管理团队能否有效管理该资产。
- 资产的典型产品生命周期，以及以类似方式使用的类似资产的使用寿命的已发布信息。这可能包括与使用类似资产运营类似业务的公司财务报表披露的使用寿命进行比较。
- 技术、工艺、商业和其他类型的过时。
- 资产运营所在行业的稳定性，以及来自该资产或与该资产相关的产品或服务的市场需求的变化。
- 实际或潜在竞争者的预期行动。
- 维护资产运营能力所需的维护水平，以及管理层是否准备实施该水平的维护。例如，管理层可能不得不在广告上投入资金以维护商标价值。
- 主体控制资产的期间，以及对于资产使用的任何法定或类似限制，例如租赁或许可证或区域限制的到期日。
- 资产的使用寿命是否取决于主体其他资产的使用寿命。例如，如果商标或品牌代表的产品的生产停止，则商标或品牌的使用可能会停止。

[IAS 第 38 号第 90 段]。

15.192 确定为具有不确定使用寿命的无形资产不摊销。[IAS 第 38 号第 89、107 段]。不确定与无限不同。不确定表示对于资产预期对报告主体的现金流量作出贡献的期间没有可预见的限制。无形资产的使用寿命仅反映为了维护

ⓒ 2012 普华永道（PricewaterhouseCoopers）版权所有。

on the period of time over which it is expected to contribute to the cash flows of the reporting entity. The useful life of an intangible asset reflects only the level of future maintenance (and management's ability and intention to carry out such maintenance) that is necessary to preserve the asset's operating capability as assessed when initially estimating the asset's useful life. The estimation of useful life does not take into account any planned future expenditure in excess of that which is required to maintain the asset's operating capability. [IAS 38 para 91].

15.193 An indefinite life for an intangible asset will generally require a business, industry and products with a track record of stability and high barriers to market entry. Added to this, of course, is the commitment of the management to continue to invest for the long term to extend the period over which the intangible asset is expected to continue to provide economic benefits. Indefinite lives may be justified for certain long established brands and publishing titles that have demonstrated their ability to survive changes in the economic environment. Finite lives may be appropriate for other brands and publishing titles that are relatively new, dependent on an individuals' reputation (movie star) or which operate in more volatile sectors, where they are more likely to be affected by changes in fashions or technology.

Example – Useful life of customer relationships

Entity A, acquired entity B, which operates a TV channel. Entity B negotiates the sale of air time directly with advertisers who are mostly big companies. Advertisement contracts are negotiated annually and management considers it likely that the relationships will continue indefinitely.

Entity A's management has concluded that the criteria have been met in order to recognise such customer relationships as intangible assets separately from goodwill and proposes to treat the relationships as having an indefinite useful life.

An indefinite useful life is attributed to an asset when there is no foreseeable limit to the period over which the asset is expected to generate cash inflows. [IAS 38 para 88]. It is unlikely that customer relationships have indefinite useful lives, because ownership of the customers may change, strategies may change and further competitors may enter entity B's market.

© 2012 PricewaterhouseCoopers LLP. All rights reserved.

在初始估计资产的使用寿命时所评价的资产运营能力而必需的未来维护水平（以及管理层实施该水平维护的能力和意图）。使用寿命的估计不考虑超出维护资产运营能力所需支出的有计划的未来支出。［IAS 第 38 号第 91 段］。

15. 193　无形资产的不确定寿命一般要求业务、行业和产品具有对稳定性的记录和较高的市场进入壁垒。除此之外，管理层当然还要致力于持续长期投入以延长无形资产预期持续提供经济利益的期间。对于已经证明能够在经济环境的变化中生存下来的某些长期存在的品牌和出版标题，可以证明它们具有不确定寿命。确定寿命对于其他品牌和出版标题可能是适宜的：相对较新、倚赖于个人声望（电影明星），或在更加不稳定的领域运营而更可能受到时尚或技术变化的影响。

示例——客户关系的使用寿命

主体 A 收购了运营一个电视频道的主体 B。主体 B 直接与多为大公司的广告商协商广告时间的销售。广告合同每年协商一次，管理层认为这些关系可能会在不确定的期间内持续。

主体 A 的管理层断定，该类客户关系符合确认为不同于商誉的无形资产的标准，并且提出将这些关系处理为具有不确定的使用寿命。

当对于资产预期产生现金流量的期间没有可预见的限制时，该资产具有不确定的使用寿命。［IAS 第 38 号第 88 段］。客户关系不可能具有不确定的使用寿命，因为客户的所有权可能会变化、战略可能会改变，以及更多的竞争者可能会进入主体 B 的市场。

ⓒ 2012 普华永道（PricewaterhouseCoopers）版权所有。

Entity A's management should consider all the relevant factors, such as historical experience, contracts periods, competitors and life cycle, to determine the useful lives of the customer relationships. This should be based on reliable assumptions about the period over which economic benefits are expected to be obtained from the relationships.

Management should be able to estimate the useful lives of the customer relationships, considering all relevant factors as described above.

15.194 Computer software and many other types of intangible asset are susceptible to technological obsolescence because of rapid changes in technology. It is likely, therefore, that their useful lives will be short. [IAS 38 para 92]. Uncertainty justifies estimating useful lives on a prudent basis, but does not justify choosing a life that is unrealistically short. [IAS 38 para 93].

15.195 The useful lives of certain intangible assets are also restricted by the period for which contractual or other legal rights are held. The useful life of such assets is the shorter of the periods determined by economic factors and contractual or other legal factors. [IAS 38 para 95]. For some intangible assets, the legal rights either remain in force indefinitely or can be continually renewed (for example, trademarks that secure brand names). For others, the legal rights that protect a product's position in the market expire after a fixed period (that is, they are non-renewable), beyond which competitors can introduce similar products (for example, drug patents). A licence may give an entity the right to carry out a business activity for a fixed period and, although the entity can apply for renewal, there is no guarantee that it will be renewed (for example, broadcasting licences).

15.196 Where contractual or legal rights are granted for a finite period, the useful life of the related intangible asset can extend beyond that period only if the legal rights are renewable and there is evidence to support renewal by the entity without significant cost. [IAS 38 para 94]. The useful life in other cases is restricted by the expiry date of the existing legal right. The evidence that the standard requires is as follows:

- Evidence, possibly based on experience, that the contractual or legal rights will

© 2012 PricewaterhouseCoopers LLP. All rights reserved.

主体 A 的管理层应当考虑所有相关因素，例如历史经验、合同期限、竞争者和生命周期，以确定客户关系的使用寿命。这应当基于对预期从这些关系获得有关经济利益的期间的可靠假设。

考虑上述所有相关因素后，管理层应当能够估计客户关系的使用寿命。

15.194　由于技术的迅速变化，计算机软件和许多其他类型的无形资产容易在技术上过时。因此，它们的使用寿命可能会很短。[IAS 第 38 号第 92 段]。不确定性证明审慎估计使用寿命是正确的，但不能证明选择短得不现实的寿命是正确的。[IAS 第 38 号第 93 段]。

15.195　某些无形资产的使用寿命也受到持有合同或其他法律权利的期限的限制。该类资产的使用寿命是由经济因素和合同或其他法律因素决定的期限中的较短者。[IAS 第 38 号第 95 段]。对于一些无形资产来说，法律权利或者能在不确定的期间内保持效力，或者能够持续续期（例如保护品牌名称的商标）。对于其他无形资产来说，保护产品在市场中的地位的法律权利在固定期限后到期（即不可续期），此外竞争者可以推出类似产品（例如药品专利）。许可证可以授予主体在固定期限内实施某项业务活动的权利，虽然主体能够申请续期，但不能保证会续期（例如播放许可证）。

15.196　如果获得的合同或法律权利的期限是确定的，则仅在以下情况下相关无形资产的使用寿命可以超过该期限：法律权利可续期，并且有证据支持主体无需重大成本的续期。[IAS 第 38 号第 94 段]。其他情况下的使用寿命由现有法律权利的到期日限制。该准则需要的证据如下：

■ 可能是基于经验的证明合同或法律权利将会续期的证据，包括在需要第三

ⓒ 2012 普华永道（PricewaterhouseCoopers）版权所有。

be renewed. This includes evidence that where the consent of a third party is required, such consent will be forthcoming.

- Evidence that any conditions necessary to obtain renewal will be satisfied. This would includes evidence that no conditions that have to be complied with in respect of renewal have been or will be breached, for example, evidence that a train operating entity has met operational targets that are a condition of renewal of its operating licence.

- Evidence that the cost to the entity of renewal is not significant compared to the future economic benefits that are expected to flow to the entity from renewal.

[IAS 38 para 96].

15.197 Where the cost of renewal is significant in comparison to the future economic benefits expected to flow to the entity, the renewal cost represents, in substance, the cost of acquiring a new intangible asset at the renewal date. [IAS 38 para 96]. The carrying amount of the replaced intangible asset should be fully amortised by the renewal date and the renewal cost is then capitalised as a new intangible asset if the recognition criteria are met. Paragraph 94 of IAS 38 clarifies that the useful life of reacquired rights (for example, franchise rights previously granted by the acquirer to the acquiree) in a business combination is the remaining contractual period for which the right was granted and should not include renewal periods.

15.198 There are illustrative examples in IAS 38 that cover assessing of the useful life of intangible assets. These cover both the basic principles and some more complicated situations, such as where an intangible asset has an indefinite useful life. Some of the examples from the standard and the principles that each one illustrates are summarised below:

Example 1 – Determining the useful life of customer list

An entity acquires a customer list and expects to derive benefit from the list for between one and three years. It should amortise the cost over its best estimate of the estimated life, which may be say, 18 months. This example merely illustrates the principle of spreading the depreciable amount over the useful life.

© 2012 PricewaterhouseCoopers LLP. All rights reserved.

方同意的情况下能得到该同意的证据。

■ 获得续期所必需的条件将会满足的证据,包括以下证据:为了续期必须遵守的条件都未违反或不会违反,例如,一家运营列车的主体已经实现作为运营许可证续期条件之一的运营目标。

■ 与通过续期预期流向主体的未来经济利益相比,主体续期成本不高的证据。

[IAS 第 38 号第 96 段]。

15.197　如果续期成本相对于预期流向主体的未来经济利益来说是重大的,那么该续期成本在本质上代表在续期日获得新无形资产的成本。[IAS 第 38 号第 96 段]。被代替无形资产的账面价值应当在续期日前完全摊销，而续期成本如果满足确认标准则资本化为新的无形资产。IAS 第 38 号第 94 段明确说明，在业务合并中重获的权利（例如，购买方之前向被购买方授予的特许权）的使用寿命是所获权利的合同期限的剩余部分，不应包含续约期限。

15.198　在 IAS 第 38 号中举例说明了对无形资产使用寿命的评价，包括基本原则和一些更复杂的情况，例如无形资产具有不确定使用寿命的情况。一些来自准则的例子以及每个例子说明的原则概述如下：

示例 1——确定客户名单的使用寿命

主体购买了客户名单，希望在一至三年内从名单获得利益。它应当在最佳估计寿命内摊销成本，比如说 18 个月。这个例子仅说明将可折旧金额在使用寿命内分摊的原则。

ⓒ 2012 普华永道（PricewaterhouseCoopers）版权所有。

Example 2 – Patent with committed residual value

Entity A acquires a patent whose economic life is 15 years. Entity A expects to use the patent for 5 years and intends to sell it after 5 years to entity B. Entity B has committed to buy the patent for 60% of the cost to entity A. Entity A amortises the depreciable amount of the intangible asset over 5 years, which is the useful life to entity A. The depreciable amount is 40% of the asset's cost, because the residual value is 60%.

The principle illustrated here is that depreciable amount is the amount to be amortised (that is, the cost less residual value). Although IAS 38 requires a residual value of nil to be assumed for intangible assets, this is an exception as a third party has committed to buy the asset after five years – see paragraph 15. 202.

Example 3 – Legal life of copyright in excess of the economic life

An entity acquires a copyright that has a remaining legal life of 50 years. The entity determines that the copyright has an economic life of only 30 years, that is, it will only generate economic benefits for 30 years. The entity must amortise the copyright over 30 years. Useful economic life is defined as the period over which the entity is expected to use the asset and this is limited to 30 years. The entity will not use the asset after 30 years and must derecognise it at the point when no future economic benefits are expected from its use. – see paragraph 15. 213.

Example 4 – Assured renewal of broadcasting license

An entity has acquired a broadcasting licence that expires in 5 years' time. The licence is renewable at little cost and has already been renewed twice in the past. There are no factors to suggest that the licence will not be renewed again and the entity intends to do so. The licence is expected to contribute to the entity's cash flows indefinitely.

The intangible asset's useful life is treated as indefinite and the licence would not be amortised. An intangible asset with a limited legal life can be treated as indefinite if it can be renewed by the entity without substantial cost and such renewal is probable. – see paragraph 15. 196.

© 2012 PricewaterhouseCoopers LLP. All rights reserved.

示例 2——具有承诺残值的专利

主体 A 购买了经济寿命为 15 年的专利。主体 A 希望使用专利 5 年，在 5 年后卖给主体 B。主体 B 承诺以主体 A 的购买成本的 60% 购买该专利。主体 A 在 5 年（也就是对于主体 A 来说的使用寿命）内摊销无形资产的可折旧金额。可折旧金额是资产成本的 40%，因为残值为 60%。

这里阐释的原则是可折旧金额是将被摊销的金额（即成本减残值）。虽然 IAS 第 38 号要求假设无形资产的残值为零，但这是例外，因为第三方已经承诺在五年后购买资产——参见第 15.202 段。

示例 3——超过经济寿命的版权法定寿命

主体购买了具有 50 年剩余法定寿命的版权。主体确定该版权仅具有 30 年的经济寿命，也就是说，它仅能在 30 年里产生经济利益。主体必须在 30 年内摊销版权。经济使用寿命定义为资产预期由主体使用的期限，在本例中为 30 年。主体在 30 年后不会使用该资产，必须在预期不会从其使用获得未来经济利益时终止确认该资产——参见第 15.213 段。

示例 4——已确保的播放许可证续期

主体购买了期限为 5 年的播放许可证。许可证的续期成本很低，过去已经续期两次。没有因素表明许可证不会再次续期，并且主体准备续期。许可证预期不确定地对主体的现金流量作出贡献。

该无形资产的使用寿命被视为不确定，许可证将不会摊销。具有有限法定寿命的无形资产可以视为不确定，前提是主体能够续期且无需重大成本，并且该续期很有可能实现——参见第 15.196 段。

ⓒ 2012 普华永道（PricewaterhouseCoopers）版权所有。

Example 5 – Broadcasting license with no assurance of renewal

Details are the same as in example 4, except that the renewal is not assured or even probable. The broadcasting authority has decided that in future it will auction the licences when they come up for renewal, rather than renew them automatically. The broadcasting authority made its decision when the licence had three years to run.

The licence is amortised over the remaining three years, because renewal is uncertain and so is the cost of renewal.

Example 6 – Change in anticipated future cash flows of indefinite life trademark

A trademark that was acquired ten years ago has been assessed previously as having an indefinite life. However, increased competition has reduced the expected future cash inflows by 20%. The trademark and the associated business are still expected to continue indefinitely because the business will still generate net cash inflows for the entity even though cash inflows will be reduced by 20%. The intangible asset is still regarded as having an indefinite useful life, because despite the reduction in profitability it still meets the conditions for such treatment. Any change in circumstances of an indefinite lived intangible asset should be carefully considered to see whether indefinite life treatment is still warranted.

Example 7 – Change of useful life of trademark from indefinite to finite

A trademark was acquired several years ago and has been treated as having an indefinite useful life as, up until now, management had expected to continue the related business indefinitely and all the other conditions for treatment as an intangible with an indefinite useful life had been met. However, management has now taken the decision to discontinue the business over the next 4 years. In these circumstances the intangible asset should be amortised over the remaining 4 years during which it will be used by the entity. The principle here is that if the assessment of an intangible asset's useful life changes from indefinite to finite, it should be amortised over that remaining finite useful life. Prior to commencing

© 2012 PricewaterhouseCoopers LLP. All rights reserved.

示例 5——没有续期保证的播放许可证

细节与示例 4 相同，但续期没有保证或不是很可能实现。播放管理机构已经决定，在许可证续期时进行拍卖，而不是自动续期。播放管理机构在许可证期限还剩三年时作出该决定。

因为续期不确定，续期成本也不确定，许可证应在剩余的三年中摊销。

示例 6——寿命不确定的商标的预期未来现金流量的变化

十年前获得的商标以前已经评价为具有不确定寿命。然而，日益激烈的竞争已经将预期的未来现金流量减少了 20%。预计商标和相关业务仍然不确定地持续，因为业务仍然为主体产生净现金流入，即使现金流入将减少 20%。因为尽管盈利能力下降，但它仍然符合这样处理的条件，无形资产仍然视为具有不确定的使用寿命。应当仔细考虑使用寿命不确定的无形资产的环境变化，以确定是否仍然能够保证将其视为不确定使用寿命的处理。

示例 7——商标使用寿命从不确定到确定的变化

主体几年前获得了一项商标。管理层直至现在，一直期望不确定地保持相关业务，并且已经符合处理为具有不确定使用寿命的无形资产的所有其他条件，因此，主体已将其处理为具有不确定的使用寿命。然而，管理层已经决定在今后四年内中终止该业务。在这种情况下，无形资产应当在主体使用它的剩余四年中摊销。这里的原则是如果无形资产使用寿命的评价从不确定变为确定，则应当在剩余的确定使用寿命中摊销。在开始摊销前，管理层必须首先进行减值分析——参见第 15. 201 段。

ⓒ 2012 普华永道（PricewaterhouseCoopers）版权所有。

amortisation, management must first perform an impairment analysis-see paragraph 15. 201.

15. 199 The useful life of a finite life intangible asset should be reviewed at least at each financial year end. Changes in useful lives should be accounted for as changes in estimates in accordance with IAS 8, ' Accounting policies, changes in accounting estimates and errors' . [IAS 38 paras 104 to 106]. A change in estimate is accounted for prospectively with the effect of the change being recognised in the current and future periods. [IAS 8 para 38].

15. 200 Where an intangible asset is not being amortised because its useful life is considered to be indefinite, an entity should carry out a review in each accounting period to confirm whether or not events and circumstances still support the assumption of an indefinite life. If they do not, the change from the indefinite to finite useful life should be accounted for as a change in estimate under IAS 8 and accounted for as set out in the preceding paragraph. [IAS 38 para 109].

15. 201 A change from an indefinite to a finite useful life is an impairment indicator under IAS 36. Therefore, if the useful life is changed from indefinite to finite the entity must carry out an impairment test under IAS 36 and charge any shortfall between recoverable amount and carrying amount as an impairment loss. [IAS 38 para 110, IAS 36 para 12(f)]. In addition, where an intangible asset has an indefinite useful life it must be reviewed for impairment annually-see 'Impairment' below (para 15. 211).

Residual value

15. 202 The residual value of an intangible asset with a finite useful life should be assumed to be zero, unless:

- a third party has committed to purchase the asset at the end of its useful life; or
- there is an active market for the intangible asset; and
  - residual value can be determined by reference to that market; and

© 2012 PricewaterhouseCoopers LLP. All rights reserved.

15.199　寿命确定的无形资产的使用寿命应当至少在每年财务年度末进行复核。根据 IAS 第 8 号“会计政策、会计估计变更和差错”，使用寿命的变化应当处理为估计的变化。[IAS 第 38 号第 104 至 106 段]。估计的变化以未来适用法进行会计处理，变化的影响在当期和未来期间确认。[IAS 第 8 号第 38 段]。

15.200　如果无形资产使用寿命为不确定而没有摊销，则主体应当在每个会计期间进行复核，以确认事项和环境是否仍然支持不确定寿命的假设。如果不支持，则从不确定到确定使用寿命的变化应当根据 IAS 第 8 号处理为估计的变化，并且按照上一段的描述进行会计处理。[IAS 第 38 号第 109 段]。

15.201　根据 IAS 第 36 号，从不确定到确定使用寿命的变化是减值迹象。因此，如果使用寿命从不确定变为确定，则主体必须根据 IAS 第 36 号进行减值测试，并将可收回金额低于账面价值的金额记为减值损失。[IAS 第 38 号第 110 段，IAS 第 36 号第 12（f）段]。另外，如果无形资产具有不确定使用寿命，则必须每年进行减值复核。参见以下的“减值”部分（第 15.211 段）。

残值

15.202　具有确定使用寿命的无形资产残值应当假设为零，除非：

- 第三方已经承诺在其使用寿命结束时购买资产；或
- 无形资产存在活跃市场，并且：
  - 可以根据该市场确定残值；

ⓒ 2012 普华永道（PricewaterhouseCoopers）版权所有。

- the market is likely to exist at the end of the asset's useful life.

[IAS 38 para 100].

If a third party has committed to buy the asset at the end of its useful life, its residual value would be the amount payable by the third party adjusted to exclude future inflation. A residual value of greater than zero assumes that an entity will not use the asset for the whole of its economic (as opposed to useful) life. [IAS 38 para 101].

15.203 Residual value is defined as the estimated amount that an entity would currently obtain from the asset's disposal, after deducting the estimated costs of disposal, if the asset were already of the age and in the condition expected at the end of its useful life. [IAS 38 para 8]. The words 'currently obtain' make clear that the amount is based on current prices. The value takes account of inflationary increases since acquisition, but does not take account of expected future inflation. The residual value also assumes an asset that has reached the end of its useful life and has been operated in a similar manner to the actual asset under consideration. [IAS 38 para 102].

15.204 Residual values should be reviewed at least at each financial year end. [IAS 38 para 102]. Changes in residual values should be accounted for as changes in estimates in accordance with IAS 8. Changes in estimates of residual value will only occur if one of the two exceptions applies.

15.205 Residual values may increase to an amount equal to or greater than the intangible asset's carrying amount. The amortisation charge would be nil, unless and until the residual value falls below the carrying amount. [IAS 38 para 103]. This situation will only occur if one of the two exceptions to the residual value assumed to be zero rule applies. The likelihood of no amortisation for a finite lived intangible asset is remote.

Amortisation methods

15.206 There are a variety of amortisation methods including the straight-line method, the diminishing balance method and the unit of production method. [IAS 38 para 98]. The amortisation method should reflect the pattern in which future

© 2012 PricewaterhouseCoopers LLP. All rights reserved.

■ 该市场在资产使用寿命结束时可能会存在。

［IAS 第 38 号第 100 段］。

如果第三方已经承诺在使用寿命结束时购买资产，则其残值应该是调整未来通货膨胀因素后第三方愿意支付的款项。大于零的残值假设主体不会在其整个经济寿命（而不是使用寿命）中使用该资产。［IAS 第 38 号第 101 段］。

15.203　残值定义为假设资产已经到达年限并处于使用寿命结束时的预期状态，主体目前应该会从资产处置中获得的扣除估计处置成本后的估计金额。［IAS 第 38 号第 8 段］。“目前获得”表明该金额以当前价格为基础。价值考虑了购买以来的通货膨胀导致的增长，但不考虑预期的未来通货膨胀。残值也假设资产已经到达使用寿命结束时点，并且已经以与该实际资产类似的方式运营。［IAS 第 38 号第 102 段］。

15.204　残值应当至少在每个财务年度末进行复核。［IAS 第 38 号第 102 段］。残值的变化应当根据 IAS 第 8 号作为估计的变化进行会计处理。残值估计的变化仅在两项例外之一适用时发生。

15.205　残值可以增加至等于或大于无形资产的账面价值。除非残值跌至账面价值以下，否则摊销费用应该为零。［IAS 第 38 号第 103 段］。仅当残值假设为零规则的两项例外之一适用时，这种情况才会发生。不摊销具有确定寿命的无形资产的可能性极小。

摊销方法

15.206　无形资产有多种摊销方法，包括直线法、余额递减法，以及单位产量法。［IAS 第 38 号第 98 段］。摊销方法应当反映具有确定使用寿命的无形资产的未来经济利益预期消耗的方式。如果该方式不能可靠确定，则必须使

ⓒ 2012 普华永道（PricewaterhouseCoopers）版权所有。

economic benefits of the intangible asset with a finite useful life are expected to be consumed. If that pattern cannot be reliably determined the straight-line method must be used. [IAS 38 para 97].

15. 207 The straight-line method of amortisation involves allocating an asset's cost or revalued amount, less its residual value, over the asset's useful life so as to charge each accounting period on a systematic basis. Each period is charged with the same amount, unless the useful life or the residual value changes.

15. 208 The amortisation method is selected on the basis of the expected pattern of consumption of expected future economic benefits from an intangible asset. The use of the word 'expect' entails judgement specific to the entity (IFRIC November 2009 and January 2010). If the consumption of future economic benefit is through the passage of time (for example, patents and licenses that operate for a fixed number of years), the straight-line method will often be the most appropriate method to use. However, if the consumption of future economic benefit is through usage or production (for example, when each car passes through a toll road or when minerals are extracted), the unit of production method is likely to be the most appropriate amortisation method. The difference of amortisation methods used for similar arrangements is inherent to the entity's expectation of consumption of economic benefits from the asset. It is also contingent upon the entity's ability to reliably measure the asset's expected usage or production. If the pattern of consumption cannot be reliably determined, the default method will be the straight-line method. Where significant judgements are made when determining the amortisation method used, this should be disclosed in the notes to the financial statements. Table 15. 5 above is an example where the unit of production method is used and Table 15. 9 below is an example of the straight-line method.

15. 209 The amortisation method should be applied consistently from period to period, unless there is a change in the expected pattern of consumption of those future economic benefits. The amortisation method for an intangible asset with a finite useful life should be reviewed at least each financial year end. [IAS 36 para 104]. Changes in the method used should be accounted for as a change in accounting estimate under IAS 8. It is unlikely that the pattern of consumption of an

© 2012 PricewaterhouseCoopers LLP. All rights reserved.

用直线法。[IAS 第 38 号第 97 段]。

15.207　直线法摊销是将减去残值后的资产成本或重估金额在资产的使用寿命中分配，从而系统地记入每个会计期间。除非使用寿命或残值发生变化，每个期间应记录相同金额。

15.208　摊销方法的选择基于来自无形资产的预期未来经济利益消耗的预期方式。“预期”这个词包含了主体的特定判断（IFRIC 2009 年 11 月和 2010 年 1 月）。如果未来经济利益的消耗是通过时间的消逝（如在固定年限内运营的专利权和经营权），直线法通常是最适宜的。然而，如果未来经济的利益消耗是基于使用或生产（如当每辆汽车通过收费公路或当矿物被开采出来），单位产量法可能是最适宜的。相似的安排使用不同的摊销方法是与主体对来自资产的经济利益消耗的预期内在相关的。它也受到主体是否有能力可靠计量资产的预期使用或生产的影响。如果消耗方式不能可靠决定，默认的摊销方法是直线法。当决定摊销方法时需要作出重要判断，这需要在财务报表附注中进行披露。上表 15. 5 是使用单位产量法的示例，下表 15. 9 是直线法的示例。

15.209　除非未来经济利益消耗的预期方式发生变化，摊销方法应该于各个期间一致应用。具有确定使用寿命的无形资产的摊销方法应当至少在每个财务年度末复核。[IAS 第 36 号第 104 段]。方法的变化应当根据 IAS 第 8 号作为会计估计的变化进行会计处理。无形资产的消耗方式在使用寿命期间不太可能发生很大变化，因此摊销方法的变化应当很少发生。

ⓒ 2012 普华永道（PricewaterhouseCoopers）版权所有。

intangible asset would vary significantly over its useful life and so changes in method should be rare.

Further examples

15. 210 Examples of other methods of amortisation and depreciation and of the application of the rules relating to residual values and useful lives are contained in chapter 16 on property, plant and equipment. Those examples are also relevant to intangible assets in most situations. An example of disclosure of amortisation rates and methods is given in Table 15. 9.

Table 15. 9 – Disclosure of amortisation rates and methods

Vodacom Group Limited – Report and accounts – 31 March 2010

Significant accounting policies (extract)

Intangible assets

The following are the main categories of intangible assets:

Intangible assets with an indefinite useful life

Intangible assets with an indefinite useful life are capitalised as cost and are not amortised, but are tested for impairment on an annual basis.

Goodwill

Goodwill arising on the acquisition of an entity represents the excess of the cost of acquisition over the Group's interest in the net fair value of the identifiable assets, liabilities and contingent liabilities of the entity recognised at the date of acquisition. Goodwill is initially recognised as an asset at cost and is subsequently measured at cost less any accumulated impairment losses, if any. Goodwill is held in the currency of the acquired entity and revalued to the closing rate at each reporting date.

Intangible assets with a finite useful life

Intangible assets with finite useful lives are stated at cost, less accumulated amortisation and accumulated impairment losses, if any. The amortisation period and method of intangible assets with a finite useful life are reviewed at least annually. Changes in the expected useful life or the expected pattern of consumption of future economic benefits embodied in the asset are accounted for by changing the amortisation period or method, as appropriate, and are treated as changes in accounting estimates. The amortisation expense is recognised in profit or

© 2012 PricewaterhouseCoopers LLP. All rights reserved.

更多示例

15.210　其他摊销和折旧方法以及与残值和使用寿命相关的规则的应用示例包含在有关物业、厂房和设备的第16章中。在大多数情况中，这些示例也适用于无形资产。表15.9中提供了披露摊销率和方法的示例。

表15.9——披露摊销率和方法

沃达丰集团有限公司——报告和账目——2010年3月31日

重大会计政策（摘要）

无形资产

以下是无形资产的主要类别：

具有不确定使用寿命的无形资产

具有不确定使用寿命的无形资产以成本资本化、不摊销，但是每年进行减值测试。

商誉

在企业收购中产生的商誉代表购买成本超出在购买日确认的该企业可辨认资产、负债和或有负债的净公允价值中属于本集团权益的部分。商誉以成本初始确认为资产，以成本减去累计减值损失（如有）计量。商誉以被购买公司的币种记录，在每个报告日以收盘汇率重估。

具有确定使用寿命的无形资产

具有确定使用寿命的无形资产以成本减去累计摊销和累计减值损失（如有）记录。具有确定使用寿命的无形资产的摊销期间和方法至少每年进行复核。预期使用年限或资产体现的未来经济利益的预期消耗方式的变化通过合理地改变摊销期间或方法进行会计处理，并被视为会计估计变更。摊销费用在估计使用寿命内按照直线法计入损益。摊销从无形资产可供使用时开始，至资产被分类为持有待售时或终止确认时结束。

ⓒ 2012 普华永道（PricewaterhouseCoopers）版权所有。

Con.

loss on a straight-line basis over the estimated useful lives, and commences when the intangible asset is available for use and ceases at the earlier of the date the asset is classified as held for sale or the date it is derecognised.

Licences

Licences, which are acquired to yield an enduring benefit, are amortised from the date of commencement of usage rights over the shorter of the economic life or the duration of the licence agreement.

Trademarks, patents and other

Trademarks, patents and other intangible assets acquired are amortised over their estimated useful lives. Expenditure incurred to develop, maintain and renew internally generated trademarks and patents is recognised as an expense in the period incurred.

Customer bases

Customer bases acquired are amortised over their estimated useful lives.

Computer software

Computer software that is not considered to form an integral part of any hardware equipment is recorded as intangible assets and amortised over its estimated useful life.

Critical accounting judgements including those involving estimations

Intangible assets with a finite useful life

Other intangible assets include the Group's aggregate amounts spent on the acquisition of licences, customer bases, computer software, trademark, patents and other. These assets arise from both separate purchases and from acquisition as part of business combinations.

The relative size of the Group's intangible assets, excluding goodwill, makes the judgements surrounding the estimated useful lives critical to the Group's financial position and performance.

At 31 March 2010, intangible assets, excluding goodwill, amounted to R3,722 million (2009: R4,364 million; 2008: R2,328 million) and represented 8.9% (2009: 9.2%; 2008: 6.8%) of the Group's total assets.

Estimation of useful life

The useful lives used to amortise intangible assets relate to the future performance of the assets acquired and management's judgement of the period over which economic benefits will be derived from the assets. The residual values of intangible assets are assumed to be zero.

© 2012 PricewaterhouseCoopers LLP. All rights reserved.

续表

许可证

购买的用于产生持久利益的许可证从使用权生效之日起以经济寿命和许可证协议期限的较短者摊销。

商标、专利和其他

购买的商标、专利和其他无形资产在估计使用寿命期间摊销。开发、维护和续期内部产生的商标和专利的支出于发生期间确认为费用。

客户基础

购买的客户基础在估计使用寿命期间摊销。

计算机软件

不视为任何硬件设备的组成部分的计算机软件确认为无形资产并在估计使用寿命期间摊销。

关键会计判断，包括包含估计的判断

具有确定使用寿命的无形资产

其他无形资产包括本集团累计用于购买许可证、客户基础、计算机软件、商标、专利和其他的金额。这些资产有通过单独购买产生的，也有作为业务合并的一部分购买产生的。

本集团无形资产（不包括商誉）的相对规模使得围绕估计使用寿命的判断对于本集团的财务状况和表现来说相当关键。

于2010年3月31日，无形资产（不包括商誉）合计R37.22亿（2009年：R43.64亿；2008年：R23.28亿），占本集团总资产的8.9%（2009年：9.2%，2008年：6.8%）。

使用寿命的估计

用来摊销无形资产的使用寿命与取得的资产的未来表现以及管理层对于能够从该资产获得经济利益的期间的判断相关。无形资产残值假设为零。

ⓒ 2012 普华永道（PricewaterhouseCoopers）版权所有。

Con.

The basis for determining the useful lives for the most significant categories of intangible assets is as follows:

Licences

The estimated useful life is, generally, the term of the licence, unless there is a presumption of renewal at a negligible cost. Using the licence term reflects the period over which the Group will receive economic benefits. For technology-specific licences with a presumption of renewal at a negligible cost, the estimated useful life reflects the Group's expectation of the period over which the Group will continue to receive economic benefits from the licence.

Trademark, patents and other

The estimated useful life represents management's view of the expected period over which the Group will receive benefits from the trademark, patents and other intangible assets with a finite useful life.

Customer bases

The estimated useful life principally reflects management's view of the average economic life of the customer base and is assessed by reference to customer churn rates or is obtained through an independent actuarial valuation. An increase in churn rates may lead to a reduction in the estimated useful life and an increase in the amortisation charge.

Computer software

For computer software licences, the useful life represents management's view of the expected period over which the Group will receive benefits from the software, but not exceeding the licence term. For unique software products controlled by the Group, the life is based on historical experience with similar products as well as anticipation of future events, which may impact their life, such as changes in technology.

The estimated useful lives of intangible assets with a finite useful life are as follows:

	2010 Years	2009 Years	2008 Years
Licences	8 – 30	8 – 30	8 – 30
Trademark, patents and other	5 – 14	10 – 12	10 – 14
Customer bases	4 – 10	8	8
Computer software	3 – 10	2 – 8	2 – 8

Historically, changes in useful lives have not resulted in material changes to the Group's amortisation charge.

© 2012 PricewaterhouseCoopers LLP. All rights reserved.

续表

确定几大类无形资产的使用寿命的原理如下：

许可证

估计使用寿命通常是许可证的期限，除非可以推测能够以较少成本续期。使用许可证期限反映了本集团将获得经济利益的期间。对针对特定技术并推测能够以较少成本续期的许可证，估计使用寿命反映了本集团预期将持续从该许可证获得经济利益的期间。

商标、专利和其他

估计使用寿命代表了管理层认为本集团将从这些具有确定使用寿命的商标、专利和其他无形资产获得利益的预期期间。

客户基础

估计使用寿命主要反映了管理层对于客户基础的平均经济寿命的观点，是参考客户流失率评估的，或者是通过独立精算评估取得的。流失率的增长可能导致估计使用寿命的降低以及摊销费用的增加。

计算机软件

对于计算机软件许可证，使用寿命代表了管理层认为本集团将从这些软件获得利益的预期期间，但不能超过许可证年限。对于本集团控制的独一无二的软件产品，其寿命是基于类似产品的历史经验以及对未来事项的预期确定的。对未来事项的预期会影响它们的使用寿命，比如技术变化。

具有确定使用寿命的无形资产的估计使用寿命如下：

	2010 年数	2009 年数	2008 年数
许可证	8 – 30	8 – 30	8 – 30
商标、专利及其他	5 – 14	10 – 12	10 – 14
客户基础	4 – 10	8	8
计算机软件	3 – 10	2 – 8	2 – 8

历史上使用寿命的变化没有导致过本集团摊销费用的重大变化。

ⓒ 2012 普华永道（PricewaterhouseCoopers）版权所有。

Impairment

15.211 Impairment of intangible assets is dealt with by IAS 36, 'Impairment of assets'. [IAS 38 para 111]. An entity should assess at each reporting date whether there is any indication that an intangible asset is impaired. If such an indication exists the entity should estimate the asset's recoverable amount. The asset should be written down to its recoverable amount – see chapter 18.

15.212 Indefinite life intangible assets are tested for impairment annually, whether or not there is any indication of impairment. [IAS 36 para 10]. A change in the estimate of an intangible asset's useful life from indefinite to finite is an indication of impairment and an impairment test is required at that point. [IAS 36 para 10].

Derecognition of intangible assets

15.213 An intangible asset should be derecognised when:

- it is disposed of; or
- no future economic benefits are expected from its use or disposal.

[IAS 38 para 112].

15.214 The gain or loss on derecognition (that is, on disposal or retirement from use) of an intangible asset is the difference between the net disposal proceeds and the carrying amount. [IAS 38 para 113]. The consideration receivable is recognised at fair value. Therefore, if payment is deferred, the consideration is recognised at the cash price equivalent. The difference between this figure and the actual amounts receivable is treated as interest receivable under IAS 18, 'Revenue', and IAS 39, 'Financial instruments: Recognition and measurement', over the period of credit given. The gain or loss on derecognition should be recognised in the income statement for the period in which derecognition occurs. [IAS 38 paras 113, 116]. The only exception is where IAS 17, 'Leases', requires a different treatment of a sale and leaseback.

© 2012 PricewaterhouseCoopers LLP. All rights reserved.

减值

15.211　无形资产减值根据 IAS 第 36 号“资产减值”处理。[IAS 第 38 号第 111 段]。主体应当在每个报告日评价是否有迹象表明无形资产存在减值。如果该迹象存在，则主体应当估计资产的可收回金额。资产应当减记至可收回金额——参见第十八章。

15.212　具有不确定寿命的无形资产，无论是否存在减值迹象，都应每年进行减值测试。[IAS 第 36 号第 10 段]。无形资产使用寿命估计从不确定到确定的变化是减值迹象，在该时点也需要进行减值测试。[IAS 第 36 号第 10 段]。

终止确认无形资产

15.213　在以下情况下应当终止确认无形资产：

- 无形资产被处置；或

- 预期从其使用或处置不会产生未来经济利益。

[IAS 第 38 号第 112 段]。

15.214　无形资产终止确认（即处置或不再使用）的利得或亏损是处置净收入和账面价值之间的差额。[IAS 第 38 号第 113 段]。应收对价以公允价值确认。因此，如果延迟付款，则对价以等值现金价格确认。该数字和实际的应收金额之间的差额根据 IAS 第 18 号“收入”和 IAS 第 39 号“金融工具：确认和计量”在给予的信用期限内处理为应收利息。终止确认利得或亏损应当在终止确认发生期间在利润表中确认。[IAS 第 38 号第 113、116 段]。唯一的例外是 IAS 第 17 号“租赁”要求对售后租回进行不同的处理。

ⓒ 2012 普华永道（PricewaterhouseCoopers）版权所有。

15. 215 Gains and losses on disposal of intangible assets should not be recognised as revenue, but are usually included in other income as gains and losses. [IAS 38 para 113]. Where the amount of the gain or loss is of such size, nature or incidence that its disclosure is relevant to an understanding of the entity's performance for the period, the nature and amount of the item should be disclosed separately. IAS 1, 'Presentation of financial statements', gives disposals of items of property, plant and equipment as an example of circumstances that may give rise to separate disclosure of gains or losses and the same would apply to disposals of intangible assets. [IAS 1 paras 86, 87].

15. 216 Disposals of intangible assets may occur in a variety of ways and include disposals by sale, entering into a finance lease (as lessor) and by donation. The date of disposal is determined by using the criteria in IAS 18 for recognising the sale of goods. IAS 18 is dealt with in chapter 9. IAS 17 applies to disposals by sale and operating leaseback and is dealt with in chapter 19. [IAS 38 para 114].

15. 217 Intangible assets that are scrapped or abandoned should be derecognised, as there are no future economic benefits expected from the asset's continuing use or from its disposal. [IAS 38 para 112b].

Example – Derecognition of capitalised expenditure

An entity is developing a new IT system that met the recognition criteria for capitalisation as an internally generated intangible asset in the previous year. Management decides to terminate the development of the IT system in the current year as the entity can no longer foresee economic benefits from the asset's continuing use. The entity, therefore, cancels the contract to develop the IT system and dismisses the staffs that were involved in the development project. The partially-completed IT system has no alternative use and has no sales value.

The entity should, therefore, derecognise the asset in the current year.

Intended disposals of intangibles

15. 218 IAS 38 specifically excludes from its scope intangible assets that are

ⓒ 2012 PricewaterhouseCoopers LLP. All rights reserved.

15.215 无形资产处置的利得和亏损不应确认为收入，但通常作为利得和亏损包含在其他收益中。［IAS 第 38 号第 113 段］。如果利得或亏损金额的规模、性质或影响使得其披露对于理解主体的当期业绩相关，则该项目的性质和金额应当单独披露。IAS 第 1 号“财务报表列报”将不动产、厂房和设备项目的处置作为可能导致单独披露利得或亏损的情况的示例，这也适用于无形资产的处置。［IAS 第 1 号第 86、87 段］。

15.216 无形资产的处置可以通过多种方式进行，包括销售、融资租赁（作为出租人）和捐赠。处置日期通过使用 IAS 第 18 号中确认货物销售的标准确定。IAS 第 18 号在第九章中阐释。IAS 第 17 号适用于通过销售和经营租回进行的处置，在第十九章中阐释。［IAS 第 38 号第 114 段］。

15.217 废弃的无形资产应当终止确认，因为从该资产的继续使用或处置中预期不会产生未来经济利益。［IAS 第 38 号第 112b 段］。

示例——终止确认资本化支出

主体正在开发新 IT 系统，该系统符合在上一年资本化为内部产生的无形资产的确认标准。管理层在今年终止该 IT 系统的开发，因为主体不再能够预见该资产的继续使用会产生经济利益。因此主体取消了开发 IT 系统的合同，并解雇了参与开发项目的员工。部分完成的 IT 系统没有其他用途，没有销售价值。

因此，主体应当在今年终止确认该资产。

无形资产的有意处置

15.218 IAS 第 38 号特别从其范围中排除了根据 IFRS 第 5 号“持有待售非流

ⓒ 2012 普华永道（PricewaterhouseCoopers）版权所有。

classified as held-for-sale under IFRS 5, ' Non-current assets held-for-sale and discontinued operations'. When intangible assets meet the conditions to be classified as held-for-sale under IFRS 5, they are accounted for in accordance with that standard. See chapter 26.

Disclosure

15.219 IAS 38 requires the following disclosures for each class of intangible asset. The disclosure should distinguish between internally generated intangible assets and other intangible assets:

- Whether the useful lives are indefinite or finite, and if finite:
  - The useful lives or the amortisation rates used.
  - The amortisation methods used (for example, straight-line method or declining balance method).
- The gross carrying amount (cost or revalued amount) at both the beginning and end of the period.
- The cumulative amount of provisions for amortisation (aggregated with accumulated impairment losses) at the beginning and end of the period.
- A reconciliation of the carrying amount at the beginning and end of the period, separately disclosing:
  - Total additions showing separately:
    - Additions from internal development.
    - Additions from separate acquisition.
    - Additions through business combinations.
  - Assets classified as held-for-sale or included in a disposal group classified as held-for-sale in accordance with IFRS 5 (disclosed separately from other assets in the balance sheet).

© 2012 PricewaterhouseCoopers LLP. All rights reserved.

动资产和终止经营”分类为持有待售的无形资产。当无形资产符合根据 IFRS 第 5 号分类为持有待售的条件时，则根据该准则进行处理。参见第二十六章。

披露

15.219　IAS 第 38 号要求对每类无形资产进行以下披露。披露应当区分内部产生的无形资产和其他无形资产：

- 使用寿命不确定还是能确定。如果是能确定：
  - 使用寿命或所用的摊销系数。
  - 所用的摊销方法（例如，直线法或余额递减法）。
- 期初和期末的账面总值（成本或重估金额）。
- 期初和期末的累计摊销准备金额（加上累计减值损失）。
- 期初和期末的账面价值调节。分别披露：
  - 总增加。分别列出：
    - 来自内部开发的增加。
    - 来自单独购买的增加。
    - 来自业务合并的增加。
  - 分类为持有待售的资产，或包含在根据 IFRS 第 5 号分类为持有待售的处置组中的资产（与资产负债表中的其他资产分开披露）。

ⓒ 2012 普华永道（PricewaterhouseCoopers）版权所有。

  - Other disposals.
  - Revaluation increases or decreases.
  - Impairment losses recognised or reversed directly in equity.
  - Impairment losses recognised in profit or loss.
  - Reversals of past impairment losses written back to profit or loss.
  - Amortisation for the period.
  - Exchange differences arising on the translation of the financial statements into the presentation currency (if applicable) and on the translation of a foreign operation into the entity's presentation currency.
  - Other changes during the period.
- The carrying amount (that is the net book amount) at the beginning and end of the financial year.
- The line items in the statement of comprehensive income that include any amortisation of intangible assets.

[IAS 38 para 118].

Comparatives are required for all of the disclosures.

15.220 Further disclosures are required in respect of impairment in accordance with IAS 36, see chapter 18. [IAS 38 para 120]. Those disclosure requirements include giving details of events and circumstances that caused material impairment losses and further analysis of impairment losses by reportable segment, where an entity gives segmental information in accordance with IFRS 8, 'Operating segments'. Further disclosures required by IAS 23, 'Borrowing costs', in respect of capitalisation of borrowing costs, where applicable, are described in chapter 16.

15.221 Further disclosures are required by IAS 36 for each cash-generating unit (CGU) that contains goodwill or intangible assets with indefinite useful lives and the amounts of such assets are significant in relation to the entity's total goodwill or intangible assets with indefinite lives. The disclosure requirements include giving details of the carrying amounts of goodwill and intangible assets with indefinite

© 2012 PricewaterhouseCoopers LLP. All rights reserved.

- 其他处置。
- 重估增加或减少。
- 在权益中直接确认或冲回的减值损失。
- 在损益中确认的减值损失。
- 计入利润表的对过去减值损失的冲回。
- 当期摊销。
- 将财务报表折算为列报货币（如适用）以及境外经营折算为主体列报货币产生的折算差额。
- 当期的其他变化。

- 财务年度开始和结束时的账面价值（即账面净额）。
- 综合收益表中包含无形资产摊销的报表项目。

[IAS 第 38 号第 118 段]。

所有披露要求提供比较数据。

15.220　IAS 第 36 号要求对减值进行更多披露，参见第十八章。[IAS 第 38 号第 120 段]。披露要求包括提供导致重大减值损失的事项和情况的详细资料，以及当主体根据 IFRS 第 8 号“经营分部”提供分部信息时按照报告分部进行的减值损失的进一步分析。如适用，IAS 第 23 号“借款费用”要求对借款费用资本化进行的更多披露在第十六章中说明。

15.221　IAS 第 36 号要求对满足下述情况的每个现金产出单元（CGU）进行更多的披露：包含商誉或具有不确定使用寿命的无形资产，且这些资产的金额与主体的商誉或具有不确定寿命的无形资产总额相比较为重大。披露要求包括提供分配给该现金产出单元的商誉和具有不确定使用寿命的无形资产的账面价值的详细资料以及确定现金产出单元可收回金额（即使用价值或公允

ⓒ 2012 普华永道（PricewaterhouseCoopers）版权所有。

useful lives allocated to the CGU and the basis on which the CGU's recoverable amount has been determined (that is, value in use or fair value less costs to sell). There are then detailed disclosures depending on which basis has been used. Further detailed disclosure is required if a reasonably possible change to a key assumption used in determining recoverable amount would cause the CGU's carrying amount to exceed its recoverable amount. [IAS 36 para 134]. Details of these disclosure requirements are given in chapter 18.

15.222 If the amounts of goodwill and intangible assets with indefinite lives allocated on a CGU by CGU basis is not significant in relation to the entity's total goodwill or intangibles with indefinite lives, this fact should be disclosed, together with the aggregate amount allocated to those units. In addition, if the recoverable amounts of any of the CGUs are based on the same key assumptions and the amount of goodwill or the amount of intangibles with indefinite lives allocated to those CGUs is significant to the corresponding totals for the entity, further disclosures are required. [IAS 36 para 135]. See chapter 18.

15.223 An example that illustrate some (but not all) of the above disclosures is given in Table 15.11.

Table 15.11 – Disclosure of intangible assets combination

S. W. I. F. T. SCRL – Report and accounts – 31 December 2010

Summary of significant accounting policies (extract)

Intangible assets

Intangible assets include acquired software licences and capitalised development costs. Intangible assets are carried at cost less accumulated amortisation and impairment losses. Those are amortised using the straight-line method commencing when the asset is available for its intended use for the operations of the Company. Amortisation rates are detailed in Note 15.

Research and Development costs are accounted for in accordance with IAS 38-Intangibles. Expenditures on research or on the research phase of an internal project are recognised as an expense when incurred. The intangible assets arising from the development phase of an internal project are recognised if the conditions as outlined in IAS 38 are complied with. This implies that the technical feasibility of completing the intangible asset for it to be available for sale or use can be demonstrated and that the intangible asset will generate probable future economic benefits. The intangible assets arising from development are amortised over the

© 2012 PricewaterhouseCoopers LLP. All rights reserved.

价值减去处置费用）的基础。之后的详细披露取决于使用的是哪个基础。如果在确定可收回金额时，使用的关键假设随着合理的可能变化而导致现金产出单元的账面价值超过其可收回金额，则要求进行更多的详细披露。[IAS 第 36 号第 134 段]。这些披露要求的细节在第十八章提供。

15.222 如果基于现金产出单元分配给一个现金产出单元的商誉和具有不确定寿命的无形资产的金额与主体的商誉或具有不确定寿命的无形资产总额相比并不重大，则应当披露该事实以及分配给那些单元的总金额。另外，如果其中某些现金产出单元的可收回金额是基于相同的关键假设，并且分配给这些单元的商誉金额或具有不确定寿命的无形资产的金额与主体的相应总额相比较为重大，则要求进行更多披露。[IAS 第 36 号第 135 段]。参见第十八章。

15.223 表 15.11 中提供了一个阐明以上一些（但不完全涵盖）披露的示例。

表 15.11——无形资产组合的披露

S. W. I. F. T. SCRL——报告和账目——2010 年 12 月 31 日

重大会计政策概述（摘录）

无形资产

无形资产包括外购的软件许可证和资本化的开发成本。无形资产以成本减累计摊销和减值损失计量。当资产能够按照指定用途用于公司运营时，开始使用直线法摊销。摊销率在附注 15 中详述。

研究和开发成本根据 IAS 第 38 号“无形资产”处理。研究支出或内部项目研究阶段的支出在发生时确认为费用。如果符合 IAS 第 38 号列述的条件，则确认来自内部项目开发阶段的无形资产。这表示完成无形资产使其能够销售或使用的技术可行性能够被证明，并且该无形资产将产生可能的未来经济利益。开发产生的无形资产在经济使用寿命内摊销。在每个资产负债表日，公司根据 IAS 第 36 号“资产减值”评价是否存在减值迹象。如果该迹象存在，则资产减记至可收回金额。

ⓒ 2012 普华永道（PricewaterhouseCoopers）版权所有。

Con.

useful economic lives. At each balance sheet date, the Company assesses whether there is any indication of impairment in accordance with IAS 36-Impairment of Assets. If any such indication exists, assets are written down to recoverable amount.

15 Intangible assets

(in thousands)	Concessions, patents and licences EUR	Capitalised development costs EUR	Work in progress EUR	Total intangible assets EUR
2009				
Opening net book value	24, 310	1, 764	1, 466	27, 540
Foreign currency translation	1	–	–	1
Additions	3, 596	1, 084	1, 792	6, 472
Transfers	681	873	(1, 466)	88
Disposals	4	–	–	(4)
Amortisation charges	(11, 767)	(1, 105)	–	(12, 872)
Amortisation rates	20% –33%	33%	–	
Closing net book value	**16, 817**	**2, 616**	**1, 792**	**21, 225**
At 31 December 2009 Cost	113, 342	4, 065	1, 792	119, 199
Accumulated amortisation	(96, 525)	(1, 449)	–	(97, 974)
Net book value	**16, 817**	**2, 616**	**1, 792**	**21, 225**
2010				
Opening net book value	16, 817	2, 616	1, 792	21, 225
Foreign currency translation	–	–	–	–
Additions	12, 044	(123)	–	11, 921
Transfers	1, 115	677	(1, 792)	–
Disposals	–	–	–	–
Amortisation charges	(10, 869)	(1, 474)	–	(12, 343)
Amortisation rates	5%	33%	–	
Closing net book value	**19, 107**	**1, 696**	**–**	**20, 803**
At 31 December 2009 Cost	120, 909	4, 619	–	125, 528
Accumulated amortisation	(101, 802)	(2, 923)	–	(104, 725)
Net book value	**19, 107**	**1, 696**	**–**	**20, 803**

The additions for 2010, amounting to EUR 11. 9 million, mainly relate to the acquisition of the AMH business from SunGard (EUR 9. 9 million).

© 2012 PricewaterhouseCoopers LLP. All rights reserved.

续表

15. 无形资产

（单位：千）	特许权、专利和许可证 欧元	资本化的开发成本 欧元	在产品 欧元	全部无形资产 欧元
2009				
期初账面净值	24, 310	1, 764	1, 466	27, 540
外币折算	1	–	–	1
增加	3, 596	1, 084	1, 792	6, 472
转移	681	873	(1, 466)	88
处置	4	–	–	(4)
摊销费用	(11, 767)	(1, 105)	–	(12, 872)
摊销系数	20% –33%	33%	–	
期末账面净值	**16, 817**	**2, 616**	**1, 792**	**21, 225**
2009 年 12 月 31 日成本	113, 342	4, 065	1, 792	119, 199
累计摊销	(96, 525)	(1, 449)	–	(97, 974)
账面净值	**16, 817**	**2, 616**	**1, 792**	**21, 225**
2010				
期初账面净值	16, 817	2, 616	1, 792	21, 225
外币折算	–	–	–	–
增加	12, 044	(123)	–	11, 921
转移	1, 115	677	(1, 792)	–
处置	–	–	–	–
摊销费用	(10, 869)	(1, 474)	–	(12, 343)
摊销系数	5%	33%	–	
期末账面净值	**19, 107**	**1, 696**	**–**	**20, 803**
2009 年 12 月 31 日成本	120, 909	4, 619	–	125, 528
累计摊销	(101, 802)	(2, 923)	–	(104, 725)
账面净值	**19, 107**	**1, 696**	**–**	**20, 803**

2010 年累计 1, 190 万欧元的增加主要与从 SunGard 收购 AMH 业务相关（990 万欧元）。

ⓒ 2012 普华永道（PricewaterhouseCoopers）版权所有。

15.224 Where intangible assets are stated at revalued amounts under the revaluation model, the following should also be disclosed:

- For each class of intangible asset:
  - The effective date of the revaluation.
  - The carrying amount of revalued intangible assets.
  - The carrying amount determined under the cost model (historical cost less depreciation measurement basis).
- The revaluation surplus relating to intangible assets, showing the opening and closing balance for the period, the change for the period and any restrictions on the distribution of the balance to shareholders.
- The methods and significant assumptions used in estimating fair values.

[IAS 38 para 124].

Classes of revalued assets may be aggregated into larger classes for disclosure purposes, but should not be aggregated if this would result in an aggregated class that included both assets measured under the revaluation model and assets measured under the cost model. [IAS 38 para 125].

15.225 Where the useful life of an intangible asset is indefinite an entity must disclose:

- The asset's carrying amount.
- The reasons that support the assessment of the useful life as indefinite, including details of the significant factors that were taken into account in the assessment.

[IAS 38 para 122(a)].

Paragraph 15.191 contains a list of factors that might be relevant in assessing useful lives and that, therefore, may need to be disclosed where applicable. [IAS 38 para 123].

15.226 Where an individual intangible asset is material to an entity's financial statements, additional disclosure in relation to that asset is required. This disclosure is:

© 2012 PricewaterhouseCoopers LLP. All rights reserved.

15.224　如果无形资产在重估模式下以重估金额计量，则应当也披露以下内容：

■ 对于每类无形资产：

　■ 重估的生效日期。

　■ 重估无形资产的账面价值。

　■ 在成本模式下确定的账面价值（历史成本减折旧的计量基础）。

■ 与无形资产相关的重估盈余，列示当期的期初和期末余额、当期变动以及对于向股东分配该余额的限制。

■ 估计公允价值时使用的方法和重要假设。

［IAS 第 38 号第 124 段］。

为了披露目的，重估资产的类别可以合并成大类。但是如果这会导致合并后的类别同时包括按照重估模式计量的资产和按照成本模式计量的资产，则不应合并。［IAS 第 38 号第 125 段］。

15.225　如果一项无形资产的使用寿命不确定，则主体必须披露：

■ 该资产的账面价值。

■ 支持将使用寿命评估为不确定的理由，包括在评价中考虑的重要因素的详细资料。

［IAS 第 38 号第 122（a）段］。

第 15.191 段包含与评估使用寿命可能相关的要素清单，因此在适用情况下可能需要披露。［IAS 第 38 号第 123 段］。

15.226　如果单一无形资产对于主体的财务报表很重大，则要求对该资产进行额外披露，包括：

ⓒ 2012 普华永道（PricewaterhouseCoopers）版权所有。

- A description of the individual intangible asset.
- The carrying amount.
- The asset's remaining amortisation period.

[IAS 38 para 122(b)].

This might apply, for example, where an entity has development expenditure relating to a major project or an acquired brand, trademark or publishing title that represents a significant proportion of the entity's total assets.

15.227 For assets acquired by way of government grant that are recognised initially at fair value the following disclosures should be made:

- The fair value that was initially recognised for the assets.
- The asset's carrying amount.
- Whether the assets are measured after initial recognition using the cost or the revaluation model.

[IAS 38 para 122(c)].

15.228 In relation to intangible assets generally, the following disclosures are also required:

- The existence and carrying amounts of intangible assets where there are restrictions on title.
- The carrying amounts of intangible assets pledged as security for liabilities.
- The amount of contractual commitments for the acquisition of intangible assets. An example of disclosure is given in Table 15.12 below.
- Details as required by IAS 8 of the nature and amount of each change in accounting estimate that has a material effect in the current period or is expected to have a material effect in future periods and that relates to:
  - The assessment of an intangible asset's useful life.
  - The amortisation method.

© 2012 PricewaterhouseCoopers LLP. All rights reserved.

■ 对该单一无形资产的描述。

■ 账面价值。

■ 该资产的剩余摊销期间。

[IAS 第 38 号第 122（b）段]。

例如，这可能适用于以下情况：主体有占主体总资产很大比例的一个主要项目的开发支出或是外购品牌、商标或出版标题。

15.227　对于通过政府补助获得的以公允价值初始确认的资产，应当进行以下披露：

■ 该资产初始确认的公允价值。

■ 该资产的账面价值。

■ 该资产在初始确认后使用的是成本模式还是重估模式计量。

[IAS 第 38 号第 122（c）段]。

15.228　对于无形资产，一般也需要进行以下披露：

■ 存在所有权限制的无形资产及其账面价值。

■ 抵押为负债担保物的无形资产的账面价值。

■ 购买无形资产的合同承诺金额。下表 15.12 提供了披露示例。

■ IAS 第 8 号所要求的在当期具有重大影响或预计在未来期间具有重大影响的与下述相关的每项会计估计变化的性质和金额的详细资料：

  ■ 无形资产使用寿命的评估。

  ■ 摊销方法。

ⓒ 2012 普华永道（PricewaterhouseCoopers）版权所有。

- Residual values.

[IAS 38 paras 121, 122(d), (e)].

Table 15.12 – Contracts for purchasing rights, co-productions and programmes

RTL Group S. A. – Report and accounts – 31 December 2010

9. Commitments and Contingencies (extract)

	2010	2009
	€m	€m
Guarantees and endorsements given	**153**	48
Contracts for purchasing rights, (co-)productions and programmes	**1,985**	2,188
Operating leases	546	595
Purchase obligations in respect of transmission and distribution	**308**	255
Other long-term contracts and commitments	**290**	308

15.229 The amount of research and development expenditure that has been recognised as an expense in the period should be disclosed. [IAS 38 para 126].

15.230 Users of financial statements may also find the following disclosures relevant to their needs. The standard encourages these disclosures, but does not require them.

- A description of any fully amortised intangible asset that is still in use.
- A brief description of significant intangible assets that are controlled by the entity but that are not recognised because either:
  - they do not meet the recognition criteria in the standard; or
  - they were acquired or generated before the issue of the 1998 version of IAS 38.

[IAS 38 para 128].

© 2012 PricewaterhouseCoopers LLP. All rights reserved.

■ 残值。

[IAS 第 38 号第 121、122（d）、(e）段]。

表 15.12——购买权利、合作作品和节目的合同

RTL 集团公司——报告和账目——2010 年 12 月 31 日

9. 承诺和或有事项（摘录）

	2010 百万英镑	2009 百万英镑
担保和背书保证	**153**	48
购买权利、(合作）作品和节目的合同	**1,985**	2,188
经营租赁	**546**	595
对于传播和经销的购买义务	**308**	255
其他长期合同和承诺事项	**290**	308

15.229 已经确认为当期费用的研究和开发支出金额应当披露。[IAS 第 38 号第 126 段]。

15.230 财务报表使用者也可能觉得以下披露与其需求相关。该准则鼓励进行这些披露，但并不强制要求。

■ 对仍然在用的已摊销完毕的无形资产的描述。

■ 对由主体控制但由于以下原因不确认的重要无形资产的简要描述：

■ 不符合准则中的确认标准；或

■ 在 IAS 第 38 号 1998 年版发布前已购买或产生。

[IAS 第 38 号第 128 段]。

ⓒ 2012 普华永道（PricewaterhouseCoopers）版权所有。

Chapter 20 Inventories

Contents

© 2012 PricewaterhouseCoopers LLP. All rights reserved.

第二十章 存货

目 录

ⓒ 2012 普华永道（PricewaterhouseCoopers）版权所有。

Introduction

20.1 This chapter addresses the accounting treatment and disclosure of inventories in accordance with IAS 2, 'Inventories'. It deals with the carrying value of inventories and complex transactions involving inventory such as inventories on consignment and sale and repurchase of inventories.

[The next paragraph is 20.41.]

Objective and scope

20.41 The objective of IAS 2 is to set out the accounting treatment for inventories. The standard notes that the key consideration in accounting for inventories is determining the amount of cost to be recognised as an asset and carried forward, until the related revenue is recognised. The standard provides guidance on determining the amount of such costs and their subsequent recognition as an expense. It also gives guidance on cost formulas used to assign costs, such as overheads, to inventory and on write-downs to net realisable value. [IAS 2 para 1].

20.42 IAS 2 applies to all inventories, (that is raw materials, consumable supplies, work in progress and finished goods) except the following, which are wholly excluded from its scope:

- Work in progress arising from construction contracts, including directly related service contracts (dealt with by IAS 11, 'Construction contracts').
- Financial instruments (dealt with in IAS 39, 'Financial instruments: Recognition and measurement').
- Biological assets related to agricultural activity and agricultural produce at the point of harvest (dealt with by IAS 41, 'Agriculture').

[IAS 2 para 2].

20.43 In addition, the standard does not apply to the measurement of the

© 2012 PricewaterhouseCoopers LLP. All rights reserved.

引言

20.1　本章针对按照《国际会计准则第 2 号——存货》（“IAS 2”）对存货进行会计处理和披露。本章对存货的账面价值以及如委托代售存货及存货的出售和回购等复杂的交易进行探讨。

[下一段为第 20.41 段。]

目的和范围

20.41　IAS 2 的目的是陈述对存货的会计处理。该准则指出，存货会计处理的关键问题是决定多少成本金额可被确认为资产，并直到该金额被转记及确认为收入。该准则为此类成本金额的确定及随后被确认为费用提供了指引。该准则也为分配成本至该成本存货的成本计量方法以及将其减记至可变现净值提供了指引。[IAS 2 第 1 段]。

20.42　除了如下所列的存货类型不在其范围之内，IAS 2 适用于所有存货科目（即原材料、低值易耗品、在产品和产成品）：

- 建筑合同包括直接相关的服务合同所形成的在建工程（遵循《国际会计准则第 11 号——建筑合同》（“IAS 11”））。
- 金融工具（遵循《国际会计准则第 39 号——金融工具：确认和计量》（“IAS 39”））。
- 与农业活动相关的生物资产，及收获时的农产品（遵循《国际会计准则第 41 号——农业》（“IAS 41”））。

[IAS 2 第 2 段]。

20.43　此外，该准则也不适用于以下存货类型的计量（但适用于所有其他方

ⓒ 2012 普华永道（PricewaterhouseCoopers）版权所有。

following types of inventories (but does apply in all other respects, for example, disclosure):

- Inventories held by producers of agricultural and forest products, agricultural produce after harvest, and minerals and mineral products, to the extent that they are measured at net realisable value in accordance with well-established practice in those industries. Where such inventories are measured at net realisable value, changes in that value are recognised in profit or loss in the period of change.
- Inventories held by commodity broker-traders who measure their inventories at fair value less costs to sell. Where such inventories are measured on that basis, changes in value are also recognised in profit or loss in the period of change.

[IAS 2 para 3].

20.44 Agricultural activity includes raising livestock, forestry, annual or perennial cropping, orchards and plantations, floriculture and aquaculture. IAS 41, 'Agriculture', is applied to agricultural produce, which is the harvested product of an entity's biological assets, at the point of harvest. The harvest is the detachment of produce from a biological asset or the cessation of a biological asset's life process. IAS 41 requires harvested produce to be measured at fair value less costs to sell at the point of harvest. At that point, the fair value less costs to sell of the harvested produce is taken as cost for the purpose of IAS 2, which applies thereafter. [IAS 41 para 13, IAS 2 para 20]. Refer to paragraph 20.47 for further information.

20.45 The extent to which IAS 2 applies to inventories of harvested produce, minerals and mineral products, depends on the accounting policy adopted by the entity for such inventories. There may be a well-established practice in those industries of carrying inventories at net realisable value, because sale is assured under a forward contract or a government guarantee, or because there is an active market in the produce and a negligible risk that the produce will not be sold. In that situation, an entity may choose to carry the inventories at net realisable value and the measurement provisions of IAS 2 do not therefore apply. The inventories are measured at net realisable value and changes in that value are recognised in profit or loss in the period in which they arise. [IAS 2 para 4]. If, on the other

© 2012 PricewaterhouseCoopers LLP. All rights reserved.

面，如披露）：

- 按照存在已久的行业惯例，生产者持有的而按可变现净值计量的农林产品、收获后农产品、矿物及矿产品等存货。此存货以可变现净值计量的情况下，其价值的变动应在变动当期确认为损益。

- 商品经纪人持有而按公允价值减去出售费用后做计量的存货。在该存货按此基础计量的情况下，其价值的变动也应在变动当期确认为损益。

［IAS 2 第 3 段］。

20.44　农业活动包括牲畜饲养、林业、一年生或多年生作物的耕种、果园及农场、花木培植和水产养殖。IAS 41 适用于农产品，即主体生物资产在收割时的收获品。收获是指农产品从生物资产上分离，或生物资产生活周期的结束。IAS 41 要求收获品以其收割时的公允价值减去销售费用计量。在该时点收获品的公允价值减去销售费用将在随后适用的 IAS 2 中作为成本。［IAS 41 第 13 段；IAS 2 第 20 段］。进一步信息请参见第 20.47 段。

20.45　IAS 2 是否适用于收获品、矿物和矿产品等存货，取决于主体为这些存货采用的会计政策。因为通过远期合同或政府担保可以保证，或者是因为产品有一个活跃的市场及滞销风险可略而不计。这些行业的惯例可能是以可变现净值对存货进行计量，在这种情况下，主体可以选择以可变现净值对这些存货进行计量，而 IAS 2 中的计量条款则不再适用。存货将以可变现净值计量，且该净值的变动在当期确认为损益。［IAS 2 第 4 段］。相反，如果主体选择以成本对这些存货进行计量，则应适用该准则的计量规则，即存货应以成本和可变现净值两者中的较低者计量。［IAS 2 第 9 段］。

ⓒ 2012 普华永道（PricewaterhouseCoopers）版权所有。

hand, the entity chooses to carry the inventories at 'cost', the standard's measurement rules apply, that is, the inventories are measured at the lower of such cost and net realisable value. [IAS 2 para 9].

20.46 Broker-traders are those who trade in commodities on their own behalf or for others. Their inventories are normally traded in an active market and are purchased with a view to resale in the near future, generating a profit from fluctuations in price or broker-traders' margin. Industry practice is often to carry such inventories at fair value less costs to sell and so an entity may adopt this policy. Where this is so, the standard's measurement provisions (lower of cost and net realisable value) do not apply and changes in fair value are recognised in profit or loss in the period in which they arise. [IAS 2 para 5].

20.47 It is important to distinguish the difference between the exceptions made for (a) mineral inventories and agricultural inventories after harvest, and (b) agricultural inventories at the point of harvest and inventories of broker-traders. Mineral inventories and agricultural inventories after harvest are carried in accordance with industry practice at net realisable value at certain stages of production. This basis would be appropriate when agricultural crops have been harvested or minerals extracted and the sale of the inventory is assured under a forward contract or a government guarantee, or because there is an active market in the produce and there is a negligible risk that the produce will not be sold. Agricultural produce at the point of harvest and inventories of broker-traders are carried at fair value less costs to sell as they are held with the purpose of selling in the near future and generating a profit from fluctuations in price or broker-traders' margin. These measurement bases are not the same. Net realisable value is the estimated selling price in the ordinary course of business less the estimated costs of completion and the estimated selling costs. Fair value is the amount for which an asset could be exchanged, or a liability settled, between knowledgeable, willing parties in an arm's length transaction. In other words, net realisable value is the amount that an entity expects to realise from the sale of inventory in the ordinary course of business. Fair value (less selling costs) is the amount that could be obtained for the same inventory from a knowledgeable willing party in the marketplace. The difference is that net realisable value is an entity-specific value, whereas fair value is not. Net realisable value for inventories may not equal fair

© 2012 PricewaterhouseCoopers LLP. All rights reserved.

20.46　经纪人是为自己或他人做商品交易的人。其存货通常都在活跃市场中交易，且为了在近期再售的目的而购入并从价格波动中获取利润或经纪人盈余。行业惯例通常将此类存货以公允价值减去销售费用进行计量，因此主体可以采用这种会计政策。如此，该准则的计量规定（成本和可变现净值两者中的较低者）不再适用，而公允价值的变动在当期确认为损益。[IAS 2 第 5 段]。

20.47　区分例外：(a) 矿产品存货及收获后的农产品存货和 (b) 收获时的农产品存货及经纪人的存货之间的差异很重要。特定生产阶段的矿产品存货和收获后的农产品存货在生产周期阶段以可变现净值计量：当销售已收获的农作物或已开采的矿产品已通过远期合同或政府担保得到保证时，或当因活跃市场的存在滞销风险可略而不计时。而收获时的农产品和经纪人的存货应以公允价值减去销售费用计量，因为是为了近期再售目的而持有并从价格波动中获取利润或经纪人盈余。两种例外的计量的基础并不相同。可变现净值是指在正常经营过程中，以估计售价减去估计完工成本和估计销售费用后的价值。公允价值是指在公平交易中，熟悉情况的交易双方自愿进行资产交换或债务清偿的金额。换言之，可变现净值是主体在正常经营过程中预计从存货的销售中可实现的金额。公允价值（减去销售费用）是市场上熟悉情况的自愿的双方对同一存货进行交易中可取得的金额。差别就在于可变现净值是只针对于某一主体的价值，而公允价值不是。存货的可变现净值不一定等于公允价值减去销售费用。[IAS 2 第6、7 段]。

ⓒ 2012 普华永道（PricewaterhouseCoopers）版权所有。

value less costs to sell. [IAS 2 paras 6, 7].

20.48 Fair values are the appropriate measurement bases for broker-traders, because they have access to ready markets. Net realisable value is appropriate for producers, because they may not have such access.

Example 1 – Difference between net realisable value and fair value less costs to sell

An entity holds mineral inventories. It could sell the stock on the open market for C10 per tonne after selling costs. The entity is currently in a forward contract to sell the stock at C12 per tonne. In this situation, fair value less selling costs is C10 per tonne, but net realisable value is C12 per tonne.

Example 2 – Net realisable value and fair value less costs to sell may differ between a producer and a broker trader entity

A producer in country X holds agricultural produce that it can sell locally for C1 per tonne or to a broker in country Y for C5 per tonne. The broker can sell the produce in the market in country Y for C8 per tonne. In this situation, to the extent that the producer will sell to the broker, both the fair value and the net realisable value for the producer is C5 per tonne. For the broker, the fair value and the net realisable value is C8 per tonne. In this situation, the values are different as between the producer and the broker, because the producer does not have access to the market in country Y and must sell either on the local market or to the broker.

Recognition

20.49 Inventories comprise assets that are:

- Held for sale in the ordinary course of business.
- In the process of production for such sale.
- In the form of materials or supplies to be consumed in the production process or in the rendering of services.

[IAS 2 para 6].

© 2012 PricewaterhouseCoopers LLP. All rights reserved.

20.48 对于经纪人而言，因为有现成的市场，公允价值是合适的计量基础。对于生产者而言，因为可能没有现成的市场，可变现净值是合适的。

示例1——可变现净值和公允价值减去销售费用之间的差异

某主体持有矿产品存货。它可以在公开市场上把这些存货以扣除销售费用后每吨10元的价格出售。该主体目前有一笔远期合同会以每吨12元的价格出售该存货。在这种情况下，公允价值减去销售费用为每吨10元，而可变现净值为每吨12元。

示例2——对生产者和经纪人主体而言，可变现净值和公允价值减去销售费用可能存在差异

X国的某生产者持有一农产品，它可以以每吨1元在当地销售，或以每吨5元销售给Y国的某经纪人。该经纪人可以以每吨8元在Y国的市场销售这种产品。在这种情况下，如果生产者将销售给经纪人，对生产者而言公允价值和可变现净值都是每吨5元。对经纪人而言，其公允价值和可变现净值为每吨8元。在这种情况下，因为生产者没有进入Y国市场的渠道而必须在本地市场销售或是销售给经纪人，对生产者和经纪人而言价值是不同的。

确认

20.49 存货包括如下资产：

- 在正常经营过程中持有待售的资产。
- 为销售而仍在生产过程中的资产。
- 在生产或提供服务的过程中将消耗的原料或物料。

[IAS 2 第6段]。

ⓒ 2012 普华永道（PricewaterhouseCoopers）版权所有。

20.50 An entity should initially recognise inventory when it has control of the inventory, expects it to provide future economic benefits and the cost of the inventory can be measured reliably. [Framework paras 49(a), 89].

20.51 Inventories include goods purchased and held for resale, such as merchandise purchased by a retailer or land and other property held for resale.

20.51.1 Property should be recognised as inventory under the following circumstances:

- Property purchased for the specific purpose of resale.
- Property constructed for the specific purpose of resale (work in progress under the scope of IAS 18, 'Revenue').
- Property transferred from investment property to inventories. This is permitted when an entity commences the property's development with a view to sale.

In the case of the third bullet point, the property's cost for subsequent recognition as inventory should be its carrying value at the date of change in use.

20.51.2 The inventory of manufacturing entities is raw materials and consumable supplies, work in progress and finished goods awaiting sale. The cost of services rendered by a service entity is recognised as inventory, where the entity has not recognised the related revenues. [IAS 2 para 8]. This amount should, however, be minimal, given the requirement to recognise service revenues on the percentage-of-completion basis.

Measurement

20.52 Initial measurement of inventories should be at cost. Subsequent to initial recognition, inventories should be measured at the lower of cost and net realisable value. [IAS 2 para 9].

20.53 Where items of inventory are not ordinarily interchangeable, or where goods or services are produced and segregated for specific contracts, their costs should be individually identified. [IAS 2 para 23]. These items should be considered individually, as to compare the total net realisable value of such items

© 2012 PricewaterhouseCoopers LLP. All rights reserved.

20.50 主体对存货进行初始确认应该是当其对存货有控制权，预期存货带来未来经济利益且存货的成本能可靠计量时。[《框架》第49（a）、89段]。

20.51 存货包括购置以备再售的商品，例如零售商购入的商品或持有以备再售的土地及其他不动产。

20.51.1 在下列情况下,应将不动产确认为存货:

- 为了特定的再售目的而购入的不动产。
- 为了特定的再售目的而建造的不动产（《国际会计准则第18号——收入》范围内的在产品）。
- 从投资性不动产转为存货的不动产。当主体为了出售而开始开发某项不动产时允许采取这种方式。

在上述第三点的情况下，将不动产后续确认为存货时的成本应为其在改变用途之日的账面价值。

20.51.2 生产型主体的存货为原材料和低值易耗品、在产品和待售产成品。服务型主体确认的存货为其在尚未确认相关收入时所提供服务的成本。[IAS 2第8段]。但是，由于服务收入是按完工百分比的基础而确认的要求，此金额应当很小。

计量

20.52 存货应以成本为初始计量。初始确认后，存货应以成本和可变现净值两者中较低者来计量。[IAS 2第9段]。

20.53 对于通常不能相互替代的存货项目,或者为特订合同生产和区别的货物或劳务,其成本应进行个别辨认。[IAS 2第23段]因为比较这些项目的可变现净值总额与其成本总额,会导致可预见损失和未变现利润互相抵销的这一不可接受的情况,这些项目应该被单独计量。

ⓒ 2012 普华永道（PricewaterhouseCoopers）版权所有。

with the total cost would result in an unacceptable setting off of foreseeable losses against unrealised profits.

20.54 However, when there are large numbers of items of inventory that are ordinarily interchangeable ('fungible' items), separate identification of costs would not be appropriate. In such cases the first-in, first-out (FIFO) or weighted average cost method may be used. [IAS 2 para 25]. IAS 2 prohibits the use of the last-in, first-out (LIFO) method.

Definition of cost

20.55 Cost is defined as all costs of purchase, costs of conversion and other costs incurred in bringing the inventories to their present location and condition. IFRS does not permit direct costing methods that expense all overheads.

20.56 Costs of purchase comprise the purchase price including import duties and other taxes (so far as not recoverable from the tax authorities), transport and handling costs and any other directly attributable costs, less trade discounts, rebates and similar items. [IAS 2 paras 10, 11]. In its rejections, IFRIC has confirmed that cash discounts received and settlement discounts should be deducted from the cost of inventories. However, rebates that specifically and genuinely refund selling expenses should not be deducted from the cost of inventories.

Example 1 – Point at which import duties are included in inventory valuation

A car dealer imports cars, bringing them initially into a customs-free zone. The cars remain there until they are sold and delivered to customers, at which point import duties will become payable by the importer.

Should the estimated import duties on inventory held in a customs-free zone be included in the cost of inventories?

No, import duties are not included in the inventory valuation for inventory held in a customs-free zone. Import duties do not arise from shipping the cars to the customs-free zone. Therefore, they are not included in the inventory valuation at that point. Import duties payable are included in the cost of inventory when the cars leave that zone.

© 2012 PricewaterhouseCoopers LLP. All rights reserved.

20.54　但是，当大量的存货项目通常可以相互替代（可互换项目）时，其成本则不应进行个别辨认。在这种情况下，可以采用先进先出（FIFO）法或是加权平均成本法。[IAS 2 第 25 段]。IAS 2 禁止采用后进先出（LIFO）法。

成本的定义

20.55　成本的定义为所有的采购成本、加工成本以及使存货达到目前场所和状态而发生的其他成本。国际财务报告准则不允许采用将所有间接经常费用费用化的直接成本计算法。

20.56　采购成本由包括进口关税和其他税项（只要其不能从税务机关退回）的采购价格、运输费、装卸费以及其他直接相关的成本，并扣除商业折扣、回扣和其他类似项目。[IAS 2 第 10、11 段]。在其拒绝解释的说明中，国际财务报告解释委员会已经确定存货成本应扣除所收到的现金折扣及结算折扣。但是，特定及真正为退返销售费用的回扣不应从存货成本中扣除。

示例 1——存货估价应包括进口关税的时点

某轿车分销商在进口轿车时，最初将其运至免税区。轿车将一直保留在该区域直至被出售并交付给客户，进口关税将在交付时点成为该进口商的应付款。

这种免税区存货的成本应否包括估计进口关税？

不，在免税区存货的估价中不包括进口关税。进口关税并非由将轿车运至免税区而引起。因此，在该时点不应将其计入存货的估价，存货成本应在轿车离开免税区时包括。

ⓒ 2012 普华永道（PricewaterhouseCoopers）版权所有。

Example 2 – Bonus related to sale of inventory

A car dealer receives bonuses from car manufacturers when it reaches certain sales targets of motor vehicles. The sales-related bonuses are received only after the cars have been sold, that is, when they are no longer in inventory.

When can the car dealer recognise the bonus?

The bonus from the manufacturers is a contingent asset and should be recognised only when it becomes virtually certain. As it is a sales-related bonus in respect of inventory that has been sold, it is appropriate to take the credit to income as a reduction in cost of sales.

Example 3 – Costs incurred in bringing inventories to their present location and condition

An entity has development land on which it intends to build houses for sale. It is to pay the local authority to build an access road from A to B, where A is on local authority land and B is on the edge of the land owned by the entity. The entity will not own the access road or have exclusive rights to use it. However, the entity considers that there is an economic benefit from the cost of building the access road, because the homes that it builds on the development site will be more attractive to customers if there is a good access road. Can the cost of building the access road be capitalised? If so, is it a separate asset or is it added to the cost of the development?

Under IAS 2, cost should include all costs of purchase, costs of conversion and other costs incurred in bringing the inventories to their present location and condition. [IAS 2 para 10]. The cost of paying the local council to build an access road should be capitalised as part of the development, provided that it is clear that the entity will gain economic benefits from the access road. This would be so, for example, if the entity needs the access road built to obtain planning permission for the development, or if the entity can sell the houses more easily or for a higher value.

If, however, the money paid to the local authority resulted in no future economic benefits to the entity (for example, if the access road did not lead to the development site) and was more in the nature of a gift or goodwill

© 2012 PricewaterhouseCoopers LLP. All rights reserved.

示例 2——与存货销售相关的奖金

某轿车经销商在达到特定销售目标时将从轿车生产厂家收取奖金。只有在出售轿车后，而不再属于存货时，才会收到与销售相关的奖金。

轿车经销商在何时可确认该奖金？

生产厂家所提供的奖金是一项或有资产，只有在其变得基本确定时才应被确认。由于这是一项针对已售出存货的与销售相关的奖金，应将此贷项作为销售成本的抵减计入收入。

示例 3——使存货达到目前场所和状态所发生的费用

某主体有一块开发性土地并计划在其上修建代售的房屋。它需要向当地政府支付款项以修建一条从 A 到 B 的道路，其中 A 属于当地政府的土地而 B 位于属于该主体的土地边缘。该主体既不会拥有该道路也不会拥有其独家使用权。但是，该主体认为花费修建该道路是有经济利益的，因为如果有好的道路，在开发场地所修建的住宅对客户而言将更具有吸引力。修建这条道路的成本可否资本化？如果可以资本化，它是一项单独的资产还是该包含在开发成本中？

根据 IAS 2 的规定，成本应包括所有的采购成本、加工成本以及使存货达到目前场所和状态而发生的其他成本。[IAS 2 第 10 段]。如果很明确该主体能从该道路获得经济利益，则为修建该道路而支付给地方政府的费用应资本化作为开发成本的一部分。例如，如果主体需要修建该道路以获得开发的规划许可，或如果主体能够更容易或以更高的价格销售住宅，那么资本化该笔支付给地方政府的费用是适当的。

但是，如果付给当地政府的钱并未给该主体带来未来经济利益（例如，如果该条道路并非通往该开发场地），而更多的是一种礼品性质或是表达善意，那么应将其冲减至利润表中。

ⓒ 2012 普华永道（PricewaterhouseCoopers）版权所有。

gesture, then it should be written off to income statement.

20.57 Costs of conversion comprise:

- Costs that are specifically attributable to units of production, for example, direct labour, direct expenses and sub-contracted work.
- A systematic allocation of fixed and variable production overheads incurred in converting raw materials into finished goods. Fixed production overheads are indirect costs of production that remain relatively constant regardless of the level of production, such as rent, local taxes such as business rates, depreciation and maintenance of factory buildings and equipment and the cost of factory management and administration. Variable production overheads are those that vary directly with the volume of production, such as indirect materials and indirect labour.
- Other overheads, if any, attributable in the particular circumstances of the business to bringing the inventory to its present location and condition.

[IAS 2 paras 12, 15].

20.58 The allocation of fixed production overheads should be based on the entity's normal level of productive capacity. This level of capacity is the average production expected to be achieved over a number of periods in normal circumstances taking account of production loss due to planned maintenance. Actual production levels may be used where they approximate to normal capacity. Allocation of fixed production overheads is not increased where production is abnormally low or plant is idle. However, in periods of abnormally high production the allocation is decreased so that inventory is not measured above cost. For example, normal production is 10 and normal overhead (fixed) is 10 so that 1 is allocated to each item. If there are three items in inventory, 3 of overhead is carried forward. If, however, 15 are actually produced, then only 0.667 (that is 10/15) should be allocated to each item. So if there are three items in inventory at end of the year, 2 of overheads are carried forward. Allocating 1 to each inventory item, where 15 are produced would be recording inventory above cost.

20.58.1 Unallocated overheads are expensed in the period in which they are incurred. Variable production overheads are allocated to each unit of production on

© 2012 PricewaterhouseCoopers LLP. All rights reserved.

20.57 加工成本包括：

- 与生产量直接相关的成本，如直接人工、直接费用和分包工作。

- 在将原材料加工为产成品过程中系统分配的固定和变动间接生产费用。固定间接生产费用是指不受产量变动影响的间接生产费用，如租金、本地税金（如营业税）、厂房和设备的折旧和维修费用、工厂管理费用和行政费用等。变动间接生产费用指直接受产量变动影响的间接生产费用，如间接材料和间接人工等。

- 与业务具体情况直接相关的、使存货达到当前场所和状态而发生的其他间接费用（若有）。

[IAS 2 第 12、15 段]。

20.58 固定间接生产费用的分配应以主体的正常生产能力水平为基础。此生产能力水平，是指在正常生产条件下，且在若干时期预计能够达到的平均生产量，其中考虑了因为计划维修而损失的生产能力。也可以是指接近正常生产能力的实际生产水平。在产量特别低或厂房闲置的情况下并不会增加固定间接生产费用的分配。但是，在产量特别高的期间，分配额将减少从而存货不会以高于成本的金额计量。例如，正常生产量是 10 且正常间接经常费用（固定）是 10，从而每个项目的分配额为 1。如果有三个存货项目，则间接费用中有 3 应被结转至存货。但是，如果实际产出为 15，那么每个项目的分配额为 0.667（即 10/15）。那么如果年末有三个存货，则间接费用中有 2 应被分配结转至存货。在产出为 15 的情况下仍然向每个存货项目分配 1，将使存货以高于成本的金额计量。

20.58.1 未分配的间接费用应在当期费用化。变动间接生产费用应以生产设备的实际使用程度为基础分配计入单位产品。[IAS 2 第 13 段]。闲置生产能力

© 2012 普华永道（PricewaterhouseCoopers）版权所有。

the basis of the production facilities' actual use. [IAS 2 para 13]. Idle capacity variances should be presented as part of cost of sales. Where an entity operates at full capacity, these costs would normally be included in inventory and later recognised as cost of sales when the product is sold. The requirement in paragraph 13 of IAS 2 effectively accelerates recognising of these costs.

Example 1 – Allocation of overheads (production less than normal)

The following example illustrates how to allocate overhead cost to inventory at normal capacity.

The following is relevant information for entity A:

- Full capacity is 10, 000 labour hours in a year.
- Normal capacity is 7, 500 labour hours in a year.
- Actual labour hours for current period are 6, 500 hours.
- Total fixed production overhead is C1 ,500.
- Total variable production overhead is C2, 600.
- Total opening inventory is 2, 500 units.
- Total units produced in a year are 8, 500 units.
- Total units sold in a year are 8, 700 units.
- Total ending inventory is 2, 300 units.
- The cost of inventories is assigned by using FIFO cost formula.

Management should allocate fixed overhead costs and variable overhead costs to units produced at a rate of C0. 2 per hour and C0. 34 per hour respectively.

Production overhead absorption rate:

= production overhead/labour hours for normal capacity

= 1 ,500/7, 500

= C0. 2 per hour

© 2012 PricewaterhouseCoopers LLP. All rights reserved.

的变动应列报为销售成本的一部分。在主体满负荷运行的情况下，这些成本通常会先计入存货并在出售产品时再确认为销售成本。IAS 2 第 13 段的要求实际上加速了这些成本的确认。

示例 1——分配间接费用(产量低于正常水平)

以下示例说明了在正常生产能力情况下如何将间接费用成本分配至存货。

以下为主体 A 的相关信息：

- 满负荷生产能力为每年 10,000 人工时。
- 正常生产能力为每年 7,500 人工时。
- 当期实际人工时为 6,500 小时。
- 固定间接生产费用总额为 1,500 元。
- 变动间接生产费用总额为 2,600 元。
- 期初存货合计为 2,500 件。
- 一年所生产的存货合计为 8,500 件。
- 一年所销售的存货合计为 8,700 件。
- 期末存货合计为 2,300 件。
- 存货成本采用先进先出成本法进行分配。

管理层应将固定间接生产费用和变动间接生产费用分别以每小时 0.2 元和 0.34 元的比率分配至每件产出的存货。

间接生产费用吸收率为：

= 间接生产费用/正常生产能力的人工时

= 1,500 元/7,500 小时

= 0.2 元/小时

ⓒ 2012 普华永道（PricewaterhouseCoopers）版权所有。

Therefore, fixed production overheads allocated to 6,500 units produced during the year (one unit per hr) = 6,500 × C0.2 = C1,300. The remaining C200 of overheads incurred that remains unallocated is recognised as an expense.

The amount of fixed overhead allocated to inventory is not increased as a result of low production by using normal capacity to allocate fixed overhead.

Variable production overhead absorption rate:

= variable production overhead / actual hours for current period

= C 2,600/6,500

= C0.4 per hour

The above rate results in the allocation of all variable overheads to units produced during the year.

As each unit has taken 1 hour to produce (6,500 hours/6,500 units produced), total fixed and variable production overhead recognised as part of cost of inventory is:

= number of units of closing inventory × number of hours to produce each unit × (fixed production overhead absorption rate + variable production overhead absorption rate)

= 2,300 × 1 × (C0.2 + C0.4) = C1,380

The remaining C2,720 (C1,500 + C2,600 − C1,380) is recognised as an expense in the income statement as follows:

	C
Absorbed in cost of goods sold (FIFO basis) (6,500 − 2,300) = 4,200 × C0.6	2,520
Unabsorbed fixed overheads – also included in cost of goods sold	200
Total	2,720

20.59 IAS 2 does not specify in detail the factors to be considered in determining the 'normal capacity'. We consider that the governing factor is that the cost of unused capacity should be written off in the current year, where such cost does not

© 2012 PricewaterhouseCoopers LLP. All rights reserved.

因此，分配至当年生产的 6,500 件存货的固定间接生产成本（一件每小时）为 6,500 × 0.2 元，即 1,300 元。剩余已发生但未分配的间接费用 200 元确认为费用。

采用正常生产能力来分配固定间接生产费用而分配至存货的金额不会因产量低而增加。

变动间接生产费用吸收率为：

= 变动间接生产费用/当期实际小时数

= 2, 600 元/6,500 小时

= 0.4 元/小时

上述比率将导致所有的变动间接生产费用被分配至当年生产的存货。

由于每件存货的生产花费 1 小时(6,500 小时/生产的 6,500 件)，确认为存货成本一部分的总固定和变动间接生产费用为：

= 期末存货件数 × 生产每件存货的小时数 ×（固定间接生产费用吸收率 + 变动间接生产费用吸收率）

= 2,300 × 1 ×（0.2 元 + 0.4 元）= 1,380 元

如下所示，剩余的 2,720 元（1,50 元 0 + 2,600 元 – 1,380 元）在利润表中确认为费用：

	元
包括在产品销售成本中(以先进先出为基础)(6,500 – 2,300) = 4,200 × 0.6 元	2,520
未吸收的固定间接生产费用 – 亦包括在产品销售成本中	200
合计	2,720

20.59 IAS 2 中并未详列在判断“正常生产能力”时所需考虑的因素。我们认为主导因素为，在未使用生产能力的成本不能构成“正常”生产能力的一部分以及公司设施未能充分运作的情况下，应将该成本在当期冲销。在判断何

ⓒ 2012 普华永道（PricewaterhouseCoopers）版权所有。

constitute a part of 'normal' capacity and where the company does not have a fully operating facility. In determining what constitutes 'normal', the following factors may be considered:

- The volume of production that the production facilities are intended by their designers and by management to produce under the working conditions (for example, single or double shift) prevailing during the year.
- The budgeted level of activity for the year under review and for the ensuing year.
- The level of activity achieved both in the year under review and in previous years.

Although temporary changes in the load of activity can be ignored, persistent variation from the range of normal activity should lead to revision of the previous normal level of activity.

20.60 Allocation of expenses during ban periods. A particular situation occurs in some industries that, due to the nature of their activities, are not allowed to operate during the whole year. For example, fishing industry activities in most countries are regulated in terms of allowed periods of extraction of natural resources in order to ensure resources are conserved. Accordingly, governments establish periods in which fishing companies are allowed to extract these natural resources while establishing periods in which fishing is forbidden. During these periods, entities continue to incur maintenance and other expenses relating to their vessels and plants. The question that arises is whether these expenses should be expensed as incurred or whether it is allowed to capitalise them as production overheads of the finished goods produced during the year. In this case the expenses incurred during the non-fishing periods correspond to unused capacity. In fact the entity may have a fully operating fleet of vessels during the fishing season. As stated above, to determine 'normal capacity' entities should consider the volume of production that the production facilities are intended to produce under the working conditions prevailing during the year. Furthermore, normal capacity is the production expected to be achieved on average over a number of periods or *seasons* under normal circumstances. [IAS 2 para. 13]. Accordingly, we consider that entities operating under similar regimes as those of the fishing industry, should establishes their normal capacity taking into account the loss of capacity resulting from the non-fishing periods.

© 2012 PricewaterhouseCoopers LLP. All rights reserved.

为“正常”的构成因素时，可考虑如下因素：

■ 生产设施的设计人员以及管理层打算在一年普遍条件（例如，单班或双班）下可达的生产量。

■ 所审核年度以及下一年的预计产量水平。

■ 所审核年度以及前一年能达到的产量水平。

虽然可以忽略工作负荷的临时变化，但是持续超出正常范围的变化应导致对之前的正常产量水平进行修正。

20.60　在禁止期分配费用。某些行业由于其活动性质，会有不被允许在全年运营的特殊情况。例如，大多数国家为了保护自然资源，渔业有捕鱼期的法规限制。因此，政府规定了捕鱼公司可以提取自然资源以及禁止捕鱼的期间。在这些期间，主体会继续发生维修和与船及厂房相关的其他费用。问题在于这些费用是否应在发生时费用化，还是可以将其资本化为当年产成品的间接生产费用。在这种情形下，在休渔期发生的费用相当于未使用的生产能力。实际上主体可能在捕鱼期有满负荷的船队。如上所述，为确定“正常生产能力”，主体应考虑在当年普遍条件下生产设施计划生产的产量。此外，正常生产能力是指在正常生产条件下在若干时期或季节内预计能够达到的平均产量。[IAS 2 第 13 段]。因此，我们认为在类似监管下运营的主体，如渔业公司，应该在确定其正常生产能力时考虑休渔期所形成的生产能力损失。

ⓒ 2012 普华永道（PricewaterhouseCoopers）版权所有。

20.61 Classifying overheads for the purpose of the allocation takes the function of the overhead as its distinguishing characteristic (for example, whether it is a function of production, marketing, selling or administration), rather than whether the overhead varies with time or with volume. The costs of general management, as distinct from functional management, are not directly related to current production and are, therefore, excluded from cost of conversion.

20.62 A company should not include external distribution costs such as those relating to the transfer of goods from a sales depot to an external customer. It may, however, include a proportion of the costs that a company incurs in distributing goods from its factory to its sales depot, as these are costs incurred in bringing the inventory to its present location. Furthermore, distribution costs are to be taken into account when assessing the net realisable value (see para 20.84).

20.63 The treatment in IAS 23 (revised) is that borrowing costs directly attributable to the acquisition, construction or production of a qualifying asset are capitalised as part of that asset's cost.

20.64 Other overheads that might be included if they are necessary to bring the inventory to its present location and condition could include the cost of designing products for specific customers, to the extent that such costs are recoverable. [IAS 2 para 15]. The example in paragraph 20.68 below also shows that in the specific circumstances, storage costs, would qualify for inclusion in cost.

20.65 IAS 2 notes that the following costs should be excluded from cost of inventories and recognised as expenses as incurred:

- Abnormal amounts of wasted materials, labour, or other production costs.
- Storage costs, unless those costs are necessary in the production process prior to a further production stage.
- Administrative overheads that do not contribute to bringing inventories to their present location and condition.
- Selling costs.

[IAS 2 para 16].

[The next paragraph is 20.67.]

© 2012 PricewaterhouseCoopers LLP. All rights reserved.

20. 61　在分配间接费用时，划分的辨别特征应为其功能（例如，间接费用是否有生产、市场营销、销售或是管理的功能），而不是间接费用是否会因时间或产量的变动而受到影响。不同于功能管理，行政管理成本与当前生产没有直接关系，因此不包括在加工成本里。

20. 62　公司加工成本中不应包括如将商品从销售仓库运输至外部客户处的外部分销费用。但是，部分货物从其工厂运输至销售仓库所产生的费用，或许可以包括在加工成本中，因为这是使存货达到其当前场所时所发生的费用。此外，在评估可变现净值时应将运输费用考虑在内（参见第 20. 84 段）。

20. 63　按照 IAS 23（修订版），可直接归于购置、建造或生产合规资产的借款费用应资本化为该资产成本的一部分。

20. 64　其他可能包括的如果是使存货达到其当前场所和状态所必需的其他间接费用，此费用可能包括为特定客户设计产品且能收回的成本。[IAS 2 第 15 段]。下文第 20. 68 段中的示例也表明，在特定情况下储存费用也符合计入成本的条件。

20. 65　IAS 2 指出，如下成本应在发生时确认为费用而不应包括在存货成本中：

■ 非正常损耗的材料、人工或其他生产成本。

■ 储存费用，除了在生产过程中为那些达到下一个生产阶段之前所需费用。

■ 无助于使存货达到目前场所和状态的间接行政费用。

■ 销售费用。

[IAS 2 第 16 段。]

[下一段为第 20. 67 段。]

ⓒ 2012 普华永道（PricewaterhouseCoopers）版权所有。

20.67 Sometimes financial instruments are used to hedge commodity price or foreign exchange price risks when purchasing inventories. The accounting treatment of transactions involving financial instruments in the context of accounting for inventories is complex and is discussed under 'Practical application' below.

20.68 The first three examples below illustrate the type of costs that may or may not be included in inventories and the fourth example illustrates the treatment of rebates.

Example 1 – Costs that may be included in inventories

The following table highlights examples of the types of costs that can be included in the cost of inventories.

Description of costs	Include in inventory		Expense Selling and
	Direct	Indirect	admin
Production materials	√		
Production labour	√		
Employment costs of direct labour (for example, pension costs)	√		
Normal amounts of materials wastage	√		
Supervisor salaries and employment costs		√	
Other indirect labour		√	
Indirect materials		√	
Rent, maintenance, heat, light, some taxes (excluding income taxes) and other indirect costs of running factory		√	
Depreciation of production equipment and related facilities and property		√	
Amortisation of related acquired intangibles		√	
Product research			√
Abnormal amounts of wastage, labour and other costs			√
Selling costs			√
Storage costs (but see example 2)			√
General management costs			√
Borrowing costs on inventories that are manufactured in large quantities and on a repetitive basis can either to be included in inventory or expensed (policy choice). [IAS 23 para 4(b)].		√	√
Borrowing costs on other qualifying categories under IAS 23 (revised).		√	

© 2012 PricewaterhouseCoopers LLP. All rights reserved.

20.67 购买存货时，会使用金融工具来对商品价格或外汇汇率风险进行套期保值。就存货的会计处理而言，涉及金融工具交易的会计处理比较复杂，下文“在实务中的应用”部分对此进行了讨论。

20.68 如下的前三个示例说明了可否计入存货的成本类型，而第四个示例说明了回扣的处理。

示例1——可计入存货的成本

下表中强调了可计入存货的成本类型示例。

成本描述	计入存货		费用
	直接	间接	销售和管理
生产材料	√		
生产人工	√		
直接人工的就职成本（例如，养老金成本）	√		
正常损耗的材料	√		
主管的工资和就职成本		√	
其他间接人工		√	
间接材料		√	
租金、维修、加热、照明、一些税金（不包括所得税）和工厂运行的其他间接成本		√	
生产设备和相关设施以及不动产的折旧		√	
相关购入无形资产的摊销		√	
产品研发			√
非正常的耗损、人工或其他成本			√
销售费用			√
存储费用（但参见示例2）			√
一般管理成本			√
大量且重复制造的存货的借款费用可计入存货或费用化（会计政策选择）[IAS 23第4（b）段]。		√	√
根据IAS 23（修订版）符合条件的其他类别的借款费用。		√	

ⓒ 2012 普华永道（PricewaterhouseCoopers）版权所有。

Example 2 – Storage costs capitalised in cost of inventory

The production of whisky involves the distilling of aged whisky in a cask prior to bottling. Can storage cost be included in the cost of inventory?

Capitalisation of storage costs is allowed only if the storage is necessary in the production process prior to a further production stage (see para 20.65 above). Therefore, in this situation, the storage cost the entity incurs during the distilling process should be capitalised, as ageing is integral to making the finished product saleable.

Example 3 – Costs of editing, translating and collecting data for travel guides

A publisher prepares travel guides. Part of the costs of preparing the guides includes the costs of editing, translating and collecting the data for the travel guides. Can the editing and translation costs be included in the cost of inventory held by a publisher?

The costs incurred in editing, translating and collecting the data should be included in the cost of inventories, as they are direct costs related to preparing the travel guides for use. The cost of inventories comprises all costs of purchase, costs of conversion and other costs incurred in bringing the inventories to their present location and condition. [IAS 2 para 10].

Example 4 – Treatment of rebates

A car distributor values its items of inventory at the year end. Rebates are only received from the car manufacturers once a year and are only known after the year end, but relate to purchases in the current period. Should the rebates be taken through the income statement as a deduction in the cost of sales without allocation to the items in inventory at the balance sheet date or should a proportion of the rebates be allocated to the inventory items at the year end?

Paragraph 11 of IAS 2 states that trade discounts, rebates and other similar items are deducted in determining the cost of purchase of inventory. A proportion of the rebates should be allocated to inventory items at the year end. For example, if purchases during the year are 100 and there is inventory with a cost of 10 at the year end, 10% of the rebate should be applied to the inventory items at the

© 2012 PricewaterhouseCoopers LLP. All rights reserved.

示例2——资本化为存货成本的存储费用

威士忌的生产在装瓶前要先蒸馏桶里多年陈酿的威士忌。这种存储成本是否可计入存货成本中?

只有当存储是到下一生产阶段之前所必须的生产流程，才允许将存储费用资本化（参见上文第20.65段）。因此，在此情况下，由于陈酿是使得产成品可售的必要步骤，主体在蒸馏过程中发生的存储费用应当资本化。

示例3——为旅行指南编辑、翻译和收集数据的成本

某出版商正在编制旅行指南。编制指南的部分成本包括一部分编辑、翻译和收集数据的成本。这些编辑和翻译成本可否被计入该出版商所持存货的成本中?

因为编辑、翻译和收集数据所产生的成本是与编制旅行指南相关的直接成本，应被计入存货成本。存货成本包括所有的采购成本、加工成本和为使存货达到其目前场所和状态所发生的其他成本。[IAS 2第10段]。

示例4——回扣的处理

某轿车经销商在年末对其存货项目进行估价。与当期购买相关的回扣从轿车生产厂家每年只能收到一次，而且只能在年末后才能确定金额。是否应在利润表里将该回扣作为销售成本的减项而不将之分配至资产负债表日的存货项目，还是应按比例将一部分回扣分配至年末的存货项目中?

在确定存货的采购成本时，IAS 2第11段说明应扣除商业折扣、回扣和其他类似项目。在年末应按比例将一部分回扣分配至存货项目中。例如，如果本年度的采购为100而年末的存货成本为10，则10%的回扣在年末应计入分配至存货项目而90%应在利润表里销售成本的减项。由于无法将回扣分配至当年具体的存货项目，因此，应将其平均分配至当年所购买的所有已

© 2012 普华永道（PricewaterhouseCoopers）版权所有。

year end and 90% should be taken through the income statement as a deduction in the cost of sales. The reasoning is that the rebates cannot be allocated to particular items in the year, therefore, they should be spread over all the items purchased during the year, sold or unsold.

20. 69 An example of an accounting policy that gives details of costs included in inventory is shown in Table 20. 1.

Table 20. 1 – Accounting policy for cost of inventory

Henkel AG & Co. KGaA – Annual report and accounts – 31 December 2010

(6) Inventories (extract)

Manufacturing cost includes – in addition to direct costs – appropriate proportions of necessary overheads (e. g. the goods inward department, raw materials store, filling and other costs prior to the finished products store), as well as production-related administrative expenses and pension costs for employees engaged in the production process, and production-related depreciation charges. The overhead allowances are determined on the basis of average capacity utilization. Interest charges incurred during the period of manufacture are, however, not included.

20. 70 Where an entity purchases goods on deferred settlement terms, the arrangement may effectively contain a financing element if the terms are more generous than the normal trade terms given by the supplier. In such situations, the financing element, that is, the difference between the purchase price of goods under normal trade terms and the actual price paid, should be accounted for as interest expense over the period of the financing. [IAS 2 para 18]. An example is Table 20. 1A.

Table 20. 1A – Inventory purchased on deferred purchase terms

Bovis Homes Group PLC – Annual report and accounts – 31 December 2009

4. Accounting policies (extract)

Inventories (extract)

Land held for development, including land in the course of development until legal completion of the sale of the asset, is initially recorded at cost. Where, through deferred purchase credit terms, cost differs from the nominal amount which will actually be paid in settling the deferred purchase terms liability, an adjustment is made to the cost of the land, the difference being charged as a finance cost.

© 2012 PricewaterhouseCoopers LLP. All rights reserved.

售或未售的项目。

20.69 表20.1中的示例介绍了详细描述计入存货成本的会计政策。

表20.1——存货成本的会计政策

Henkel AG & Co. KGaA——年报和财务报表——2010年12月31日

（6）存货（摘录）

除了直接成本，制造成本还包括了合比例的且必须的间接费用（如商品采购部、原材料储存、灌装以及产成品储存之前的其他成本），以及与生产相关的管理费用、从事生产流程工作员工的退休金和与生产相关的折旧费用。间接费用的金额根据平均产能利用率确定。但是，生产期间所发生的利息费用不包括在内。

20.70 在主体按照延期结算条款购买商品时，如果该条款比供应商的正常贸易条款更有利，则此协议可能事实上包含融资因素。在这种情况下，此融资因素，即根据正常贸易条款商品的购买价格和实际支付的价格之间的差额，应在融资期间做为利息费用核算。[IAS 2第18段]。表20.1A为一示例。

表20.1A——按照延期购买条款所购买的存货

Bovis Homes Group PLC——年报和财务报表——2009年12月31日

4. 会计政策(摘录)

存货(摘录)

持有待开发的土地，包括资产销售完成之前仍正在开发过程中的土地，以成本进行初始记录。因为使用了延期购买信贷条款，成本和实际用以结算该条款负债而支付的金额有差异，因此土地的成本需要调整，该差额被计为财务费用。

ⓒ 2012 普华永道（PricewaterhouseCoopers）版权所有。

20.71 The production process may result in more than one product being produced at the same time. Allocation of costs to each of the 'joint products' may present problems. IAS 2 states that allocation of costs should be made on a rational and consistent basis. It suggests, for example, that such allocation may be based on the relative sales value of each product. This allocation may be made at the point in the production process where the joint products become separately identifiable or at the completion of production. [IAS 2 para 14].

20.72 In other cases the production process may result, not in joint products that are each important, but rather in a main product and a relatively unimportant by-product. Where this is the case the standard notes that such by-products are often measured at their net realisable value and this value is then deducted from the total costs to give a net cost for the main product. As a result the carrying amount of the main product is not materially different from its cost. [IAS 2 para 14]. Table 20.2 is an example of an accounting policy for by-products.

Table 20.2 – Accounting policy for by-products

Impala Platinum Holdings Limited – Report and accounts – 30 June 2010

1. Summary of significant accounting policies (extract)

1.11 Inventories (extract)

Metal inventories

Platinum, palladium and rhodium are treated as main products and other platinum group and base metals produced as by-products. Metals mined by the Group, including in-process metal contained in ore, concentrate and matte produced by the smelter and precious metal concentrate in the base and precious metal refineries, are valued at the lower of average cost of production and net realisable value. Quantities of in-process metals are based on latest available assays. The average cost of production is taken as total costs incurred on mining and refining, including depreciation, less net revenue from the sale of by-products, allocated to main products on a units produced basis. Refined by-products are valued at net realisable value. Stocks of metals purchased or recycled by the Group are valued at the lower of cost or net realisable value.

20.73 Inventories (work in progress) of service providers are costs incurred in providing the services, for which the entity has not recognised revenues. IAS 2 notes that in relation to a service provider, to the extent that it has inventories, the

© 2012 PricewaterhouseCoopers LLP. All rights reserved.

20.71　生产过程可能同时生产不止一种产品。将成本分配至各“联产品”时可能出现问题。IAS 2 指出成本应在合理和一致的基础上进行分配。例如，可以根据每种产品的相对销售价值而分配。分配的时点在生产过程中可以单独辨认联产品时或在生产结束时。[IAS 2 第 14 段]。

20.72　有些生产过程可能生产了一个主产品和一个相对而言不重要的副产品，而不是各个都重要的联产品。在这种情况下，该准则指出这些副产品通常以可变现净值计量，且其价值应从总成本中扣除以得到主产品的净成本，而使主产品的账面金额与其成本不会有显著差异。[IAS 2 第 14 段]。表 20.2 中所示为副产品会计政策的示例。

表 20.2——副产品的会计政策

Impala Platinum Holdings Limited ——年报和财务报表——2010 年 6 月 30 日

1. 重大会计政策汇总（摘录）

1.11 存货（摘录）

金属存货

铂、钯和铑被视为主产品而其他产出的铂类和贱金属为副产品。本集团所开采的金属，包括熔炉所冶炼的矿石、精砂和在产品金属以及贱金属和贵金属精炼厂里的贵金属精砂，均按照平均生产成本和可变现净值两者中较低者来进行估价。在产品金属的数量是基于最新的化验分析而确定的。平均生产成本是由采矿和精炼所发生的总成本，包括折旧，减去出售副产品的净收入得出，并按照单位产出的方式分配至主产品中。精炼副产品以可变现净值进行估价。本集团所购入的金属存货以成本或可变现净值两者中较低者进行估价。本集团的存货不包括在代炼合同下的金属。

20.73　劳务提供者的存货（在产品）是在提供劳务过程所发生的成本但主体尚未确认收入的部分。IAS 2 指出，对于劳务提供者而言，如果其有存货，那么这些存货的成本主要是直接提供劳务人员（包括监管人员）的人工和其他

ⓒ 2012 普华永道（PricewaterhouseCoopers）版权所有。

cost of these is mainly the labour and other costs of the personnel who are directly engaged in providing the service, including supervisory personnel and attributable overheads. Labour and other costs attributable to sales and general administration are not included and are recognised as expenses as incurred. The cost of inventories of a service provider does not include profit margins or non-attributable overheads that are sometimes included in the price charged to customers by service providers. [IAS 2 para 19]. In its rejections, IFRIC has indicated that the consumption of inventories by a service organisation should be accounted for in a similar way to other items of inventory.

Determining cost

20.74 IAS 2 permits the use of techniques for arriving at cost instead of using actual costs, where the techniques approximate to cost. Such techniques are often used where there are a large number of similar items and they include standard cost methods or the retail method. Standard costs take account of the normal levels of materials and supplies, labour, efficiency and capacity use and are regularly reviewed and revised where necessary. [IAS 2 para 21]. The retail method is often used in the retail industry for measuring the cost of large numbers of rapidly changing items that have similar margins and for which there is no other practicable costing method. The cost of inventory is arrived at by reducing the selling price by the percentage gross margin. The reduction takes account of any reductions already made from the original selling price (for example, where the items have been in a sale). Sometimes an average gross margin for each retail department is used. [IAS 2 para 22].

20.75 An example of a company that uses the standard cost method is given in Table 20.3.

Table 20.3 – Use of standard costs for inventory

Novo Nordisk A/S – Annual report and accounts – 31 December 2010

Accounting policies (extract)

Inventories

Inventories are stated at the lower of cost and net realisable value. Cost is determined using

© 2012 PricewaterhouseCoopers LLP. All rights reserved.

费用以及可归属的间接费用。与销售和一般管理人员相关的人工和其他费用，应在其发生时确认为费用，而不包括在劳务提供者的存货成本中。劳务提供者的存货成本不包括向客户收取的价格中有时已包括的边际利润或不归属的间接费用［IAS 2 第 19 段］。在其拒绝解释的说明中，国际财务报告解释委员会已经表明服务机构的存货消耗应采用与其他存货项目类似的会计处理方法。

成本的确定

20.74　在计算结果与成本接近时，IAS 2 允许采用成本计算方法来代替使用实际成本。这些成本计算方法包括标准成本法或零售价法，通常在有大量类似项目的情况下被采用。标准成本法考虑了材料和物料、人工、效率以及生产能力的正常水平，在需要时应定期审查并修正。［IAS 2 第 21 段］。零售价法通常在零售业中用于计量大量迅速周转的存货成本，这些存货项目具有类似的边际利润，而且没有其他切实可行的成本计算方法。存货的成本根据销售价格扣除毛利率百分比来确定。该扣除要考虑到那些从最初售价中已经扣除的其他任何项目（例如，促销存货项目进行时的折扣）。有时零售价法会使用各零售部门的平均毛利率。［IAS 2 第 22 段］。

20.75　表 20.3 中所示为使用标准成本法的公司示例。

表 20.3——对存货采用标准成本法

Novo Nordisk A/S——年报和财务报表——2010 年 12 月 31 日

会计政策（摘录）

存货

存货以成本与可变现净值两者中较低者计量。成本采用先进先出法确定。成本包括诸

ⓒ 2012 普华永道（PricewaterhouseCoopers）版权所有。

Con.

the first-in, first-out method. Cost comprises direct production costs such as raw materials, consumables and labour, as well as production overheads such as employee wages, depreciation, maintenance etc. The production overheads are measured based on a standard cost method which is reviewed regularly to ensure relevant measures of utilisation, production lead time etc.

If the expected sales price less completion costs and costs to execute sales (net realisable value) is lower than the carrying amount, a write-down is recognised for the amount by which the carrying amount exceeds its net realisable value.

Key accounting estimates and assumptions (extract)

Indirect production costs (IPCs)

Production costs for work in progress and finished goods include IPCs such as employee costs, depreciation, maintenance etc.

IPCs are measured based on a standard cost method which is reviewed regularly to ensure relevant measures of utilisation, production lead time and other relevant factors. Changes in the parameters for calculation of IPCs, including utilisation levels, production lead time etc could have an impact on the gross margin and the overall valuation of inventories.

The carrying amount of IPCs on inventory is DKK 5,090 million as at 31 December 2010. Please refer to note 15 for further information.

15 Inventories

	2010	2009
Raw materials	**1,378**	1,290
Work in progress	**6,344**	7,254
Finished goods	**3,268**	2,196
Total inventories (gross)	**10,990**	10,740
Inventory write-downs at year-end	**1,301**	724
Total inventories	**9,689**	10,016
Indirect production costs included in work in progress and finished goods	**5,090**	5,046
The movements in the inventory write-downs can be specified as follows:		
Inventory write-downs at the beginning of the year	**724**	1,038
Utilisation of inventory write-downs	**(139)**	(513)
Reversal of inventory write-downs	**(116)**	(115)
Inventory write-downs net for the year	**832**	314
Inventory write-downs at the end of the year	**1,301**	724

© 2012 PricewaterhouseCoopers LLP. All rights reserved.

续表

如原材料、低值易耗品和人工等直接生产成本以及诸如职工工资、折旧、维修费等间接生产费用。间接生产费用采用标准成本法计量，并定期审查以确保其利用率、生产提前期等是相关的。

如果预计销售价格减去完工成本和销售费用（可变现净值）小于账面余额，则需要将账面余额超出可变现净值的金额确认为减记。

关键会计估计和假设（摘录）

间接生产成本（IPCs）

在产品和产成品的成本包括如职工成本、折旧、维修费等间接生产费用。

间接生产费用采用标准成本法计量，并定期审查以确保使用率、生产提前期及其他因素是相关的。包括使用率、生产提前期等间接生产费用计算参数的变化，可能会影响毛利和存货的整体估价。

存货的间接生产费用于2010年12月31日的账面余额为50.90亿丹麦克朗。更多信息请参见附注15。

15. 存货

	2010	2009
原材料	**1,378**	1,290
在产品	**6,344**	7,254
产成品	**3,268**	2,196
存货总额(总额)	**10,990**	10,740
期末存货减记金额	**1,301**	724
存货总额	**9,689**	10,016
在产品和产成品中包括的间接生产费用	**5,090**	5,046
存货减记金额的变动明细如下：		
存货减记的期初余额	**724**	1,038
存货减记利用	(**139**)	(513)
存货减记转回	(**116**)	(115)
当年存货减记的净值	**832**	314
存货减记的期末余额	**1,301**	724

ⓒ 2012 普华永道（PricewaterhouseCoopers）版权所有。

20. 75. 1 An example of a company that uses the retail method is given in Table 20. 3A.

Table 20. 3A – Use of retail method for inventory

John Lewis Partnership plc – Annual report and accounts – 31 January 2009

1 Accounting policies (extract)

Inventory valuation

Inventory is stated at the lower of cost, which is either computed on the basis of selling price less the appropriate trading margin or as average unit cost, and net realisable value. Inventory excludes merchandise purchased by the group on a sale or return basis, where the group does not have the risks and rewards of ownership.

20. 77 The standard states that the method for determining the cost of fungible items (that is, normally interchangeable items such as identical nuts and bolts) is either the first-in, first-out method (FIFO) or weighted average cost. [IAS 2 para 25]. Under the FIFO method, it is assumed that items of inventory that were purchased first are sold first and so the items remaining in inventory are carried at more up-to-date purchase prices. Under the weighted average cost method, the cost of each item is determined from the weighted average of the cost of similar items at the beginning of the period and the cost of similar items purchased or produced during the period. The average may be calculated on a periodic basis or as each additional delivery is received. [IAS 2 para 27].

20. 78 The example below illustrates the calculation of the value of inventories on both a FIFO basis and a weighted average price basis.

Example – Determining costs of inventories using FIFO and weighted average cost valuation methods

Assume that opening inventory on 1 March 20X9 is nil. All inventory is finished good and is of the same type. Details of the inventory received and sent out are as shown below.

© 2012 PricewaterhouseCoopers LLP. All rights reserved.

20.75.1　表20.3A中所示为使用零售法的公司示例。

表20.3A——对存货采用零售法

John Lewis Partnership plc——年报和财务报表——2009年1月31日

1. 会计政策(摘录)

存货估价

存货以成本和可变现净值两者中较低者计量,其中成本是根据销售价格减去适当的交易毛利或平均单位成本计算。集团并不具有与所有权相关的风险与报酬的情况下,存货不包括集团根据不销售则返还基础而购入的商品。

20.77　该准则指出可互换项目（即，通常能相互替代的如同样的螺母和螺栓等项目）的成本确定方法为先进先出法（FIFO）或是加权平均成本法。[IAS 2第25段]。在先进先出法下，假定先购买的存货项目先售出，从而留在存货中的项目会根据较新的购买价格计量。在加权平均成本法下，每个项目的成本是根据期初类似项目的成本和当期购买或生产的类似项目的成本的加权平均数。该平均数可以定期计算或在每次收到一批货物时计算。[IAS 2第27段]。

20.78　如下示例说明了根据先进先出法及加权平均价格法而计算存货的价值。

示例——采用先进先出法和加权平均成本法确定存货的成本

假设20X9年3月1日的期初存货为零。所有存货均为产成品而且类型相同。收到及发出存货的详细信息如下所示。

© 2012 普华永道（PricewaterhouseCoopers）版权所有。

		Quantity unit	Unit cost
			C
Batch 1 received on 1 March 20X9		2	3.00
Batch 2 received on 15 March 20X9		4	4.50
On 25 March 20X9 the entity sold 5 units		(5)	
Closing inventory on 31 March 20X9		1	

	Quantity unit	Unit cost	Value
		C	C
(a) FIFO	1	4.50 (a)	4.50
(b) Weighted average	1	4.00 (b)	4.00

(a) FIFO: all units of batch 1 have been sent out first, then three units from batch 2 were despatched. One unit from batch 2 remains at C4.50.

(b) Weighted average: the average unit cost of all units received is C4.00 (2 × C3 + 4 × C4.50)/(2 + 4).

20.79 An entity must use the same cost formula (FIFO or weighted average cost) for all inventories having similar nature and use in the entity. For inventories with different nature or use, different cost formulas may be justified. The standard gives an example of certain inventories used in one operating segment that may have a different use from the same type of inventories used in a different operating segment. However, a difference in the geographical location of inventories or in the respective tax rules is, by itself, not sufficient to justify the use of different cost formulas. [IAS 2 paras 25, 26].

20.80 The example given in the standard is not entirely persuasive, as it does not say how the inventories in one operating segment differ in nature and use. However, if in one operating segment the inventories were, say, unrefined sugar that was used in a manufacturing process and in the other operating segment the inventories were refined sugar purchased for resale, that might be sufficiently different for different formulas to be used. However, a situation justifying the use of different cost formulas is likely to occur only rarely.

20.81 An example of a company that uses weighed average costs is given in

© 2012 PricewaterhouseCoopers LLP. All rights reserved.

	数量 个	单位成本 元
20X9 年 3 月 1 日收到第一批	2	3.00
20X9 年 3 月 15 日收到第二批	4	4.50
主体于 20X9 年 3 月 25 日售出 5 个	(5)	
20X9 年 3 月 31 日的期末存货	1	

	数量 个	单位成本 元	价值 元
(a) 先进先出法	1	4.50 (a)	4.50
(b) 加权平均法	1	4.00 (b)	4.00

(a) 先进先出法：第一批的所有存货都已售出，第二批的存货发出了 3 个。第二批的存货剩余一个，金额为 4.50 元。

(b) 加权平均法：所有收到存货的平均单位成本为 4.00 元(2 × 3 + 4 × 4.50)/(2 + 4)。

20.79 主体对于具备类似性质和用途的所有存货应采用相同的成本计算方法(先进先出法或加权平均成本法)。对于性质或用途不同的存货，可以采用不同的成本计算方法。该准则给出了一个示例，用于某经营分部的特定存货与用于另一经营分部的同类存货对主体有着不同的用途。然而，存货地理位置或各自纳税规则的差异其自身并不足以辩明应采用不同的成本计算方法。[IAS 2 第 25、26 段]。

20.80 该准则中给出的示例并不完全具有说服力，因为它并未说明一个经营分部中的存货的性质和用途如何不同。但是，如果一个经营分部的存货为用于生产过程的粗糖，而另一经营分部的存货是为了待售而购入的粗糖，此差异足以采用不同的方法。但是，出现可以采用不同成本计算方法的情况比较罕见。

20.81 表 20.4 中所示为使用加权平均成本法的公司示例。

ⓒ 2012 普华永道（PricewaterhouseCoopers）版权所有。

Table 20. 4.

Table 20. 4 – Use of weighted average cost for determining cost of inventory

AB Electrolux – Annual report and accounts – 31 December 2009

Note 1 Accounting and valuation principles (extract)

Inventories

Inventories and work in progress are valued at the lower of acquisition cost, at normal capacity utilization, and net realizable value. Net realizable value is defined as the estimated selling price in the ordinary course of business less the estimated costs of completion and the estimated costs necessary to make the sale at market value. The cost of inventories is assigned by using the weighted average cost formula. The cost of inventories are recognized as expense and included in cost of goods sold. Provisions for obsolescence are included in the value for inventory.

20. 82 An example of a company that uses FIFO is given in Table 20. 5.

Table 20. 5 – Use of FIFO for determining cost of inventory

Koninklijke Ahold N. V. – Annual report and accounts – 2 January 2011

3 Significant accounting policies (extract)

Inventories

Inventories are stated at the lower of cost or net realizable value. Cost consists of all costs of purchase, cost of conversion and other costs incurred in bringing the inventories to their present location and condition, net of vendor allowances attributable to inventories. The cost of inventories is determined using either the first-in, first-out ("FIFO") method or the weighted average cost method, depending on their nature or use. For certain inventories, cost is measured using the retail method, in which the sales value of the inventories is reduced by the appropriate percentage of gross margin. Net realizable value is the estimated selling price in the ordinary course of business, less the estimated marketing, distribution and selling expenses.

20. 83 A method of arriving at cost by applying the latest purchase price to the total number of units in inventory is unacceptable because it is not necessarily the same as actual cost and, in times of rising prices, will result in the taking of profit that has not been realised. A base stock method is also not an acceptable method of

© 2012 PricewaterhouseCoopers LLP. All rights reserved.

表 20.4——采用加权平均成本法确定存货成本

AB Electrolux——年报和财务报表——2009 年 12 月 31 日

附注 1. 会计和评估政策(摘录)

存货

存货和在产品以正常生产能力下的采购成本和可变现净值两者中较低者计价。可变现净值是在正常经营过程中的估计售价减去估计完工成本及使销售售价可达市场价所必须的估计费用后的价值。存货成本采用加权平均成本法计算。存货成本确认为费用并被包括在产品销售成本中。陈旧过时的准备包括在存货的计价中。

20.82 表 20.5 中所示为使用先进先出法的公司示例。

表 20.5——采用先进先出法确定存货成本

Koninklijke Ahold N. V. ——年报和财务报表——2011 年 1 月 2 日

3. 重大会计政策（摘录）

存货

存货以成本和可变现净值两者中的较低者来计量。成本包括所有的采购成本、加工成本和使存货达到目前场所和状态而发生的其他成本，并扣除属于存货的供应商折扣。存货的成本根据其性质或用途采用先进先出法（FIFO）或是加权平均成本法确定。对于特定的存货而言，其成本采用零售法来计量，即存货的销售额减去适当百分比的毛利。可变现净值是正常经营过程中的估计售价减去估计市场营销、分销及销售费用。

20.83 通过对存货总件数采用最近的购买价格得出成本的方法并不可用，因为这和实际成本并不一定相同，而在价格上涨时，将会导致确认尚未实现的利润。基本存量法也不是一种可用的存货成本计算方法，因为它经常会导致存货在资产负债表中所列报的金额与其最近的成本水平无关。根据这种方法，存

ⓒ 2012 普华永道（PricewaterhouseCoopers）版权所有。

inventory costing, as it often results in inventory being stated in the balance sheet at amounts that bear little relationship to recent cost levels. Under this method, the cost of inventories is calculated on the basis that a fixed unit value is ascribed to a predetermined number of units of inventory, any excess over this number being valued on the basis of some other method. The last in first out or 'LIFO' method is also prohibited because, like the base stock method, it results in inventory being stated in the balance sheet at amounts that bear little relationship to recent cost levels.

Net realisable value

20.84 IAS 2 requires that inventories should be measured at the lower of cost and net realisable value. [IAS 2 para 9]. If there is no reasonable expectation of sufficient future revenue to cover cost incurred, the irrecoverable cost should be charged as an expense in the period under review. Net realisable value is the estimated selling price in the ordinary course of business less the estimated costs of completion and the estimated costs necessary to make the sale. [IAS 2 para 6].

20.85 The principal situations in which net realisable value is likely to be less than cost are where there has been:

- An increase in costs to complete or selling costs or a fall in selling price.
- Physical deterioration of inventories.
- Obsolescence of products.
- A decision as part of a company's marketing strategy to manufacture and sell products at a loss.
- Errors in production or purchasing.

[IAS 2 para 28].

20.86 The write-down of inventory to net realisable value is normally made on an individual item basis. However, it may be more appropriate in certain cases to make the write-down by reference to groups of similar or related items. This would be where items relate to the same product line, have a similar purpose and end use,

© 2012 PricewaterhouseCoopers LLP. All rights reserved.

货成本的计算是先为确定数量的存货指定固定的单位价值，而任何超出这一数量的存货均以其他方法进行估价。后进先出法（LIFO）也被禁止使用，因为与基本存量法类似，它也会导致存货在资产负债表中所列报的金额与其最近的成本水平无关。

可变现净值

20.84　IAS 2 要求存货应以成本和可变现净值两者中较低者计量。[IAS 2 第 9 段]。如果不能合理预期将有足够的未来收入承担所发生的成本，应将不可回收的成本在审查期间计为费用。可变现净值是正常经营过程中以估计售价减去估计完工成本和销售所必需的估计费用后的价值。[IAS 2 第 6 段]。

20.85　可变现净值可能低于成本的主要情况为如下事件：

- 完工成本或销售费用增加或销售价格下降。
- 存货遭受毁损。
- 产品陈旧过时。
- 作为公司市场营销策略的一部分而作出亏本生产和销售产品的决定。
- 生产或采购错误。

[IAS 2 第 28 段]。

20.86　将存货减记至可变现净值通常是以逐项进行的。但是，在特定情况下将类似或相关的项目合并处理可能更为恰当，例如，当存货项目与同一生产线相关、具有类似目的和最终用途、在同一地区生产和销售、且实际上难以将其于该生产线的其他项目区别开来的情况。但是，为此而将项目按一般类别或

ⓒ 2012 普华永道（PricewaterhouseCoopers）版权所有。

are produced and marketed in the same geographical area and cannot practicably be distinguished from other items in that product line. However, it is not appropriate to group items for this purpose by reference to general categories or classifications of inventory such as finished goods or to apply write-downs generally to sectors such as operating segments. [IAS 2 para 29].

20.87 IAS 2 notes that service providers generally collect costs in respect of each service for which a separate selling price is charged. Therefore, each such service is considered separately when applying the lower of cost and net realisable value principle. [IAS 2 para 29].

20.88 The initial calculation of a write down to reduce inventory from cost to net realisable value may often be made by the use of formulas based on predetermined criteria. The formulas normally take account of the age, movements in the past, expected future movements and estimated scrap values of the inventory, as appropriate. Whilst the use of such a formula establishes a basis for making a write down that can be consistently applied, it is still necessary for the results to be reviewed in the light of any special circumstances that cannot be anticipated in the formula, such as changes in external market information or in the state of the order book.

20.89 The calculation of net realisable value should also take account of the intended use of the inventory. For example, the net realisable value of inventories held to satisfy a particular sales or service contract should be based on the contract price. Contracts for future sales or for future purchases of raw materials may give rise to provisions where such contracts are onerous. An example of the former is where a future sales contract is set at a price that is below the entity's cost of production of the relevant goods. An example of the latter is where the entity has a purchase commitment for goods or raw materials that is at a price above the price at which the entity can sell on the goods or manufacture the finished product from the raw materials. Onerous contracts are accounted for under IAS 37, 'Provisions, contingent liabilities and contingent assets', which is considered in chapter 21. [IAS 2 para 31].

20.90 Where a write down is required to reduce the value of finished goods below cost, the stocks of the parts and sub-assemblies held for the purpose of the

© 2012 PricewaterhouseCoopers LLP. All rights reserved.

存货分类（如产成品）合并起来或在如经营分部等业务中以整体进行减记是不恰当的。[IAS 2 第 29 段]。

20.87 IAS 2 指出，劳务提供者通常就每项单独计价的劳务进行成本累计。因此，在应用成本和可变现净值孰低的原则时，每一项这样的劳务应视作一个单独项目处理。[IAS 2 第 29 段]。

20.88 将存货从成本减至可变现净值的初始计算通常可能通过基于预先设定标准的公式作出。这些公式通常会视情况而定，考虑到存货的账龄、过去的变动情况、预计未来的变动情况以及估计残值。虽然使用这种公式能够建立一种使减记被一致地运用的基础，但是仍需要根据如外部市场信息的变化或订单状态的改变等公式无法预见的任何特殊情况对结果进行审查。

20.89 计算可变现净值还应考虑存货的预期用途。例如，为了满足特定销售或劳务合同而持有的存货的可变现净值应以合同价为基础计算。如未来出售或原材料采购合同是亏损性合同时可能会导致计提准备。前者的例子为某未来销售合同的定价低于主体生产该产品的成本。后者的例子为主体对商品或原材料做出的购买承诺，其价格高于主体可能出售该商品或用原材料生产该产成品的价格。IAS 37—准备、或有负债和或有资产对亏损性合同进行了规范，并在第 21 章中进行了讨论。[IAS 2 第 31 段]。

20.90 当需要将产成品的价值减记至成本以下时，需要审查为生产该产品而持有的部件和组件的库存以及已订购但未交货的存货，以确定是否也需要对

ⓒ 2012 普华永道（PricewaterhouseCoopers）版权所有。

manufacture of such products, together with inventories on order, need to be reviewed to determine if a write down is also required against such items.

20.91 Events occurring between the balance sheet date and the date of completion of the financial statements need to be considered in arriving at the net realisable value at the balance sheet date (for example, a subsequent reduction in selling prices), to the extent that such events confirm conditions existing at the end of the year. [IAS 2 para 30].

Example – Impact of post balance sheet events in determining the net realisable value of inventory

An entity supplies car parts to a major manufacturer. At the year end it had inventories of parts and the carrying value was C1m. However, after the year end the manufacturer changed the models of the cars and as a result the inventories became obsolete (the part is not interchangeable between models). Should the entity provide against the inventories at the year end?

IAS 10, 'Events after the balance sheet date', gives examples of events that require an adjustment to amounts recognised at the balance sheet date. One such example given in paragraph 9 (b) of IAS 10 refers to the sale of inventories after the balance sheet date as giving evidence of the net realisable value at the balance sheet date.

IAS 2 states in paragraph 30: "*Estimates of net realisable value are based on the most reliable evidence available at the time the estimates are made, of the amount the inventories are expected to realise. These estimates take into consideration fluctuations of price or cost directly relating to events occurring after the end of the period to the extent that such events confirm conditions existing at the end of the period*".

This raises the question of whether the condition existed at the year end. It might be argued that the change of model by the manufacturer is a condition that did not exist at the year end and, therefore, the loss is a post balance sheet event. However, it is likely that the manufacturer would have been considering the change over a long period (including the period prior to the year end) even if it did not announce the change until after the year end. In

© 2012 PricewaterhouseCoopers LLP. All rights reserved.

这些项目进行减记。

20.91　如果在资产负债表日和财务报表报出日之间所发生的事项能够证实年末即存在的状况，则在计算资产负债表日的可变现净值时应将这种事项考虑在内（例如，期后所发生的销售价格下降情况）。[IAS 2 第 30 段]。

示例——资产负债表日后事项对确定存货可变现净值的影响

某主体向一主要生产商供应轿车部件。年末时所持有部件存货的账面价值为 1 百万元。但是，年末之后生产商改变了其轿车型号，并导致这些存货变为陈旧过时（该部件不能在不同型号间互换）。该主体是否应在年末计提存货准备？

《国际会计准则第 10 号——资产负债表日后事项》（IAS 10）中给出了对资产负债表日所确认的金额进行调整的事项示例。IAS 10 第 9（b）段中所给出的一个示例指出，资产负债表日后存货的销售，提供了其在资产负债表日时可变现净值的证据。

IAS 2 第 30 段中规定："*估计可变现净值是以对存货的可变现金额进行估计时所取得的最可靠的证据为基础的。这些估计数应考虑与期末以后发生的事项直接相关的价格或成本波动，但限于其中能证实期末存在状况的事项*。"

问题在于年末是否存在这种状况。可以争论说，生产商更改型号并非是年末存在的状况，因此，该损失是一个资产负债表日后事项。但是，即使生产商直到年后才宣布此变更，它很可能已经考虑了很长时间（包括年前的期间）。此外，高存货量也可能已经显示出生产商的低需求。而资产负债表日后的公告确认了年末供大于求的情况。此状况（型号会变更的可能性及因此发生的潜在损失）很可能在年末即已存在，因此，资产负债

© 2012 普华永道（PricewaterhouseCoopers）版权所有。

addition, the high inventory levels may have indicated slow demand from the manufacturer. This is confirmed by the post balance sheet announcement confirming the over-supply at the year end. The condition (the likelihood that the models would change and the resultant potential loss) is likely to have existed at the year end and, therefore, the post balance sheet confirmation of the change of model and the resultant loss should be reflected in the carrying value of the inventories at the year end.

20.92 A write down is not necessary when the net realisable value of material inventories is less than the purchase price, provided that the finished goods into which the materials are to be incorporated can still be sold at a profit after incorporating the materials at cost price. This is illustrated in the example below. However, where a decline in the price of materials indicates that the cost of the finished goods will exceed their net realisable value, the materials should be written down. In such circumstances, the replacement cost of the raw materials will often be the best available measure of their net realisable value. [IAS 2 para 32].

Example – Determining the net realisable value of material inventories to be incorporated into finished goods

An entity manufactures telecommunication equipment in three stages. There is a market for the semi-finished product for each stage, but the entity only sells the completed product. The following are details of the cost structure of the telecommunication equipment as at 31 December 20X2 (financial year end).

	Cost/unit	Selling price/unit
Stage 1	150	120
Stage 2 – conversion costs	40	90
	190	210
Stage 3 – conversion costs	60	70
	250	280

© 2012 PricewaterhouseCoopers LLP. All rights reserved.

表日后对型号变更的确认及因此发生的损失应该在年末的存货账面金额中反映出来。

20.92 当材料存货的可变现净值低于其采购价格时，如果使用此材料生产的产成品，在包括了此材料的成本价格后，其出售仍能产生利润，则无需减记。如下示例对此进行了说明。但是，如果材料价格的下降表明产成品的成本超过可变现净值，那么该材料就应减记。在这种情况下，材料重置成本往往是计量其可变现净值的最佳基础。[IAS 2 第 32 段]。

示例——确定将被用于产成品生产的材料存货的可变现净值

某主体通过三个阶段生产通讯设备。每阶段的半成品均有市场，但是该主体只出售产成品。如下所列为 20X2 年 12 月 31 日（财务年度末）此通讯设备成本结构的详细信息。

	单位成本	单位销售价格
第 1 阶段	150	120
第 2 阶段——加工成本	40	90
	190	210
第 3 阶段——加工成本	60	70
	250	280

ⓒ 2012 普华永道（PricewaterhouseCoopers）版权所有。

Assuming that the selling costs are immaterial, what is the net realisable value of the semi-finished product in stage 1 as at 31 December 20X2?

Although the selling price per unit at stage 1 is 120, the calculation of the net realisable value of work in progress should consider the expected selling price of the finished products in which it will be incorporated. [IAS 2 para 32]. The profit margin on the estimated cost of completion should, therefore, be considered when calculating the net realisable value of work in progress if the entity has the ability to dispose of the finished product at a price that exceeds the production cost.

Therefore, the net realisable value of the semi-finished product at stage 1 is:

Selling price of completed product	280
less stage 3 conversion costs	(60)
less stage 2 conversion costs	(40)
Net realisable value at stage 1	180

20.93 After a write down has been made, net realisable value should be re-assessed in each subsequent period. If the circumstances that caused the write-down cease to exist, such that all or part of the write down is no longer needed, it should be reversed to that extent. Similarly, if there is clear evidence that the net realisable value has increased because of changed economic circumstances, the write down is reversed. The new carrying value of the inventory would then be the lower of cost and the revised net realisable value. [IAS 2 para 33].

Derecognition

20.94 Inventories should be derecognised when they are sold. At that point they are recognised as an expense in the income statement, in the same period as the revenue from their sale is recognised. An entity should also derecognise inventory when it has no future economic value, for example obsolete inventory. Similarly, although the inventory is not derecognised, write-downs to net realisable value result in the amount of the inventory that has been written down being recognised

© 2012 PricewaterhouseCoopers LLP. All rights reserved.

假设销售费用并不重大,在20X2年12月31日,第1阶段半成品的可变现净值是多少?

尽管第1阶段的单位销售价格为120，计算时，在产品可变现净值应考虑用其生产的产成品的预计销售价格。[IAS 2 第32段]。因此，如果主体能够以超出其生产成本的价格出售产成品，则在计算在产品可变现净值时应该考虑完工成本的利润率。

因此,第1阶段半成品的可变现净值为:

完工产品的销售价格	280
减第3阶段的加工成本	(60)
减第2阶段的加工成本	(40)
第1阶段的可变现净值	180

20.93　减记后，在随后的每个期间都应对可变现净值重新估计。如果造成减记的条件不复存在，因而不再需要全部或部分的减记，则应将其相应转回。类似地，如果有确凿的证据表明因经济环境的变化而导致可变现净值增加，减记应予以转回。之后存货的新账面金额应该是成本与修订了的可变现净值两者中的较低者。[IAS 2 第33段]。

终止确认

20.94　存货在售出后应予以终止确认。在该时点，应将其在利润表中确认为一项费用，这与因其销售而确认的收入在同一期间。当存货不再具有未来经济利益时，如陈旧过时的存货，主体也应将其终止确认。类似地，尽管存货并未被终止确认，但是减记至可变现净值的金额应在当期确认为一项费用。如果且当减记被转回时，此转回应在当期的利润表中确认，而相应地增加存货的金额。此转回将与当期确认为费用的存货金额冲销（并需披露转回的金额——

© 2012 普华永道（PricewaterhouseCoopers）版权所有。

as an expense in the period in which the write-down occurs. If and when a write down is reversed, the reversal should be recognised in the income statement in the period in which the reversal occurs and the amount of inventories is increased accordingly. The reversal is netted against the amount of inventories recognised as an expense in the period (with disclosure of the amount of the reversal - see para 20.98 below). [IAS 2 para 34].

Example – Reversal of write down of inventory

Entity C's management determines that a provision of C12,000 against inventories recorded in previous years should be reversed because of changes in market conditions.

The tax rate is 30%. Tax relief is granted in respect of provisions recognised against specific items of inventory.
How should the reversal of the provision be presented in the financial statements?

The reversal of the provision should be included in cost of sales, as this was the line in the income statement against which the original provision had been charged. [IAS 2 para 34].

The reversal of the provision will result in an increase in the entity's tax charge for the year of C3,600 (12,000 × 30%). This charge reverses the tax relief received in prior periods. The adjustment to the tax charge should be included in the tax line item in the income statement.

20.95 In some cases inventories may be allocated to other assets, for example, inventory that is used in constructing a property for the entity's own use. In such cases, the inventory is derecognised when incorporated in the cost of construction of the other asset and recognised as part of the cost of that other asset. [IAS 2 para 35].

20.96 IAS 18, 'Revenue', sets out the conditions for when the sale of goods should be recognised. Therefore, these conditions need to be met before inventory is derecognised (unless it is being written off as obsolete). IAS 18 requires that all the following conditions are met:

- The entity has transferred to the buyer the significant risks and rewards of

© 2012 PricewaterhouseCoopers LLP. All rights reserved.

请参见下文第20.98段)。[IAS 2第34段]。

示例——存货减记的转回

主体C的管理层确定由于市场情况的变动，应该转回以前年度所记录的存货准备金额为12,000元。

税率为30%。对于具体存货项目所确认的准备享有税收减免。

在财务报表中，应如何列报对此准备的转回?

此准备的转回应计入销售成本，因为这是利润表中记录原准备的项目。[IAS 2第34段]。

此准备的转回将导致主体在该年度的所得税费用增加3,600元(12,000 × 30%)。这一费用转回了以前期间所收到的税收减免。所得税费用的调整应计入利润表中的所得税行中。

20.95 在某些情况下，存货可能被归属到其他资产中，例如主体用于建造自用不动产的存货。在这种情况下，当存货被包括在其他资产的建造成本时，应将其终止确认并确认为该项其他资产成本的一部分。[IAS 2第35段]。

20.96 《国际会计准则第18号——收入》(IAS 18) 中规定了商品销售收入确认的条件。因此，在存货被终止确认前(除非其已作为陈旧过时品减计) 应满足这些条件。IAS 18要求满足以下所有条件:

- 主体已将商品所有权上的重大风险与报酬转移给购货方。

ⓒ 2012 普华永道 (PricewaterhouseCoopers) 版权所有。

ownership of the goods.

- The entity retains neither continuing managerial involvement to the degree usually associated with ownership nor effective control over the goods sold.
- The amount of revenue can be measured reliably.
- It is probable that the economic benefits associated with the transaction will flow to the entity.
- The costs incurred or to be incurred in respect of the transaction can be measured reliably.

[IAS 18 para 14].

20.97 Certain types of more complex transactions such as consignment sales or sale and repurchase transactions require careful consideration as to whether inventory should be derecognised or not as a result of the transaction. These more complex transactions are considered under 'Practical application' below.

Disclosure

20.98 IAS 2 requires disclosure of:

- The accounting policies adopted in measuring inventories, including the cost formula (for example, FIFO or weighted average cost) used. (See Tables 20.4, 20.5 and 20.6.)
- The total carrying amount of inventories and the carrying amount in classifications appropriate to the entity. The total carrying amount is required by IAS 1 (revised), 'Presentation of financial statements', to be shown on the face of the balance sheet. [IAS 1 (revised) para 54]. (See Table 20.6 for an example of disclosure by classifications.)
- The carrying amount of inventories carried at fair value less costs to sell (typically, inventories held by commodity broker dealers). (See Table 20.6A for example.)
- The amount of inventories recognised as an expense during the period. (See

© 2012 PricewaterhouseCoopers LLP. All rights reserved.

■ 主体既没有保留通常与商品所有权相联系的持续管理权，也没有对已售出商品实施控制。

■ 收入的金额能够可靠的计量。

■ 与交易相联系的经济利益很可能会流入主体。

■ 与交易相关的已发生或将发生的成本能够可靠的计量。

[IAS 18 第 14 段]。

20.97　如委托代售或出售和回购交易等更为复杂的特定类型的交易需要仔细考虑存货是否应因交易而终止确认。在下文“在实务中的应用”部分对这些更为复杂的交易进行了讨论。

披露

20.98　IAS 2 要求披露：

■ 计量存货所采用的会计政策，包括所使用的成本计算方法（例如先进先出法或加权平均成本法）。（请参见表 20.4、表 20.5 和表 20.6。）

■ 存货的账面总金额以及按适合主体而分的各存货类的账面金额。《国际会计准则第 1 号——财务报表的列报》（修订版）[IAS 1（修订版）] 要求账面总金额列报于资产负债表的主表中。[IAS 1（修订版）第 54 段]。（分类披露的示例请参见表 20.6。）

■ 以公允价值减去销售费用后而计量的存货的账面金额（一般是商品经纪人所持有的存货）。（请参见表 20.6A 中示例。）

■ 当期确认为费用的存货金额。（请参见表 20.6 中示例。）

ⓒ 2012 普华永道（PricewaterhouseCoopers）版权所有。

Table 20. 6 for example.)

- The amount of any write down of inventories recognised as an expense in the period. (See Tables 20. 6 and 20. 6B for examples.)
- The amount of any reversal of any write down that is recognised as a reduction in the amount of inventories recognised as expense in the period in accordance with paragraph 34 of IAS 2. (See Tables 20. 6 and 20. 6B for examples.)
- The circumstances or events that led to the reversal of a write-down of inventories in accordance with paragraph 34 of IAS 2.
- The carrying amount of inventories pledged as security for liabilities. (See Table 20. 6B for an example.)

[IAS 2 para 36].

20. 99 Paragraph 37 of IAS 2 notes, in relation to the second bullet point above, that common classifications of inventories include:

- Merchandise.
- Production supplies.
- Materials.
- Work in progress.
- Finished goods.

Another common classification is 'payments on account'. This represents the payments an entity makes on account of inventories and not the payments it receives from customers. For a service provider, inventories may simply be classified as work in progress. The classifications chosen should be applied consistently. [IAS 1 (revised) para 45].

20. 100 An example of disclosure of inventory classifications is given in Table 20. 6. This example also discloses the accounting policy, inventory recognised as an expense, write downs and the reversal of previous years' write-downs.

© 2012 PricewaterhouseCoopers LLP. All rights reserved.

■ 在当期确认为费用的存货减记金额。（请参见表 20. 6 和表 20. 6B 中示例。）

■ 根据 IAS 2 第 34 段的规定，在当期转回的减记金额且用以减少当期费用化的存货金额。（请参见表 20. 6 和表 20. 6B 中示例。）

■ 根据 IAS 2 第 34 段的规定，导致存货减记转回的情况和事项。

■ 作为债务抵押品的存货的账面金额。（请参见表 20. 6B 中示例。）

[IAS 2 第 36 段]。

20. 99　IAS 2 第 37 段指出，与上述第二点相关的常见存货分类包括：

■ 商品。

■ 生产物料。

■ 材料。

■ 在产品。

■ 产成品。

另一个常见的分类是“预付账款”。这指的是主体为了存货账户而支付的款项，而不是它从客户处所收到的款项。对于劳务提供者而言，存货可以简单地划分为在产品。所选择的分类类别应一致地使用。[IAS 1（修订版）第 45 段]。

20. 100　表 20. 6 中给出了存货分类披露的示例。该示例还披露了会计政策、确认为费用的存货、减记和以前年度减记的转回。

ⓒ 2012 普华永道（PricewaterhouseCoopers）版权所有。

Table 20. 6 – Disclosure in respect of inventories

Invensys plc – Annual report and accounts – 31 March 2011

Accounting policies (extract)

Inventories

Inventories are valued at the lower of cost and estimated net realisable value. Provision is made for obsolete and slow-moving items. Cost comprises the cost of raw materials, determined on a first-in, first-out cost basis, and an appropriate proportion of labour and manufacturing overheads based on normal operating capacity, to reflect the costs incurred in bringing the product to its present location and condition.

17 Inventories

	2011	2010
	£m	£m
Raw materials and consumables	**83**	87
Work in progress	**30**	30
Finished goods	**42**	40
	155	157

Cost of inventories recognised as an expense

	2011	2010
	£m	£m
Cost of inventories recognised as an expense	**811**	833
Including:		
– Write-down of inventories to net realisable value	**2**	4
– Reversals of impairments in inventories	—	(1)

20. 100. 1 Table 20. 6A shows disclosure of amounts of inventory carried at fair value less costs to sell. Table 20. 6B discloses, in addition to several of the other disclosures already illustrated, the amount of inventory pledged as security.

© 2012 PricewaterhouseCoopers LLP. All rights reserved.

表 20. 6——有关存货的披露

Invensys plc——年报和财务报表——2011 年 3 月 31 日

会计政策（摘录）

存货

存货以成本和估计可变现净值两者中的较低者计价。对陈旧过时和滞销的项目计提了准备。成本包括按先入先出成本法确定的原材料成本以及根据正常生产能力比例的人工和生产间接费用，以反映使产品达到目前场所和状态所发生的成本。

17. 存货

	2011	2010
	百万英镑	百万英镑
原材料和低值易耗品	**83**	87
在产品	**30**	30
产成品	**42**	40
	155	157

确认为费用的存货成本

	2011	2010
	百万英镑	百万英镑
确认为费用的存货成本	**811**	833
包括：		
— 将存货减至可变现净值的减记	**2**	4
—存货减值的转回	—	(1)

20. 100. 1　表 20. 6A 显示了以公允价值减去销售费用后而计量的存货金额的披露。除了已列举的其他几项披露以外，表 20. 6B 中还披露了作为抵押品的存货金额。

© 2012 普华永道（PricewaterhouseCoopers）版权所有。

Table 20.6A – Inventory at fair value less costs to sell

BP p.l.c. – Annual report and accounts – 31 December 2009

1. Significant accounting policies (extract)

Inventories

Inventories, other than inventory held for trading purposes, are stated at the lower of cost and net realizable value. Cost is determined by the first-in first-out method and comprises direct purchase costs, cost of production, transportation and manufacturing expenses. Net realizable value is determined by reference to prices existing at the balance sheet date.

Inventories held for trading purposes are stated at fair value less costs to sell and any changes in net realizable value are recognized in the income statement.

Supplies are valued at cost to the group mainly using the average method or net realizable value, whichever is the lower.

26 Inventories

	2009	2008
Crude oil	**6,237**	4,396
Natural gas	**105**	107
Refined petroleum and petrochemical products	**12,337**	9,318
	18,679	13,821
Supplies	**1,661**	1,588
	20,340	15,409
Trading inventories	**2,265**	1,412
	22,605	16,821
Cost of inventories expensed in the income statement	**163,772**	266,982

The inventory valuation at 31 December 2009 is stated net of a provision of $46 million (2008 $1,412 million) to write inventories down to their net realizable value. The net movement in the year in respect of inventory net realizable value provisions was $1,366 million credit (2008 $1,295 million charge).

© 2012 PricewaterhouseCoopers LLP. All rights reserved.

表 20.6A——以公允价值减去销售费用后而计量的存货

BP p. l. c. ——年报和财务报表——2009 年 12 月 31 日

1. 重大会计政策（摘录）

存货

除了为交易而持有的存货以外，其他存货以成本和可变现净值两者中的较低者计量。成本采用先进先出法确定，包括直接购买成本、生产成本、运输和生产费用。可变现净值应参考资产负债表日的价格。

为交易而持有的存货以公允价值减去销售费用后而计量，可变现净值的所有变动都确认在利润表中。

对主要采用平均法或可变现净值两者中的较低者进行估价的集团，物料应以成本法计量。

26. 存货

	2009	2008
原油	**6,237**	4,396
天然气	**105**	107
精炼石油和石油化工产品	**12,337**	9,318
	18,679	13,821
物料	**1,661**	1,588
	20,340	15,409
交易存货	**2,265**	1,412
	22,605	16,821
在利润表中计入当期费用的存货成本	**163,772**	266,982

为了将存货减记至可变现净值，2009 年 12 月 31 日的存货计价已计提准备 4,600 万美元（2008：14.12 亿美元）。当年的净变动主要是转回了存货可变现净值准备的 13.66 亿美元（2008：12.95 亿美元的计提）。

© 2012 普华永道（PricewaterhouseCoopers）版权所有。

Table 20. 6B – Inventory pledged as security

Unilever PLC – Annual report and accounts – 31 December 2009

12 Inventories

	€ million	€ million
Inventories	**2009**	2008
Raw materials and consumables	**1,298**	1,437
Finished goods and goods for resale	**2,280**	2,452
	3,578	3,889

Inventories with a value of € 91million (2008: € 134 million are carried at net realisable value, this being lower than cost. During 2009, € 200 million (2008, € 246 million was charged to the income statement for damaged, obsolete and lost inventories. In 2009, € 19 million (2008, € 23 million) was utilised or released to the income statement from inventory provisions taken in earlier years.

In 2009, inventories with a carrying amount of € 10 million were pledged as security for certain of the Group's borrowings (2008: € 34 million).

20. 101 The requirement to disclose the amount of inventories recognised as an expense in the period can be interpreted in two ways. Some companies will adopt a classification of expenses according to the nature of the expense and others will choose to present expenses based on their function. Either method of presentation is permitted by IAS 1 (revised), 'Presentation of financial statements'. For example, an entity that adopts the 'nature of expense' approach would disclose wages of factory employees as staff costs, but one that adopts the 'function of expense' approach would disclose such wages as part of cost of sales.

20. 102 IAS 2 notes that entities that adopt the 'function of expense' approach would include as cost of inventories (within cost of sales) those costs previously included in inventories (that is, direct and indirect costs and overheads). The amount recognised as an expense in respect of inventories should also include unallocated production overheads and abnormal amounts of production costs of inventories. The standard also notes that in some specific circumstances of an entity other costs, such as distribution costs, may also be included. [IAS 2 para 38].

© 2012 PricewaterhouseCoopers LLP. All rights reserved.

表 20.6B——作为抵押品的存货

Unilever PLC——年报和财务报表——2009 年 12 月 31 日

12 . 存货

	百万欧元	百万欧元
存货	**2009**	2008
原材料和低值易耗品	**1,298**	1,437
产成品和待再售商品	**2,280**	2,452
	3,578	3,889

价值为 9,100 万欧元（2008：1.34 亿欧元）的存货以低于成本的可变现净值计量。在 2009 年，计入利润表的毁损、陈旧过时和丢失存货的金额为 2 亿欧元（2008：2.46 亿欧元）。在 2009 年的利润表中实现或释放的以前年度的存货准备的金额为 1,900 万欧元（2008：2,300 万欧元）。

在 2009 年，账面价值为 1,000 万欧元（2008：3,400 万英镑）的存货成为集团某些借款的抵押品。

20.101　对当期确认为费用的存货金额的披露要求可以有两种解释。有的公司按费用的性质对费用进行分类，而其他公司则选择按功能来列报费用。这两种列报方法在 IAS 1（修订版）中均允许采用。例如，采用“费用性质”法的主体会将工厂职工的工资披露为员工成本，但采用“费用功能”法的公司则会将这些工资披露为销售成本的一部分。

20.102　IAS 2 指出，采用“费用功能”法的主体将之前包括在存货中的那些成本（即直接和间接成本以及间接费用）计入到存货成本（在销售成本内）中。确认为费用的存货金额还应包括未分配的间接生产费用和异常金额的存货生产成本。该准则还指出，根据主体的特殊情况也可能需要包括其他成本，例如分销费用。[IAS 2 第 38 段]。

ⓒ 2012 普华永道（PricewaterhouseCoopers）版权所有。

20. 103 Entities that adopt the 'nature of expense' approach would disclose the amounts of operating costs, classified by their nature, applicable to revenues for the period. Thus they would disclose the cost of raw materials and consumables, labour costs and other operating costs, together with the amount of the net change in inventories for the period. [IAS 2 para 39].

20. 104 Sometimes a write-down to net realisable value may be of such significance that it should be separately disclosed under IAS 1 (revised), 'Presentation of financial statements', either in the notes or on the face of the income statement. [IAS 1 (revised) paras 97, 98]. IAS 1 (revised) is dealt with in chapter 4.

Practical application

Sale and repurchase of inventories

20. 105 IAS 18, 'Revenue', notes that sometimes the recognition criteria (see para 20. 96) are applied to two or more transactions together when they are linked in such a way that the commercial substance cannot be understood without reference to the series of transactions as a whole. It gives an example of a sale of goods where the seller, at the same time, enters into a separate contract to repurchase the goods at a later date. It states that this negates the substantive effect of the transaction and, in such a case, the two transactions are dealt with together. [IAS 18 para 13]. In a more complicated situation, inventory may be sold with an option (rather than an unconditional contract) to buy it back. The detailed terms of such options vary and, indeed, the options may sometimes be expressed at market value such that it is by no means certain that the options will be exercised. Perhaps more commonly, however, the option is constructed so that it is reasonably certain that it will be exercised. The arrangement may run for months, or even years, during which time the company that sold the inventory will use the sale proceeds as a form of finance. In such a situation, there is an overriding requirement in IAS 8, 'Accounting policies, changes in accounting estimates and errors', to develop policies that ensure that the financial statements "*... reflect the economic substance of transactions, other events and conditions, and not merely the legal form...*".

© 2012 PricewaterhouseCoopers LLP. All rights reserved.

20.103　采用“费用性质”法的主体将披露按性质进行分类、与当期收入配比的经营成本的金额。因此，它们将披露原材料和易耗品成本、人工成本和其他成本以及本期存货变动净额。[IAS 2 第 39 段]。

20.104　有时减记至可变现净值的金额可能非常重要，因而应根据 IAS 1（修订版）在附注或利润表的主表中对其单独进行披露。[IAS 1（修订版）第 97、98 段]。在第 4 章对 IAS 1（修订版）进行了讨论。

在实务中的应用

存货的出售和回购

20.105　IAS 18——收入指出，确认标准适用于当两项或以上的交易相互关联，且如果不把这一系列交易视为一个整体，就不能理解其商业实质时（请参见第 20.96 段）。它给出了一个示例，为卖方在销售商品同时也签订了一份日后重新回购该种商品的单独合同。它指出，这否定了该项交易的实质效应，在这种情况下，这两项交易应结合在一起处理。[IAS 18 第 13 段]。更为复杂的情况是，存货可能在出售时还连带一个回购的期权（而非无条件的合同）。这种期权的具体条款各不相同，而事实上，该选项有时可能按市场价值签出，因而无法确定其是否会被行权。但是，可能更常见的情形是该期权的设定使其能合理地确定将行权。这种协议的期限可能是几个月，甚至是几年，在此期间销售存货的公司将销售收入作为一种融资的形式。在这种情况下，IAS 8——会计政策、会计估计变更和差错中有一更高的要求，即主体应制定会计政策来使财务报表“*……反映交易、其他事项或事件的经济实质，而不仅仅是法律形式……*”。
[IAS 8 第 10（b）（ii）段]。

ⓒ 2012 普华永道（PricewaterhouseCoopers）版权所有。

[IAS 8 para 10(b)(ii)].

20.106 In summary, we consider that, based on the extracts from IAS 8, 'Accounting policies, changes in accounting estimates and errors', and IAS 18, 'Revenue', referred to above and the principles set out in the IASB's Framework, the true commercial effect of a transaction is a sale if the seller genuinely relinquishes control of significant benefits and transfers the exposure to significant risks associated with the asset to the buyer (for example, if the repurchase price is market value at the date of repurchase). However, a transaction structured so that in practice the purchaser secures a lender's return on the purchase price without genuine exposure to, or benefit from, changes in value of the underlying assets (for example, if the repurchase price is predetermined as original sale price plus an increment based on interest rates applied to the finance provided), should be treated as a financing arrangement.

20.107 IAS 18, 'Revenue', also notes in its appendix that sale and repurchase agreements need to be analysed to ascertain whether, in substance, the seller has transferred the risks and rewards of ownership to the buyer. When the seller has retained the risks and rewards, even if legal title has been transferred, the transaction is a financing arrangement and does not give rise to revenue. [IAS 18 App A para 5].

20.108 Where such a transaction is, in substance, a financing arrangement; the inventories are not derecognised, but instead a liability for the repurchase price (that may represent the original selling price plus interest accrued over the period to the date of repurchase) is recorded, together with the cash received.

Example – Accounting for an inventory financing arrangement

A company sells inventory in year one for C100,000 and at the same time enters into an agreement to repurchase it a year later for C110,000. The C10,000 should not be treated as part of the cost of the inventory, but represents interest and should be charged to the profit and loss account.

The company should initially show in its balance sheet inventory of C100,000 and a financing liability of C100,000. Interest should be calculated using the effective interest method as set out in paragraph 9 of IAS 39, 'Financial

© 2012 PricewaterhouseCoopers LLP. All rights reserved.

20.106　总而言之，我们认为根据上述摘录的 IAS 8 以及 IAS 18 以及 IASB《框架》的原则，如果卖方真正放弃重大权益的控制权并将与资产相关的重大风险转移给买方（例如，当回购价格是回购日的市场价值时），则这项交易的真实商业实质是销售。但是，如果一项交易的设计使得买方实际上确保了购买价格的贷款人回报而不用真正因标的资产的价值变化而承担风险或获利（例如，当回购价格被预先确定为初始价格加上根据所提供融资的利率计算的增量时），其应被视为一项融资安排。

20.107　IAS 18——收入中还在其附录中指出，要对销售和回购协议进行分析以确定卖方是否实质上已经将所有权的风险和报酬转移给买方。当卖方保留了风险和报酬时，即使所有权已经转移，此交易也只是一项融资安排而不会产生收入。[IAS 18 附录 A 第 5 段]。

20.108　当这种交易实质上是一项融资安排时，存货不会被终止确认，而是与所收到现金一起，对回购价格确认一项负债（其可能代表原销售价格加至回购日期间所发生的利息）。

示例——存货融资安排的会计处理

某公司在第一年以 100,000 元出售存货，同时还签订了一份在一年后以 110,000 元将其回购的协议。10,000 元不能被视为存货成本的一部分，而是代表利息并应被计入损益表中。

该公司最初应在其资产负债表中显示 100,000 元的存货和 100,000 元的融资负债。利息应采用《国际会计准则第 39 号——金融工具：确认和计量》（IAS 39）第 9 段中定义的实际利率法计算。[IAS 39 第 47 段]。这

ⓒ 2012 普华永道（PricewaterhouseCoopers）版权所有。

instruments: Recognition and measurement' [IAS 39 para 47]. This means that the interest is charged at a constant rate on the carrying value of the liability.

Consideration would also need to be given to whether the inventory needs to be written down to reduce it to net realisable value.

20.109 In more complex situations, it may be determined that a sale and repurchase agreement is not, in substance, a financing transaction and that the seller only retains access to an insignificant proportion of the original asset's benefits. If, for example, the buyer receives more than merely a lender's return, as significant other benefits and risks associated with the asset have been transferred to the buyer, the seller will not have retained the original asset. In this situation, and if the likelihood of the repurchase commitment being called upon is not probable, the asset should be derecognised.

20.110 Where there is a repurchase commitment that will probably be called upon, the asset should be retained on balance sheet. Such situations are particularly common in the automotive industry where the seller is a manufacturer or dealer and like many others in that industry it sells vehicles with a buy back commitment of short duration. In such a situation the treatment adopted is to retain the vehicle in its entirety in the balance sheet and treat the transaction as a short term operating lease during the buyback commitment period. Table 20.6C gives an example of this treatment.

Table 20.6C – Vehicles with buy back commitments treated as operating leases

Peugeot S.A. – Annual report and accounts – 31 December 2009

Note 1 Accounting policies (extract)

1.5. Sales and Revenue

A. Manufacturing and Sales Companies

(a) Automobile Division

Sales and revenue of the manufacturing and sales companies include revenues from the sale and leasing of vehicles and the sale of other goods and services. In accordance with IAS 18 –

© 2012 PricewaterhouseCoopers LLP. All rights reserved.

就意味着利息将根据负债的账面金额按照固定的利率来计算。

还需要考虑是否应将存货减记以将其降低至可变现净值。

20.109 在更为复杂的情况下，某出售或回购协议实质上并非融资安排，且卖方仅保留原资产利益的不重大部分。例如，当与资产相关的其他重大利益和风险已经转移给买方，买方所收到的不仅仅是贷款人的回报时，卖方不能保留原资产。在这种情况下，而且如果行使这种回购承诺的可能性不大，该资产应被终止确认。

20.110 当回购承诺很可能会被行使时，资产应被保留在资产负债表上。这种情况在汽车行业尤为常见，当卖方为生产厂商或经销商时，同该行业中的很多其他公司一样，它会在出售汽车的同时签署一项短期的回购承诺。在这种情况下，所采用的会计处理是将汽车全部保留在资产负债表上，并将这种交易在回购承诺期内视为一项短期经营租赁。表 20.6C 给出了这种处理方法的一个示例。

表 20.6C——被视为经营租赁的具有回购承诺的车辆

Peugeot S. A. ——年报和财务报表——2009 年 12 月 31 日

附注 1. 会计政策(摘录)

1.5. 销售和收入

A. 生产和销售公司

(a)汽车部门

生产和销售公司的销售和收入包括销售和租赁汽车以及销售其他商品和服务所得到的收入。根据 IAS 18 规定，在所有权的风险和回报被转移之日确认新汽车的销售。这通

ⓒ 2012 普华永道（PricewaterhouseCoopers）版权所有。

Con.

Revenue, new vehicle sales are recognised on the date the risks and rewards of ownership are transferred. This generally corresponds to the date when the vehicles are made available to non-group dealers or the delivery date, in the case of direct sales.

Sales at cost of items purchased on behalf of other parties and sales to subcontractors of raw materials, parts and mechanical components that are intended to be bought back at cost are not included in sales and revenue.

Sales of new vehicles with a buyback commitment are not recognised at the time of delivery but accounted for as operating leases when it is probable that the vehicle will be bought back. This principle applies:

— Whatever the duration of the buyback commitment.

—For both direct sales and sales financed by Banque PSA Finance and its subsidiaries.

The difference between the sale price and the buyback price is recognised as rental revenue on a straight-line basis over the duration of the buyback commitment. The vehicle is initially recognised at production cost in property, plant and equipment. Depreciation expense is calculated over the term of the lease by the straight-line method, on the basis of the vehicle's cost less its estimated residual value, representing the anticipated resale price on the used vehicle market. Any additional gain made on the final sale of the vehicle is recognised in the period in which the vehicle is sold on the used car market. If the net difference is a loss, an allowance is booked when the buyback contract is signed.

Inventory on consignment

20. 112 Arrangements where goods are supplied from a manufacturer to a dealer on a consignment basis are common in certain industries, particularly in the motor vehicle trade. The objective of both parties to a consignment arrangement is to enable the dealer to sell as many units of the product as possible. The dealer is often given some incentive by the manufacturer through various bonus schemes to ensure that the volume of items sold is as high as possible. The consignment arrangement serves to achieve this objective and benefit both parties.

20. 113 However, under such arrangements the manufacturer (or a financier) generally retains title to the goods supplied to the dealer until some predetermined event occurs. This may be when the dealer sells the goods or has held them for a

© 2012 PricewaterhouseCoopers LLP. All rights reserved.

续表

常对应的是汽车可被提供给集团外经销商之日，或在直销的情况下的交付日。
替其他方购买的以成本出售的项目以及预计将按照成本回购的出售给分包商的原材料、部件和机械部件不计入销售和收入。
当汽车很可能被回购时，带有回购承诺的新车销售在交货时并不会确认，而是作为经营租赁进行核算。此原则适用于： ——所有回购承诺期间； ——直销和由 Banque PSA Finance 及其子公司融资的销售。 销售价格和回购价格之间的差额在回购承诺期内按直线法确认为租赁收入。汽车以生产成本在不动产、工厂和设备中进行初始确认。折旧费用将以直线法在租期按汽车成本减其预计残值（即二手车市场的预计出售价格）计算。由于车辆的最终出售而获得的所有额外的利得将在车辆在二手车市场出售的期间确认。如果净差额是损失，当签订回购合同时将计提一项备抵。

委托代售存货

20.112　以委托代售的方式由生产厂商将商品供应给经销商的安排在某些行业中比较常见，尤其是机动车辆贸易行业。委托代售安排双方的目的是使经销商销售尽可能多数量的产品。生产厂商通过各种奖励机制以激励经销商，以保证所售出项目的数量尽可能地多。委托代售协议能够达到此目的并使双方都能获利。

20.113　但是，根据这种安排生产厂商（或提供融资方）通常会在预先确定的事项发生之前保留提供给经销商的商品的所有权。这可以是经销商售出货物、持有商品达到一定的时间、或其他触发经销商获取商品的事项（即当其

ⓒ 2012 普华永道（PricewaterhouseCoopers）版权所有。

set period, or some other event triggers the dealer's adoption of the goods (that is, when he pays for them and acquires title). But the date that title transfers tends to be some time after the date that the inventory item is physically transferred to the dealer. Title will generally pass on receipt of cleared funds (but not to the dealer if he has already sold the vehicle on).

20.114 The key issue is to determine the point at which the dealer has in substance acquired an asset that should be recognised on its balance sheet (that is, whether it is when legal title passes or at some other time).

20.115 In addition to setting out the general conditions for when the sale of goods should be recognised (see para 20.96 above), IAS 18, 'Revenue', deals briefly with revenue recognition for one form of consignment arrangement. It states that where the recipient of the goods (buyer) undertakes to sell goods on behalf of the shipper (seller), revenue is recognised by the shipper when the goods are sold by the recipient to a third party. [IAS 18 App A para 2(c)]. The shipper would not derecognise its inventory until that point.

20.116 IFRS does not give any other detailed guidance on accounting for consignment arrangements. Paragraph 10 of IAS 8, 'Accounting policies, changes in accounting estimates and errors', requires that in the absence of a standard or an interpretation that specifically applies to a transaction, other event or condition, management should use its judgement in applying accounting policies that result in information that satisfies the qualitative characteristics of the IASB's Framework. These characteristics include reflecting the economic substance of transactions and not merely the legal form. IAS 8, sets out a hierarchy of guidance to which management refers and whose applicability it considers when selecting accounting policies. IAS 8, specifically requires that in making the judgement in selecting accounting policies, management should consider the applicability of the requirements in IFRS dealing with similar and related issues.

20.117 Additional insight on the treatment of consignment stock may also be obtained from the guidance in IAS 39, 'Financial instruments: Recognition and measurement', concerning derecognition of financial assets, as these are substance-based. For example, the following questions have to be answered to determine whether an asset can be derecognised:

© 2012 PricewaterhouseCoopers LLP. All rights reserved.

支付费用并取得所有权）。但是所有权转移的日期一般会晚于存货项目实物被转移给经销商的日期。所有权通常在收到尾款后转移（但是如果经销商已售出车辆则不会转移给经销商）。

20.114　关键问题是确定经销商在何时已实质性地获取相关资产从而在资产负债表上予以确认（即，是合法所有权转移时或另一个时间）。

20.115　除规定了销售商品应何时予以确认的一般条件以外（参见上文第20.96段），IAS 18还简要规范了一种委托代售协议的收入确认问题。它规定，在商品的接收方（买方）替发货方（卖方）销售商品的情况下，发货方应在接收方把商品售与第三方时确认收入。[IAS 18附录A第2（c）段]。发货方在该时点之前不能终止确认其存货。

20.116　IFRS并未对委托代售协议的会计处理给出其他详细指南。IAS 18——会计政策、会计估计变更和差错第10段要求，在缺乏专门适用于某种交易、其他事项或事件的准则或解释时，管理层应当在考虑会计政策的应用时运用其判断，使相关的信息满足IASB《框架》中所规定的定性特征。这些特征包括反映交易的经济实质，而不仅仅是其法定形式。IAS 8规定了管理层在选择会计政策时可以参考并需要考虑其适用性的指南级次。IAS 8特别要求在对选择会计政策作出判断时，管理层应考虑IFRS对处理类似和相关问题要求的适用性。

20.117　IAS 39——金融工具:确认和计量有关终止确认金融资产的是根据其实质性,因此从中能对委托代售存货的会计处理获得额外的洞察。例如,在判断是否可以终止确认某项资产时必须要回答如下问题:

ⓒ 2012 普华永道（PricewaterhouseCoopers）版权所有。

1. Have the rights to the cash flows from the asset expired?

2. Has the entity transferred its contractual rights to receive the cash flows from the asset?

3. Has the entity assumed an obligation to pay the cash flows from the assets to another party?

4. Has the entity transferred substantially all the risks and rewards?

5. Has the entity relinquished control of the asset?

If the manufacturer no longer has rights to the cash flows from the asset (question 1) then it could derecognise the asset. Similarly, it could derecognise the asset if it can answer yes to questions 2 and 4 or to questions 3 and 4. If the manufacturer retains some of the risks and rewards, it can only derecognise the asset if it no longer controls the asset.

Example – Manufacturer supplies goods to a distributor on a consignment basis

A distributor purchases clothes from a manufacturer on extended credit and stores the goods in its own warehouse until they are sold to a third party. Legal title to the goods passes to the distributor when the distributor receives them. The distributor does not have to pay for the goods until it receives payment from the third party customer. If the clothes are not sold within three months, the distributor can either return them to the manufacturer or pay for them and keep them.

Until it is known that the goods have been sold (whether to a third party or to the distributor after three months), the goods should be treated as the manufacturer's inventory, that is, consignment inventory, and excluded from the distributor's balance sheet.

Arrangements where a manufacturer supplies goods to a distributor on consignment are common in certain industries. These arrangements enable the dealer to maximise sales. The manufacturer usually retains title to the product and thereby substantial risks and rewards until triggered by some event when title is transferred.

20.118 The hierarchy of guidance set out in IAS 8, 'Accounting policies,

© 2012 PricewaterhouseCoopers LLP. All rights reserved.

1. 取得资产现金流量的权利是否已经到期？

2. 主体是否已转让收取资产现金流量的合同权利？

3. 主体是否承担了将资产现金流量支付给另一方的义务？

4. 主体是否已经转让了几乎所有的风险和报酬？

5. 主体是否已经出让了资产的控制权？

如果生产厂商不再有取得资产现金流量的权利（问题1），则可以终止确认该项资产。类似地，如果问题2和4的答案为是，或问题3和4的答案为是，那么也可以终止确认该项资产。如果生产厂商保留了一些风险和报酬，只有在它不再控制该项资产时才可以终止确认。

示例——生产厂商以委托代售的形式向经销商供应商品

某经销商以循环信用的方式从某生产厂商处购买衣服并将商品储存在自己的仓库中，直至销售给第三方。在经销商收到商品时其合法所有权即已转移。在第三方客户付款之前经销商不用为商品支付款项。如果这些衣服未在三个月内售出，经销商可以将其返还给生产厂商或在付款后将其据为己有。

在知道这些商品已出售之前（无论售予第三方还是在三个月后售予经销商），这些商品应被视为生产厂商的存货，即委托代售存货，且不能将其计入经销商的资产负债表中。

某些行业会较常见由生产厂商供应商品给经销商的委托代售安排。这种安排使经销商最大程度地提高销售额。生产厂商通常会保留产品的所有权以及其主要风险和报酬，直到触发所有权转移的事项发生时。

20.118　IAS 8 规定了管理层在选择会计政策时可以参考并考虑其适用性的指

ⓒ 2012 普华永道（PricewaterhouseCoopers）版权所有。

changes in accounting estimates and errors', to which management refers and whose applicability it considers when selecting accounting policies, includes considering the most recent pronouncements of other standard-setting bodies that use a similar conceptual framework to develop accounting standards. [IAS 8 paras 10 to 12].

[The next paragraph is 20. 134].

Financial instruments

20. 134 Commodity price and foreign exchange price movements between the date of order and settlement may expose an entity to risks when purchasing inventories. Commodity price risk arises where an entity enters into a contract to purchases a commodity whose price varies. Foreign exchange risk arises where the entity pays for the inventory in a foreign currency.

20. 135 To mitigate or hedge commodity price risk, the entity may enter into a forward contract to buy the commodity at a fixed price at a future date. If the contract is entered into and continues to be held for the purpose of the delivery of the commodity in accordance with the entity's expected purchase or usage requirements, the entity does not recognise the forward contract as a derivative. If the entity has a practice of settling net (either with the counterparty or by entering into offsetting contracts or by taking delivery of the commodity and selling it within a short period after delivery for the purpose of generating a profit from short term fluctuations in price or dealer's margin), then the forward contract will have to be recognised as a derivative. This is because such a contract to buy or sell non-financial items (for example, inventory) would be within the scope of IAS 39, 'Financial instruments: Recognition and measurement'. In practice many contracts to buy or sell a commodity fall within IAS 39's scope. See further Financial instruments chapter 6. [IAS 39 paras 5, 6, IG A. 1].

Example 1 – Own use exemption for a contract to buy a commodity

An entity enters into a fixed-price forward contract to purchase one million kilograms of iron ore in accordance with its expected usage requirements. The contract permits the entity to take physical delivery of the iron ore at the end

© 2012 PricewaterhouseCoopers LLP. All rights reserved.

南级次，其中包括考虑使用类似概念框架而制定会计准则的其他准则制定机构的最新通告。[IAS 8 第 10 到 12 段]。

[下一段为第 20.134 段]。

金融工具

20.134　订单日和结算日之间商品价格和外汇价格的变动可能会使得主体在购买存货时面临风险。当主体签订合同购买价格可变动的商品时，即会出现商品价格风险。当主体以外币为存货支付款项时，即会出现外汇风险。

20.135　为了规避商品价格风险或对其进行套期，主体可以签订在未来某一日期以固定价格购买商品的远期合同。如果签订并继续持有合同是以交付商品为目的并符合主体所预期的购买或使用要求，主体不会将该远期合同确认为一项衍生工具。如果主体有以净值结算的惯例（无论是与交易对方还是通过签订抵销合同，或是通过收取商品并在交付后的短期内将其出售，以从价格或交易商保证金的短期波动中获取利润），则该远期合同必须被确认为一项衍生工具。这是因为这种购买或出售非金融项目（例如存货）的合同在《国际会计准则第 39 号——金融工具：确认和计量》的范围内。在实务中很多购买或销售商品的合同都在 IAS 39 的范围内。更多讨论请参见《金融工具》第六章。[IAS 39 第 5、6 段，IG 第 A.1 段]。

示例 1——购买商品的合同的自用例外

某主体根据其预计使用需求签订了一份购买一百万公斤铁矿石的固定价格远期合同。合同允许主体在 12 个月末时对铁矿石收取实物，或是根据铁矿石的公允价值变化支付或收取现金结算净额。

ⓒ 2012 普华永道（PricewaterhouseCoopers）版权所有。

of 12 months or to pay or receive a net settlement in cash, based on the change in iron ore's fair value.

If the entity intends to settle the contract by taking delivery and has no history for similar contracts of settling net in cash or of taking delivery of the iron ore and selling it within a short period after delivery for the purpose of generating a profit from short-term fluctuations in price or dealer's margin the contract is not recognised as a derivative under IAS 39, even though it meets the definition of a derivative. Instead, it is considered an executory contract. The definition of and accounting for derivatives is dealt with in chapter 6.

Example 2 – Practice of net settlement for forward contracts to purchase oil held as inventory

An entity enters into a forward contract to purchase oil. The entity has an established pattern of settling such contracts net before delivery by contracting with a third party. The entity settles any market value difference for the contract price directly with the third party.

The forward contract to purchase oil is recognised as a derivative. IAS 39, 'Financial instruments: Recognition and measurement' applies to a contract to purchase a non-financial asset if the contract meets the definition of a derivative and the contract does not qualify for the exemption for delivery in accordance with the entity's expected purchase or usage requirements. [IAS 39 paras 9, 5]. The entity does not expect to take delivery. A pattern of entering into offsetting contracts that effectively accomplishes settlement on a net basis means that the transaction does not qualify for the exemption for delivery in accordance with the entity's expected purchase or usage requirements.

[The next paragraph is 20.137].

20.137 An entity may enter into a contract to purchase inventory in a currency other than the entity's functional currency. In effect, the contract is a host contract to purchase inventory and a swap or forward contract to exchange one currency for another (an embedded derivative). Embedded derivatives are considered in chapter 6.

[The next paragraph is 20.140].

© 2012 PricewaterhouseCoopers LLP. All rights reserved.

如果主体打算对合同进行实物交割且对于类似的合同，没有以现金净额结算或收取铁矿石并在交付后的短期内将其出售，以从价格或交易商保证金的短期波动中获取利润的历史，那么即使该合同符合衍生工具的定义，也不会根据 IAS 39 确认为一项衍生工具。相反，应将其视为一项执行合同。在第六章中对衍生工具的定义和会计处理进行了讨论。

示例 2——对购买存货石油的远期合同有以净额结算的惯例

某主体签订了一项购买石油的远期合同。该主体已经形成通过和第三方签约的方式在交货前以净额结算这些合同的模式。该主体直接与第三方结算合同价格和市场价值的差值。

此购买石油的远期合同应确认为一项衍生工具。如果购买非金融资产的合同符合衍生工具的定义且合同不符合根据主体预期的购买或使用要求进行交货的例外，则适用 IAS 39——金融工具：确认和计量。[IAS 39 第 9、5 段]。该主体不打算实物交割。签订能有效地达到净额结算的抵销合同的模式意味着该项交易不符合根据主体预期的购买或使用要求进行交货的例外。

[下一段为第 20. 137 段]。

20. 137　主体可能签订以其功能货币以外的货币购买存货的合同。实际上，此合同是一项购买存货的主合同和用一种货币兑换另一种货币的互换或远期合同（嵌入衍生工具）。在第六章中对嵌入衍生工具进行了讨论。

[下一段为第 20. 140 段]。

ⓒ 2012 普华永道（PricewaterhouseCoopers）版权所有。

20. 140 Where an entity enters into a contract to purchase inventory in a currency other than its functional currency, it can hedge the purchase with a separate hedging instrument. Where the criteria in paragraph 88 of IAS 39, 'Financial instruments: Recognition and measurement' are met, an entity is permitted to account for the hedging instrument using hedge accounting. The criteria are dealt with in chapter 6.

20. 141 Hedges of foreign currency purchases of inventory can be designated as cash flow hedges or fair value hedges. [IAS 39 IG F3. 3]. This is because the purchase of inventory can either be a highly probable forecast transaction or an unrecognised firm commitment. A hedge of the foreign currency risk of a highly probable forecast transaction would be designated as a cash flow hedge. [IAS 39 para 86(b)]. A hedge of the foreign currency risk of a firm commitment may be accounted for as a fair value hedge or as cash flow hedge. [IAS 39 para 87].

20. 142 A cash flow hedge of a highly probable purchase of foreign currency inventory is accounted for as follows:

- The hedging instrument is measured at fair value. Gains/losses on the effective portion of the hedging instrument are taken to other comprehensive income. The ineffective portion of the gain or loss on the hedging instrument is recognised in profit or loss.

- For hedges of highly probable forecast transactions that give rise to *non-financial* assets (such as inventory), the entity should adopt either of the following approaches as its accounting policy and apply that policy consistently:

- It should reclassify gains and losses previously recognised in other comprehensive income to profit or loss in the same periods as the inventory affects profit or loss (that is, in the periods in which the inventory is written off as part of cost of sales). Any losses that are deemed irrecoverable should be recognised in profit or loss immediately.

- It should remove the gain or loss previously recognised in other comprehensive income and include it in the initial cost or other carrying amount of the inventory.

[IAS 39 paras 95, 98, 99].

© 2012 PricewaterhouseCoopers LLP. All rights reserved.

20.140　当主体签订了以其功能货币以外的货币购买存货的合同时，它可以通过一项单独的套期工具来对该项采购进行套期。在符合 IAS 39 第 88 段所规定条件的情况下，允许主体对套期工具采用套期会计。在第六章对这些条件进行了讨论。

20.141　对以外币购买存货的套期可以被指定为现金流量套期或公允价值套期。[IAS 39 IG 第 F3.3 段]。这是因为存货的购买既可以是一项极可能发生的预期交易，也可以是一项未确认的确定承诺。极可能发生的预期交易的外汇风险套期应该被指定为现金流量套期。[IAS 39 第 86（b）段]。确定承诺的外汇风险套期可以作为公允价值套期核算，或是作为现金流量套期核算。[IAS 39 第 87 段]。

20.142　对极可能发生的外币存货采购的现金流量套期按如下方式进行会计处理：

- 套期工具以公允价值计量。套期工具有效部分的利得/损失计入其他综合收益。套期工具的利得或损失的无效部分应计入损益。

- 对于形成非金融资产（如存货）的极可能发生的预期交易的套期，主体应采用如下任意一种方法作为其会计政策并一致地采用：

- 应将之前已确认为其他综合收益的利得和损失在存货影响损益的同一期间（即存货被减记为销售成本的一部分的期间）重分类计入损益。被认定为不可收回的任何损失应立即计入损益。

- 应将之前以确认为其他综合收益的利得或损失转出，计入存货的初始成本或其他账面余额。

[IAS 39 第 95、98、99 段]。

ⓒ 2012 普华永道（PricewaterhouseCoopers）版权所有。

20. 143 A fair value hedge of an unrecognised firm commitment of an inventory purchase is accounted for as follows:

- The cumulative change in the fair value of the firm commitment attributable to foreign exchange risk is recognised as an asset or liability on the balance sheet with the corresponding gain or loss recognised in the profit and loss account.
- The change in the fair value of the derivative hedging instrument is also recognised in the profit and loss account and offsets the above gain or loss on the firm commitment.
- When the firm commitment is met and the inventory is purchased, the cumulative change in the fair value of the firm commitment attributable to the foreign exchange risk that is on the balance sheet is adjusted against the initial carrying amount of the inventory.

[IAS 39 paras 93, 94].

20. 144 Hedging foreign currency risk attributable to inventory is possible because the fair value changes attributable to the foreign currency risk can be isolated and measured. However, it is not possible to hedge a particular ingredient or component of an item of inventory, because changes in price of the ingredient generally do not have a predictable, separately measurable effect on the price of the inventory. For this reason, an inventory can only be designated as a hedged item in its entirety for all risk or for foreign currency risk. [IAS 39 paras 82, AG100]. For example, inventories of manufactured tyres cannot be hedged for changes in the price of rubber, because the tyre includes other components and the change in fair value of rubber is not necessarily representative of the change in fair value of the tyre.

Reservation of title

20. 145 In some jurisdictions it is quite common for companies that sell goods to other companies to have reservation of title clauses included in their contracts. This enables the selling company to retain legal ownership of those goods until the purchaser has paid for them. The main effect of trading with reservation of title is that the position of the unpaid seller may be improved if the purchaser becomes

© 2012 PricewaterhouseCoopers LLP. All rights reserved.

20.143　对未确认存货购买承诺的公允价值套期按如下方式进行会计处理：

- 归属于外汇风险的确定承诺公允价值的累计变动在资产负债表中确认为一项资产或负债，相应的利得或损失计入损益表。
- 衍生套期工具的公允价值变动也计入损益表，并抵销上述确定承诺的利得或损失。
- 在确定承诺已履行且存货已采购后，存货的初始账面余额应根据已在资产负债表中确认的归属于外汇风险的确定承诺公允价值的累计变动而调整。

[IAS 39 第 93、94 段]。

20.144　因为归属于外汇风险的公允价值变动可以被隔离并计量，对归属于存货的外汇风险进行套期是可能的。但是，不可能对某一存货项目的特别要素或组成部分进行套期，因为要素价格的变动一般不会对这个存货的价格产生可以预测的、可单独计量的影响。因此，存货只能被整体指定为对所有风险的被套期项目或被指定为对外汇风险的被套期项目。[IAS 39 第 82 段，AG 第 100 段]。例如，生产出的轮胎存货不能够对橡胶的价格变动进行套期，因为轮胎还包括其他组成部分而橡胶的公允价值变动并不一定能够代表轮胎的公允价值变动。

保留所有权

20.145　在有些辖区，销售商品给其他公司时，合同中包括条款以保留所有权的情况相当常见。这使得卖方公司能够在买方付款前保留那些商品的法定所有权。以保留所有权的方式进行交易的主要效果是，如果买方破产，对尚未收款的卖方，其偿付顺序可能会得以改善。但是，是否存在有效的保留所有权取决于具体合同的结构。

© 2012 普华永道（PricewaterhouseCoopers）版权所有。

insolvent. However, whether an effective reservation of title exists depends upon the construction of the particular contract.

20.146 Even if there is an effective reservation of title clause, on a going concern basis it is common practice for the purchaser to recognise such inventories in its balance sheet, although the supplier retains legal title to the goods. The liability to the supplier is also recognised.

20.147 There is no specific guidance in IFRS on this issue. However, the Framework emphasises that to represent faithfully transactions and events it is necessary that they are accounted for in accordance with their substance and economic reality and not merely their legal form. [Framework para 35].

20.148 Where the financial statements are materially affected by the accounting treatment adopted in relation to sales or purchases subject to reservation of title, we recommend that consideration should be given to disclosing the treatment in a note indicating the amount of liabilities that are subject to reservation of title clauses be given, where quantifiable. However, in practice, this note is often not given where the purchasing company is a going concern such that the likelihood of the reservation of title clause crystallising is remote. Whether or not disclosure is necessary in order to give a fair presentation will be a matter for judgement. A fair presentation requires an entity to provide additional disclosures when compliance with the specific requirements in IFRSs is insufficient to enable users to understand the impact of particular transactions, other events and conditions on the entity's financial position and financial performance. [IAS 1 (revised) para 17(c)]. An example might be where the company did not have legal title to assets and disclosure of this fact was necessary for a fair presentation to be given.

Inventory or investment property

20.149 A property under construction originally classified as inventory, as it is held for sale in the ordinary course of business, can only be transferred to investment property when, and only when, there is a change in use evidenced by the commencement of an operating lease to another party. [IAS 40 para 57(d)].

© 2012 PricewaterhouseCoopers LLP. All rights reserved.

20.146 即便有条款有效地让供应商保留了这些商品的合法所有权，在持续经营的情况下，实务中买方会将这些存货确认在其资产负债表上。对供应商的负债同时也会同时确认。

20.147 在国际财务报告准则中没有这一问题的具体指南。但是,《框架》中强调,为真实地反映交易和其他事项,会计处理必须根据其实质和经济现实,而不仅仅是其法律形式。[《框架》第35段]。

20.148 在为保留所有权的销售或采购所采用的会计处理对财务报表有重大影响的情况下，应考虑在附注中披露该处理，并在可以定量的情况下显示由于保留所有权条款形成的负债金额。但是，在实务中，采购公司在持续经营从而使得保留所有权条款得以实施的可能性很小的情况下，往往不会给出此附注。是否需要披露而实现公允列报必须是一个需要判断的事项。当主体遵循国际财务报告准则的具体要求不足以让使用者理解特定交易、其他事项或情况对主体的财务状况和财务业绩的影响时，公允列报要求提供附加披露。[IAS 1（修订版）第17（c）段]。比如，公司不具有资产的法定所有权，必须披露此事实才能实现公允列报。

存货或投资性房地产

20.149 为在正常经营过程中销售而持有因此最初分类至存货的在建房地产，仅当与另一方开始一项经营租赁以证明其用途发生变更时，才可以转至投资性房地产。

ⓒ 2012 普华永道（PricewaterhouseCoopers）版权所有。

Example 1 – Renting before completion of entire property

Entity A, a property developer with a history of developing properties for sale immediately after completion, constructs a residential property for sale. To increase the possibility of selling the entire property after completion, the entity decides to lease out individual apartments when completed. The tenants move in before the property is completed in its entirety and before it is sold. How should entity A account for the property?

Entity A should continue to classify the property as inventory, as this is consistent with the entity's principal activities and its strategy for the property even after the commencement of the leases. The leases are intended to increase the possibility to sell the property rather than to earn rental income on a continuing basis, and the property is not held for capital appreciation. The entity's intention to sell the property immediately after completion has not changed, as the property continues to be held exclusively with the view to subsequent disposal in the ordinary course of business; it does not, therefore, meet the definition of an investment property. [IAS 40 para 9(a)].

Example 2 – Renting until market activity improves

Entity B, a property developer with a history of developing properties for sale immediately after completion, constructs a residential property for sale. However, as property prices are at a multi-year low and there are few buyers/transactions in the market, entity B decides to rent out the property until market activity improves. Entity B believes it will be better able to find a buyer for the property at that time. How should entity B account for the property?

Entity B needs to carefully assess whether the property should continue to be classified as inventory or be transferred to investment properties in accordance with paragraph 57 (d) of IAS 40. The property should continue to be classified as inventory if this is consistent with entity B's strategy for this property. However, it should be transferred to investment property if there is a change in management's intention to hold the property for future rentals or for capital appreciation (for example, until market prices recover).

© 2012 PricewaterhouseCoopers LLP. All rights reserved.

示例 1——整体房地产完工前出租

主体 A 是一家房地产开发商，过去曾开发过完工后立即销售的房地产，目前建造一处以销售为目的的住宅房地产项目。为提高房地产整体完工后的销售几率，该主体决定单个公寓完工后将其对外出租。公寓承租人在该房地产整体完工前且尚未销售时就已经搬入。主体 A 应如何对该房地产进行会计处理?

即使租赁已经开始，主体 A 仍应继续将该房地产分类至存货，这与该主体的主要经营活动以及对该房地产的战略一致。该租赁的意图是为了提高房地产销售的几率，而不是长期赚取租金，同时持有该房地产的意图也不是资本升值。该主体打算在完工后立即销售房地产的意图并未发生改变，因为继续持有该房地产的唯一意图是为了后续在正常经营过程中处置；因此，它并不符合投资性房地产的定义。[IAS 40 第 9（a）段]。

示例 2——市场环境改善前出租

主体 B 是一家房地产开发商,过去曾开发过完工后立即销售的房地产,目前建造一处以销售为目的的住宅房地产项目。但是,因为房地产价格多年来持续低迷,并且市场上鲜有买家/交易,主体 B 决定对外出租该房地产直至市场环境改善。主体 B 相信那时将更容易找到该房地产的买家。主体 B 应如何对该房地产进行会计处理?

主体 B 需要仔细评估该房地产是否应该继续被分类至存货,还是根据 IAS 40 第 57(d)段转换成投资性房地产。如果与主体 B 对该房地产的战略一致,则该房地产应该继续被分类至存货。但是,如果管理层持有该房地产的意图发生变化,变为出租或者为了资本升值(例如,直到市场价格回升),则该房地产应被转换成投资性房地产。

ⓒ 2012 普华永道（PricewaterhouseCoopers）版权所有。

Determining the correct classification of such a property requires judgement. The inception of a lease with third parties in itself does not automatically require the reclassification as investment property, although it may be indicative of a change in management's intention.

The property may, therefore, continue to be classified as inventory to the extent it is available for immediate sale in its present condition, at a current market price, in the ordinary course of business. Factors to consider include:

- Is the property actively marketed for sale?
- Is the property available for sale at a price that is reasonable relative to its current market value?
- Does a market exist for properties with sitting tenants, with longer lease terms, such that the property is in a condition to be sold immediately?
- Where there is no market for properties with sitting tenants, are the terms of any leases less than the length of the period that other similar properties take to be sold in the ordinary course of business under current market conditions?

If the entity is unwilling to sell the property at the current depressed market price, it is likely that the property's intended use has changed to meet the definition of an investment property – held to earn rental income and for capital appreciation. Factors to consider are:

- Has the board decided to postpone the sale of the property until the market price recovers?
- Is there a change in the business plan that takes into account the rental income earned and the necessary future maintenance expenses?
- Is the property no longer actively marketed for sale?
- Is there still an active market for similar properties?
- Is the property available for sale only at a price that is not reasonable relative to its current market value?

© 2012 PricewaterhouseCoopers LLP. All rights reserved.

确定这类房地产的正确分类需进行判断。与第三方的租赁的开始本身并非自动要求重分类至投资性房地产，尽管这可能表明管理层意图的改变。

因此,只要该房地产在目前状况下,在正常经营过程中以目前的市场价格可以立即出售,它就可能继续被分类为存货。考虑因素包括:

- 是否针对该房地产进行了积极的销售?
- 该房地产是否能够以与其目前市场价值合理相关的价格出售?
- 拥有现居租户、更长租赁期间的房地产是否存在市场，使得该房地产处于能够立刻出售的状态?
- 当拥有现居租户的房地产不存在市场时，租赁协议时间是否短于其他类似房地产在现有市场条件下的正常经营过程中销售所需要的时间?

如果该实体不愿意以目前低迷的市场价格出售房地产,该房地产的预计使用用途很可能已经变为符合投资性房地产的定义——为赚取租金和为资本增值而持有的房地产。考虑因素包括:

- 董事会是否已决定推迟该房地产的销售，直至市场价格回升?
- 经营计划是否发生改变以考虑获得的租金收入以及未来必要的维修费用?
- 该房地产是否不再进行积极的销售?
- 类似的房地产是否仍然存在积极的市场?
- 该房地产是否仅能以一个与其市场价值不合理相关的价格出售?

ⓒ 2012 普华永道（PricewaterhouseCoopers）版权所有。

Example 3 – Change in intended use

Entity C, a property developer with a history of developing properties for sale immediately after completion, constructs a residential property for sale. However, as property prices are at a multi-year low, entity C decides to no longer pursue the plan to sell the property after completion and to reconsider the decision to sell at a later stage when the market improves. The intended change in use is evidenced by a formal decision of the board and a change in entity C's business plan. Entity C intends to rent the property out to third parties on longer lease terms. However, at the year end, no lease contract has been signed. How should entity C account for the property?

Entity C should continue to classify the property as inventory. Paragraph 57 of IAS 40 precludes the transfer of such a property to investment property until there is an actual change in use; this is evidenced by the commencement of an operating lease with a tenant. [IAS 40 para 75(c)]. The intention to rent out the building after completion – with no lease contract yet in place – may indicate a change in the intended use but is, in itself, not sufficient to qualify for a change in classification.

Example 4 – Timing of transfers to inventories

Entity D is engaged in two lines of business: property development for sale; and investment property held for rental purposes. Two of the properties currently classified as investment property are to be sold in the near future. Property X is going to be redeveloped prior to sale. The redevelopment will significantly improve and enhance the property. Property Y will also be sold, but significant redevelopment is not necessary (although some basic repairs will be undertaken). Entity D wishes to transfer both properties from investment property to inventory at the date the developments commence in accordance with paragraph 57(b) of IAS 40. How should entity D account for the properties?

Entity D should transfer property X to inventories at the commencement of the redevelopment; property Y should continue to be classified as investment property until the criteria in IFRS 5 are met, at which point the property

© 2012 PricewaterhouseCoopers LLP. All rights reserved.

示例 3——使用意图改变

主体 C 是一家房地产开发商，过去曾开发过完工后立即销售的房地产，目前建造一处以销售为目的的住宅房地产项目。但是，因为房地产价格多年来持续低迷，主体 C 决定不再执行原计划即完工后出售该房地产，同时也重新考虑待市场好转后再出售的决定。董事会的正式决议以及主体 C 业务计划的变更证实了该房地产用途发生了改变。主体 C 计划延长向第三方出租该房地产的时间。但是，本期期末尚未签订任何租赁合同。主体 C 应该如何对该房地产进行会计处理？

主体 C 应该继续将该房地产分类至存货。IAS40 第 57 段不允许上述类型的房地产转换为投资性房地产，除非用途发生实际的改变：通过与一承租人开始一项经营租赁来证明。[IAS40 第 75（c）段]。完工后对外出租大楼的意图——在未有租赁合同时——也许说明了预期用途会发生改变，但是这本身并不足以作为分类改变的证据。

示例 4——转换为存货的时点

主体 D 从事两种业务：为销售而进行的房地产开发；以及持有投资性房地产以出租。分类至投资性房地产的两处房地产最近将被出售。房地产 X 将在出售前进行重新开发，这将大幅提高和改善该房地产的状况。房地产 Y 也将被出售，但是无需进行大规模的重新开发（尽管要进行一些基础维修工作）。主体 D 想根据 IAS40 第 57（b）段在开发开始之日，将这两处房地产由投资性房地产转换为存货。主体应如何对这两处房地产进行会计处理？

主体 D 应在重新开发开始之日，将房地产 X 转换为存货；房地产 Y 应继续分类至投资性房地产，直至满足 IFRS 5 的条件将该房地产分类为持有待售。IAS 40 第 57（b）段要求，投资性房地产转换成存货仅当该房地

ⓒ 2012 普华永道（PricewaterhouseCoopers）版权所有。

should be classified as held for sale. Paragraph 57(b) of IAS 40 requires an investment property to be transferred to inventories only when the property is being developed with a view to sale. Developments in this context should substantially modify or otherwise enhance the property; basic repairs typically would not qualify as a substantial modification.

© 2012 PricewaterhouseCoopers LLP. All rights reserved.

产为出售而开始开发。在本文中的开发应当是实质性地改变或者改善房地产的状况；基础维修通常不能视为实质性改变。

ⓒ 2012 普华永道（PricewaterhouseCoopers）版权所有。

PwC Assurance Service Contacts
联系普华永道审计业务部

北京 Beijing
梁伟坚 Thomas Leung
电话 Tel：+86（10）6533 2838
电子邮件 Email：thomas. w. leung@ cn. pwc. com

青岛 Qingdao
张国俊 Kevin Zhang
电话 Tel：+86（532）8089 1818
电子邮件 Email：kevin. zhang@ cn. pwc. com

重庆 Chongqing
李松波 Bobby Lee
电话 Tel：+86（23）6393 7388
电子邮件 Email：bobby. lee@ cn. pwc. com

上海 Shanghai
李丹 Daniel Li
电话 Tel：+86（21）2323 3388
电子邮件 Email：daniel. li@ cn. pwc. com

大连 Dalian
关兆文 Dorman Kwan
电话 Tel：+86（411）8379 1666
电子邮件 Email：dorman. kwan@ cn. pwc. com

深圳 Shenzhen
张展豪 Albert Cheung
电话 Tel：+86（755）8261 8833
电子邮件 Email：albert. cheung@ cn. pwc. com

广州 Guangzhou
张展豪 Albert Cheung
电话 Tel：+86（755）8261 8833
电子邮件 Email：albert. cheung@ cn. pwc. com

苏州 Suzhou
汪超 Arthur Wang
电话 Tel：+86（512）6273 1998
电子邮件 E－mail：arthur. wang@ cn. pwc. com

杭州 Hangzhou
潘振翔 Steve Pan
电话 Tel：+86（21）2323 2626
电子邮件 Email：steve. pan@ cn. pwc. com

天津 Tianjin
郑广安 Kwong On Cheng
电话 Tel：+86（22）2318 3003
电子邮件 Email：kwong. on. cheng@ cn. pwc. com

南京 Nanjing
钱进 Jevens Qian
电话 Tel：+86（21）2323 3579
电子邮件 Email：jevens. qian@ cn. pwc. com

厦门 Xiamen
张祚诚 Douglas Chang
电话 Tel：+86（592）210 7888 * 1616
电子邮件 Email：douglas. dc. chang@ cn. pwc. com

宁波 Ningbo
徐宏 Toby Xu
电话 Tel：+86（21）2323 3399
电子邮件 Email：toby. xu@ cn. pwc. com

西安 Xi'an
叶骏 Joe Ye
电话 Tel：+86（29）8720 3998
电子邮件 Email：joe. ye@ cn. pwc. com

PwC Accounting Consulting Services Contacts
联系普华永道会计咨询服务

黄家勇 Wilfred Wong
电话 Tel：+852 2289 1322
电子邮件 Email：wilfred. wong@ hk. pwc. com

陈保郎 Baolang Chen
电话 Tel：+86（21）2323 2555
电子邮件 Email：baolang. chen@ cn. pwc. com

金以文 Yvonne Kam
电话 Tel：+86（21）2323 3267
电子邮件 Email：yvonne. kam@ cn. pwc. com

陈燕华 Tracy Chen
电话 Tel：+86（21）2323 3070
电子邮件 Email：tracy. yh. chen@ cn. pwc. com

PwC China, Hong Kong, Macau , Taiwan and Singapore Office Locations and Contacts
普华永道在中国大陆、香港、澳门和台湾及新加坡的事务所

北京 Beijing
中国北京市
朝阳区东三环中路 7 号
北京财富中心写字楼 A 座 26 楼
邮政编码 100020
26/F Office Tower A
Beijing Fortune Plaza
7 Dongsanhuan Zhong Road
Chaoyang District
Beijing 100020, PRC
电话 Tel: +86 (10) 6533 8888
传真 Fax: +86 (10) 6533 8800

重庆 Chongqing
中国重庆市渝中区邹容路 68 号
大都会商厦 19 楼 1905 室
邮政编码 400010
Room 1905
19/F Metropolitan Tower
68 Zou Rong Road
Chongqing 400010, PRC
电话 Tel: +86 (23) 6393 7888
传真 Fax: +86 (23) 6393 7200

大连 Dalian
中国大连市西岗区中山路 147 号
森茂大厦 8 楼
邮政编码 116011
8/F Senmao Building
147 Zhongshan Road
Xigang District
Dalian 116011, PRC
电话 Tel: +86 (411) 8379 1888
传真 Fax: +86 (411) 8379 1800

广州 Guangzhou
中国广州市天河区珠江新城
珠江西路 10 号
普华永道中心 18 楼
邮政编码 510623
18/F PwC Center
10 Zhujiang Xi Road
Pearl River New City
Tianhe District
Guangzhou 510623, PRC
电话 Tel: +86 (20) 3819 2000
传真 Fax: +86 (20) 3819 2100

杭州 Hangzhou
中国杭州市下城区环城北路 208 号
坤和中心 3205 室
邮政编码 310006
Room 3205, Canhigh Center
208 Huancheng Road North
Xiacheng District
Hangzhou 310006, PRC
电话: +86 (571) 2807 6388
传真: +86 (571) 2807 6300

香港 Hong Kong
中国香港中环太子大厦 22 楼
22/F Prince's Building
Central
Hong Kong, PRC
电话 Tel: +852 2289 8888
传真 Fax: +852 2810 9888

澳门 Macau
中国澳门苏亚利斯博士大马路 323 号
中国银行大厦 29 楼
29/F Bank of China Building
323 Avenida Doutor Mario Soares
Macau, PRC
电话 Tel: +853 8799 5111
传真 Fax: +853 8799 5222

青岛 Qingdao
中国青岛市市南区延安三路 234 号
海航万邦中心 1 号楼 37 楼
邮政编码 266071
37/F Tower One, HNA IMC Center
234 Yanan Third Road, Shinan District
Qingdao 266071, PRC
电话 Tel: +86 (532) 8089 1888
传真 Fax: +86 (532) 8089 1800

南京 Nanjing
中国南京市鼓楼区中央路 201 号
南京国际广场南塔 12A 层 01 室
邮政编码 210009
Room 12A01, South Tower
Nanjing International Center
201 Zhongyang Road
Gulou District
Nanjing 210009, PRC
电话 Tel: +86 (25) 6608 6288
传真 Fax: +86 (25) 6608 6210

上海 Shanghai
中国上海市黄浦区湖滨路 202 号
企业天地 2 号楼
普华永道中心 11 楼
邮政编码 200021
11/F PwC Center
2 Corporate Avenue
202 Hu Bin Road
Huangpu District
Shanghai 200021, PRC
电话 Tel: +86 (21) 2323 8888
传真 Fax: +86 (21) 2323 8800

宁波 Ningbo
中国宁波市江东区民安东路 268 号
宁波国际金融服务中心 E 座 1203 室
邮政编码 315040
Room 1203, Tower E
Ningbo International Financial Center
268 Min An Road East
Jiangdong District
Ningbo 315040, PRC
电话 Tel: +86 (574) 8187 1788
传真 Fax: +86 (574) 8187 1700

深圳 Shenzhen
中国深圳市罗湖区深南东路 5016 号
京基 100 – A 座 34 楼
邮政编码 518001
34/F Tower A, Kingkey 100
5016 Shennan East Road
Luohu District
Shenzhen 518001, PRC
电话 Tel: +86 (755) 8261 8888
传真 Fax: +86 (755) 8261 8800

新加坡 Singapore
新加坡 048424 邮区
PWC 大厦
克罗士街 8 号 17 楼
8 Cross Street # 17－00
PWC Building
Singapore 048424
电话 Tel：+65 6236 3388
传真 Fax：+65 6236 3300

天津 Tianjin
中国天津市和平区
南京路 189 号
津汇广场 2 座 36 楼
邮政编码 300051
36/F The Exchange Tower Two
189 Nanjing Road
Heping District
Tianjin 300051, PRC
电话 Tel：+86（22）2318 3333
传真 Fax：+86（22）2318 3300

苏州 Suzhou
中国苏州市苏州工业园区
旺墩路 188 号建屋大厦 1501 室
邮政编码 215028
Room 1501, Genway Tower
188 Wang Dun Road
Suzhou Industrial Park
Suzhou 215028, PRC
电话 Tel：+86（512）6273 1888
传真 Fax：+86（512）6273 1800

厦门 Xiamen
中国厦门市思明区鹭江道 8 号
国际银行大厦 11 楼 B 室
邮政编码 361001
Unit B, 11/F
International Plaza
8 Lujiang Road
Siming District
Xiamen 361001, PRC
电话 Tel：+86（592）210 7888
传真 Fax：+86（592）210 8800

台湾 Taiwan
中国台北市信义区 110
基隆路一段 333 号 27 楼
International Trade Building,
27F, 333 Keelung Road, Section 1,
Taipei 110, Taiwan
电话 Tel：+886 2 27296666
传真 Fax：+886 2 27576371

西安 Xi'an
中国西安市南关正街 88 号
长安国际中心 D 座 7 楼
邮政编码 710068
7/F, D Block, Chang'an Metropolis Center
88 Nanguan Street
Xi'an 710068, PRC
电话 Tel：+86（29）8469 2688
传真 Fax：+86（29）8469 2600

如欲了解更多资讯，敬请登陆公司网站：
For more information, please visit our websites at：
pwccn. com
pwchk. com

图书在版编目（CIP）数据

国际财务报告准则实务指引．第十五章，无形资产、第二十章，存货：汉英对照/金以文等编译．—北京：中国财政经济出版社，2012.9
（普华永道国际财务报告准则实务指引系列）
ISBN 978－7－5095－3494－6

Ⅰ．①国…　Ⅱ．①金…　Ⅲ．①会计准则－世界－汉、英　Ⅳ．①F233.1

中国版本图书馆 CIP 数据核字（2012）第 047859 号

责任编辑：蔡丽兰　　　　责任校对：胡永立

中国财政经济出版社出版

URL：http：//www.cfeph.cn

E－mail：cfeph@cfeph.cn

（版权所有　翻印必究）

社址：北京市海淀区阜成路甲 28 号　邮政编码：100142
营销中心电话：88190406　财经书店电话：64033436
北京财经印刷厂印刷　各地新华书店经销
787×1092 毫米　16 开　21.25 印张　358 000 字
2012 年 9 月第 1 版　2012 年 9 月北京第 1 次印刷
定价：55.00 元
ISBN 978－7－5095－3494－6/F·2953
（图书出现印装问题，本社负责调换）
本社质量投诉电话：010－88190744